# The Remedy and Prevention of Mobbing in Higher Education

# The Remedy and Prevention of Mobbing in Higher Education

## Two Case Studies

### Kenneth Westhues

With contributions by
Jo A. Baldwin, Barry W. Birnbaum, James Gollnick,
Anson Shupe, James Van Patten, Stan C. Weeber, and
Committee A, American Association of University Professors

THE EDWIN MELLEN PRESS
Lewiston ● Queenston ● Lampeter

**Library of Congress Cataloging-in-Publication Data**

This book has been registered with the Library of Congress.

The remedy and prevention of mobbing in higher education : two case studies /
 Kenneth Westhues.

ISBN 0-7734-5720-8

A CIP catalog record for this book is available from the British Library.

Front Cover: Alexander, Socrates, and other Greek thinkers in conversation. Detail from
Raphael, The School of Athens (1509-1510), Vatican.

Copyright © 2006  Kenneth Westhues

The Edwin Mellen Press                 The Edwin Mellen Press
Box 450                                         Box 67
Lewiston, New York                     Queenston, Ontario
USA  14092-0450                        CANADA  L0S 1L0

The Edwin Mellen Press, Ltd.
Lampeter, Ceredigion, Wales
UNITED KINGDOM SA48 7DY

Printed in the United States of America

# Table of Contents

## Conclusion

# Introduction:

# Substance and Methodology

This collection of original papers on extreme cases of mobbing in higher education addresses two basic questions about this pathology. The first is substantive: what is it? The second is methodological: how does one study it? These are the foundational questions in any new field of scientific inquiry. For the new field of mobbing in the academic workplace, this book offers answers to both questions. It also suggests in a tentative, open-ended way numerous hypotheses about causes and consequences, remedy and prevention.

Near the top of the list of intended readers are researchers in this area: sociologists, psychologists, and scholars of other stripes who have accepted the challenge of explaining the bizarre organizational process Heinz Leymann (see 1990) first identified in Sweden in the 1980s. At the very top of the list, however, are college and university administrators, given their urgent practical interest in this subject. Their energies and budgets are needlessly sapped, their own careers are jeopardized, and their institutions are undermined, when professors get mobbed. Administrators will find herein clues to keeping their institutions free of this pathology. This book is intended for ordinary professors, too, who need to learn about academic mobbing in order to protect themselves from becoming targets and restrain themselves from being caught up in academic mobs. Professors already targeted can glean from this volume tactics for fighting back. In sum, this book is for anyone concerned with preventing administrative disasters in higher education, anybody who wants to keep colleges and universities on course toward achieving their noble objectives of seeking and sharing truth.

## Extreme Cases Show What Mobbing Is

Most academics in the USA and Canada, including many readers of this book, have but a hazy notion of *workplace mobbing* and approach these pages with doubts about whether this new concept deserves a place in their vocabularies. Is it perhaps just a trendy buzzword from management gurus, likely to be replaced by a new "theory x" or "theory y" next year? Or is it a word all academics need to learn, to safeguard themselves and their institutions from devastating harm? The *New York Times* reviewer of the major Italian film, *Mi piace lavorare – Mobbing* (2004), felt obliged to explain to his American readers, "*Mobbing* is a slang expression used in Italy for harassment in the workplace" (Deming 2005).

Far from being a slang expression, *mobbing* is the scientific term Leymann drew from the ethological studies of Nobel Laureate Konrad Lorenz (1967), to describe fanatic ganging up of managers and/or co-workers against a targeted worker, subjection of the target to a barrage of hostile communications, humiliations, threats, and tricks, toward the end of driving the target out of his or her job. Scholarly research on mobbing has burgeoned in Europe over the past quarter-century, lawmakers and journalists have picked up on it, and the English word *mobbing* has gradually been incorporated into most European languages, from Swedish and Finnish in the North to Spanish and Italian in the South. Ironically, it is only in recent years that research on mobbing, along with the word itself, has begun to be known in the English-speaking world.

Readers interested in conceptual discussion of mobbing and review of the existing research literature are referred to Leymann's original studies (1996, for example), to my earlier books and articles (1998, 2002, 2004, 2005a, 2005b), and to reports by other researchers (like Zapf 1999, Davenport *et al.* 1999, and Shallcross 2003). The present book conveys the substance of mobbing, what it is, as directly and explicitly as possible, by describing, comparing, and contrasting extreme examples of the phenomenon in two different institutions.

For grasping what a tornado *really* is, armchair studies of wind and weather patterns are important, but equally so is firsthand, on-the-ground inspection of neighborhoods where tornadoes have touched down. The present book takes the latter approach, focussing attention on archetypes of the phenomenon: recent, dramatic examples of academic mobbing at Medaille College in Buffalo, New York, and the University of Toronto, Ontario.

What makes these examples extreme? That tenured high-achievers on the faculty were ritually deemed corrupt, publicly discredited, dropped from the payroll, and formally dismissed, through impassioned collective attacks by administrators and colleagues – attacks that appear in retrospect to have been untruthful and wrong.

Not all mobbing cases reach the point of a full-blown *auto-da-fe*. Informal ostracization and harassment are often enough to send targets fleeing elsewhere, to wreck their health, or get rid of them in some other way. In some cases, the degradation ceremony by which the target is judged unfit to remain on campus occurs in the privacy of a dean's or vice-president's office, and the target goes quietly into early retirement or long-term disability. In other cases, the humiliation of being publicly accused and denounced drives the target to suicide, heart attack, stroke, or resignation, even before a court or tribunal finding of guilt. Only a minority of cases proceed to the point of formal, public dismissal – the academic ritual in our time that corresponds to obsolete harsher rituals like being pilloried, branded, burned at stake, hung, drawn, and quartered, defrocked or drummed out.

The cases chosen for analysis in this book are "textbook cases," extreme in the severity of institutional attack (though not in the effect on the targets; in other cases in my research, attacks of less severity have resulted in the death or permanent disability of the targeted professors).

Part One of this book concerns two bizarre cases that unfolded in tandem at Medaille College. The mobbing targets were Therese Warden, PhD in Sociology from SUNY Buffalo, a 15-year veteran of the faculty, tenured Associate Professor in the Department of Human Services, and Uhuru Watson, PhD in Political Science from SUNY Buffalo, a 22-year veteran of the faculty, tenured Associate Professor in the Department of Social Sciences. Acting President John Donohue formally dismissed Warden on February 8, 2002, and Watson on

April 26, 2002, the charge in both cases being turpitude. These dismissals were upheld by five-person, in-house grievance tribunals.

Part Two of this book concerns the most famous and complex dismissal case in Canadian academic history, that of Herbert Richardson, PhD in History and Philosophy of Religion from Harvard, tenured Professor of Religious Studies at St. Michael's College, University of Toronto, where he had taught since 1968. Toronto President Robert Prichard formally dismissed Richardson on July 9, 1993, and St. Michael's President Richard Alway followed suit on November 26, 1993. The charges were shifting and muddled, but came down at the end to dishonesty. The dismissal decision was upheld by a three-person grievance tribunal chaired by John Evans, a law professor who has since been named a judge, and was finalized on September 26, 1994.

Even by itself, each of the two parts of this book sheds light on academic mobbing, and can be read with profit separately. To gain more from this book, however, and acquire more insight into the common organizational pathology both parts illustrate, I urge readers to ponder and puzzle over the similarities and differences between the Medaille and Toronto cases. Here at the outset, this introduction can usefully highlight some of both.

*Similarities between these cases*

The numbered paragraphs below profile the Medaille and Toronto cases in terms of the checklist of sixteen mobbing indicators I formulated in 2001 for workshop presentations of my research in this area (the *"WAMI," Waterloo Anti-Mobbing Instruments*). These are the similarities (drawn in the first instance from the papers in Part One herein, and in the second instance from my 2005 book, *The Envy of Excellence*) that define the cases at these two institutions as classic examples of the general process:

1.   *By standard criteria of job performance, the target is at least average, probably above average.* Relative to colleagues in their respective institutions, Warden, Watson, and Richardson were high achievers. Warden had co-founded the AAUP chapter at Medaille, designed and administered several certificate programs, chaired her department, and been active in research. She was an acknowledged faculty leader. Watson was the first

African-American to have won tenure at Medaille. Richardson was and is among the major Protestant theologians of his generation. At the time of his dismissal, he had published more books and supervised more doctoral students than any other professor at St. Michael's, far more than the Toronto average.

2. *Rumours and gossip circulate about the target's misdeeds: "Did you hear what she did last week?"* Rumors swirled at Medaille in the months between Warden's and Watson's suspension in January of 2002, and finalizaton of their dismissals later that spring. At Toronto, Richardson had been the subject of malicious gossip for at least seven years prior to his final dismissal in 1994.

3. *The target is not invited to meetings or voted onto committees, is excluded or excludes self.* This indicator does not apply to the Medaille dismissals: Warden and Watson were active, involved members of the faculty up to the point of commencement of disciplinary action against them. This indicator applies to the Toronto dismissal in spades. Richardson had been marginalized in many ways at least since 1989, when he refused, as a Protestant theologian and Presbyterian minister, to sign a kind of loyalty oath to Catholic theology that the St. Michael's administration introduced and required of all professors.

4. *Collective focus on a critical incident that "shows what kind of man he really is."* The critical incident seized upon to justify going after Warden and Watson was their alleged breach of the confidentiality of a committee meeting held on June 8, 2001. The critical incident in Richardson's case was his alleged loss of temper in an evening class on October 30, 1991.

5. *Shared conviction that the target needs some kind of formal punishment, "to be taught a lesson."* Essential to mobbing is the perpetrators' insistence on making a federal case out of what they have considered a critical incident, treating it not as a mistake to be corrected, quirk to be tolerated, blip to be ignored, or disagreement to be worked out, but as something "too serious to be glossed over," a sign of bad character, therefore grounds for severe discipline. In both the Medaille and Toronto cases, the critical incidents identified in (4) were treated in this way.

6. *Unusual timing of the decision to punish, e. g., apart from the annual performance review.* As is usual in mobbing cases, the targets' alleged offenses at both Medaille and Toronto were

considered too grave to be folded into routine evaluative procedures, requiring instead exceptional, *ad hoc* administrative action. At Medaille, Dean Joseph Savarese commenced what he called a "lengthy investigation." At Toronto, Vice-Deans Craig Brown and Don Dewees investigated student complaints following Richardson's class of October 30, 1991; copies of the complaints were withheld from Richardson for eleven months.

7.  *Emotion-laden, defamatory rhetoric about the target in oral and written communications.* The Medaille cases provide an egregious example of this indicator: pronouncing Warden and Watson guilty of *turpitude* (which dictionaries define as inherent baseness of character, depravity, degeneracy, and immorality) for questioning the legitimacy of a committee meeting. A *Toronto Star* headline on the Richardson case read: "Professor flouted every rule, panel told." Overblown characterizations like these suggest hype and chicanery.

8.  *Formal expressions of collective negative sentiment toward the target, e. g. a vote of censure, signatures on a petition, a meeting to discuss what to do about the target.* Most of the academic mobbing cases I have studied showed some kind of groundswell of outrage against the mobbing target by students or colleagues, evidenced by a mass meeting or collective petition. The cases at Medaille and Toronto are exceptional in that the groundswell arose among administrators themselves. Savarese and Donohue at Medaille did not even pretend to be responding to faculty or student complaints against Warden and Watson. The Toronto administrators did present themselves initially as responding to widespread student dissatisfaction with Richardson, but there turned out to be little supporting evidence (three or four students out of hundreds). Once administrators attacked the targets, however, colleagues and students piled on. Five of Warden's and Watson's colleagues at Medaille signed their names to grievance decisions remarkable for their groundless invective. Two of Richardson's colleagues at St. Michael's did the same in his case, and student and public media in both Canada and the USA denounced Richardson enthusiastically.

9.  *High value on secrecy, confidentiality, and collegial solidarity among the mobbers.* In response to media inquiries about the dismissals, both Acting President Donohue at Medaille and

President Prichard at Toronto pled confidentiality and sought ratification of the dismissal decisions through internal, official channels shielded from public view – the standard administrative strategy (see Martin 2005). By contrast, Warden challenged the college's processes openly in appeals to AAUP and other faculty bodies. Over objections of the university's lawyers, Richardson won a decision that his dismissal proceeding should be public.

10. *Loss of diversity of argument, so that it becomes dangerous to "speak up for" or defend the target.* Chapter 2 herein reports how I personally witnessed the hostility to communications professor John Schedel at Medaille, when he publicly questioned the dismissals. Both there and at Toronto, most colleagues of the mobbing targets faded into the woodwork. It is hard to say to what extent the reason was apathy, and to what extent fear of being targeted themselves. The few who spoke out in the targets' defense found themselves shunned and sidelined.

11. *The adding up of the target's real or imagined venial sins to make a mortal sin that cries for action.* In these as in most mobbing cases, there was no single offense – like a plagiarized book, abandonment of classes, embezzlement or assault – serious enough to justify dismissal. It was therefore necessary to build a case: to impute to the mobbing targets nefarious motives for what the targets considered to be good deeds (like Watson's questioning of an improper committee decision or Richardson's founding of a publishing company), then to aggregate these good-deeds-turned-bad into a major offense. The construction of a menacing mountain out of benign molehills was especially striking in the Richardson case: he asked the father of one of his students to buy her a computer, took a medically authorized stress leave, failed to inform administrators properly of publishing activities they already knew about, and so on.

12. *The target is seen as personally abhorrent, with no redeeming qualities; stigmatizing, exclusionary labels are applied.* For assassination of character, few nouns serve as well as *turpitude,* the label placed on Warden and Watson at Medaille. Richardson was found guilty of "gross misconduct," an almost equally stigmatizing term. Following are some of the adjectives applied to Richardson in the decision on his dismissal: *potentially*

*exploitative, intolerable, unattractive, unprofessional, ludicrous, contemptuous, vulgar, volatile, dominating, flagrant.*

13. *Disregard of established procedures, as mobbers take matters into their own hands.* The AAUP report on the Medaille dismissals, reprinted in Part One of this book, details many procedural irregularities, notably that Warden's and Watson's trials before the grievance tribunal were held after rather than before they were dismissed. It was the same at Toronto: Richardson's trial began ten months after President Prichard had dismissed him. In the latter case, moreover, the tribunal lacked authority to overturn Prichard's decision. The most it could have done was keep Richardson at St. Michael's, but without an appointment to the university faculty.

14. *Resistance to independent, outside review of sanctions imposed on the target.* The Medaille administration rebuffed AAUP's inquiries into the dismissal, its president refusing even to meet with the investigators AAUP sent to Buffalo in January of 2003. In the Richardson case, the administration successfully prevented the introduction of many administrative documents into the dismissal hearing, arguing that they were privileged and confidential. When Richardson appealed the tribunal's decision to the Ontario Court of Justice, the university asked the court to deny the appeal and the court agreed, saying only a "patently unreasonable" decision by such a tribunal would deserve to be interfered with by the public judiciary.

15. *Outraged response to any appeals for outside help the target may make.* This indicator applies mainly to mobbings that arise first from students or professors, prior to official denunciation and punishment of the target by administrative authority. In such cases, expressions of outrage can neutralize counterpressures (like pleas from civil-liberties organizations or letters from colleagues elsewhere) in the target's defense. When, as at Medaille and Toronto, the administration takes the lead in punishing a target, or after the administration has been persuaded to impose such punishment, mobbers tend to hunker down in silence. The deed is done. The target is officially discredited. To make the eliminative decision stick, mobbers generally prefer not to hear or respond to dissenting voices.

16. *Mobbers' fear of violence from target, target's fear of violence from mobbers, or both.* The targets in these cases did not fear violence from the mobbers, but the mobbers apparently did from them. At the time of their suspension, Warden and Watson were both barred from coming onto campus, a provision allowed by college policy only if their presence on campus would constitute "an immediate physical or psychological danger." In the Toronto case, the two student complainants, according to Vice-Dean Dewees, claimed Richardson was dangerous and that they were physically afraid of him. Thankfully, no violence to persons occurred in either the Medaille or Toronto cases, though most of the contents of Warden's office were destroyed during the period when she was forbidden to set foot on campus.

From this long checklist of mobbing indicators, it becomes apparent that the similarity between the Medaille and Toronto cases extends far beyond the facts of administrative dismissal and tribunal ratification. Far from being mere terminations for cause, these were campus-based social movements with a specific and personal goal, the humiliation of the targeted professors and their social elimination from respectable company. In a word, these were cases of *mobbing,* or more precisely, *administrative mobbing.* The chapters of this book enlarge on this basic conceptualization.

*Differences between these cases*

While the Medaille and Toronto cases are alike in severity or extremity, they are different in many other ways. Indeed, it is the combination of abundant similarities and abundant differences that makes the comparative analysis of these cases so interesting, and so productive of insight into academic mobbing and the larger shape of politics in contemporary higher education.

The most noteworthy difference is in outcome.

The mobbing cases at Medaille are in that very small minority, among the hundred or so I have studied, that have been corrected. The correction is nearly full in the case of Uhuru Watson, who was reinstated to the Medaille faculty, with acceptable compensation, in June of 2004, a little over two years after being dismissed and dropped from the payroll. At about the same time, Medaille College reached with Therese Warden a settlement that, while not providing for her reinstatement, did award her a substantial sum of money. In a letter to AAUP a year later, on June 1, 2005, Medaille President Joseph Bascuas did not go so far as to apologize for what was done to these professors, but he clearly acknowledged the wrongness of their ouster:

> One year ago, the current administration of the College entered into just and mutually agreeable settlements with Drs. Watson and Warden. We did so to correct decisions that were made using (perhaps even misusing) the inadequate processes and procedures available at the time. I recommended those settlements because I had come to believe that Drs. Watson and Warden had not been afforded fair treatment and because to settle with them was the right thing to do.

The Toronto case, in striking contrast, has not been corrected, and no settlement or reconciliation has been reached between Richardson on the one hand, the Toronto and St. Michael's administrations on the other. As reported in my book on the case (2005a), the chief witness against Richardson in his dismissal hearing, a publisher named Robert West, who had also orchestrated much of the attack on Richardson, formally retracted his testimony in November of 2003. Several dozen commentators on my book have concluded from it that Richardson, as Bascuas might put it, "had not been afforded fair treatment." Yet unlike at Medaille, no correction has been made.

How can this big difference be accounted for? Without pretending to answer this question adequately, I can nonetheless suggest other important differences between the Medaille and Toronto cases that readers may keep in mind as they peruse the chapters of this book, toward piecing together an adequate explanation.

First, two significant differences between the mobbing targets:

- Warden is a woman and Watson is an African-American man. Both are thus in what are sometimes called "protected categories," segments of the population legally and culturally deemed to deserve preferential treatment on account of past discrimination. Richardson, by contrast, is a heterosexual white Christian male. I have analyzed elsewhere (1999) mobbing cases wherein biopolitics (the sex and race of the parties involved) has played a decisive role. If biopolitics played some role in all three of the dismissals showcased in the present book, as I believe it did, I am no less confident that biopolitics has played some role in the correction of two of them and noncorrection of the third.

- Warden, Watson, and Richardson fought back in different ways, in keeping with their respective values, temperaments, and resources. Sociologist Warden not only hired a lawyer but took the lead in appeals to the state and national AAUP and in mobilizing professors in greater Buffalo into a vibrant campaign for due process and shared governance in all the region's colleges – activism that has resulted in a new organization, COFAWNY, the Confederation of Faculty Associations of Western New York. Watson, in contrast, suffered deep personal wounds from being mobbed, and withdrew for long periods. Richardson, in further contrast, sought redress through official legal channels: courts in Ontario and New York.

Differences between the two institutions are undoubtedly also relevant for explaining not only the different outcomes but the contrasting ways in which the mobbings were carried out:

- The two schools are in vastly different academic leagues. Medaille is a small liberal-arts college (fewer than 100 faculty) in Tier 4 of the ranking by *US News & World Report*. Toronto placed among the top 30 universities of the world in the most recent ranking by the *Times Higher Education Supplement*. The incursions on Warden's and Watson's jobs were swift, direct, crude, and clumsy; the attack on Richardson's job was slow, circuitous, careful, and adroit.
- As one would expect in a small college, the governing board was involved in the dismissals at Medaille and their aftermath, while I have no evidence of board involvement in the Toronto case.
- Only two administrators at Medaille, the dean and acting president, were officially involved in dismissing Warden and Watson. More than a dozen administrators at St. Michael's and Toronto took part in dismissing Richardson.
- Acting President John Donohue left Medaille College a few months after dismissing Warden and Watson, and was replaced by a permanent president recruited from afar, Joseph Bascuas. All the senior administrators involved in dismissing Richardson remained in their positions for years afterward – Toronto President Prichard, for instance, until 2000. St. Michael's President Alway still headed the college in 2005.

- The rightist orthodoxy Donohue represented at Medaille (a perspective neither Warden nor Watson shared) weakened after Donohue's departure, while the Catholic orthodoxy Richardson ran afoul of at St. Michael's has endured to the present day.

Any explanation of the different outcomes of the two mobbing episodes would have to give significant weight to a crucial difference in the role of outside organizations. In the Medaille cases, the New York State branch of the AAUP came to Warden's and Watson's defense promptly and aggressively, and the national AAUP followed up with a reasonably thorough investigation, the report of which it publicized nationally in its journal, *Academe* (it is reprinted herein in Part One). AAUP then threatened to censure the college if reasonable settlements were not made with the two dismissed professors. In the Toronto case, in sharp contrast, the counterpart Canadian professors' organization, CAUT, sat on its hands. Its president was publicly quoted as saying Richardson's dismissal did not threaten the institution of tenure in Canadian universities. Nor was the Toronto faculty association of much help to Richardson. After President Prichard had formally dismissed Richardson from the Toronto faculty, the faculty association's lawyer wrote to the chair of the religious studies department, proposing that she resolve the matter informally.

A college or university, despite its commitment to seeking truth, is a political organization, and its administrators tend to tell the truth only in so far as political pressures allow and encourage it. Bascuas steadfastly rebuffed all interventions on Warden's and Watson's behalf by AAUP and others, including me, for almost two full years after he became Medaille's president in July of 2002. Why did he then, in the spring of 2004, decide that settling with them was "the right thing to do"? The answer, so the evidence suggests, is that AAUP had scheduled a vote on formal censure of the Medaille administration for its June, 2004, meeting. One suspects that Medaille's governing board had put Bascuas's own job on the line: if he could not avoid censure by the national professors' organization, the board would pull the plug on his presidency. Bascuas therefore came to terms. AAUP voted to delay censure until its next annual meeting on June 10-12, 2005, pending overhaul of the college's policies. Hence Bascuas's long, respectful letter of June 1, 2005, pleading that the dismissals had been rectified and that new policies would require a little more time.

It is an open question, of course, whether pressure from the local faculty association and CAUT might have prevented Richardson's dismissal at Toronto, or brought about its correction in the following years. A national professors' body can more easily intimidate a small college than a major university, and the latter has more resources with which to cajole and mollify outside pressure groups, and keep them off its back.

But all these similarities and differences between the Medaille and Toronto mobbings are offered cautiously, heuristically, with no attempt to arrange them into a conclusive explanation or theory. My purpose is only to help readers make good use of this book by weighing Parts One and Two against each other, gaining insight thereby into academic mobbing at a more general, abstract level, beyond the specific cases analyzed here.

## Research Methods for Practical Dialogue

The present volume is designed to illuminate not only what mobbing is but how to study it in a social scientific way. Two methodological priorities apparent in both Parts One and Two are worth pointing out in this introduction: reliance on the method of case study, and dissemination of research results in ways that encourage dialogue.

### The document-based case study

No method or procedure for researching mobbing should be ruled out, so long as it brings empirical data, the evidence of actual events, to bear systematically on relevant concepts and hypotheses. Heinz Leymann was appropriately eclectic and pluralist in his research strategies, which ranged from large-scale surveys to historical investigations to individual case studies. He designed a 45-item "Inventory of Psychological Terrorization" and had it administered via questionnaire to a national sample of 2,500 Swedish adults (1992), as well as to employees in specific companies. To estimate the percentage of suicides attributable to workplace mobbing (between 12 and 15 percent, he concluded; see 1987), he sent questionnaires to pastors in the diocese of Stockholm, reasoning that in the course of counselling bereaved survivors they would have learned the attendant circumstances of suicides. He administered a battery of medical and psychological tests to the first 64 patients in his rehabilitation center, Violen, for mobbed workers suffering post-traumatic stress disorder (see Leymann and Gustafsson 1996). He analyzed diaries of mobbing targets (see 1988). In a substantial book (1989), he sketched a theory of victimology broad enough to encompass not only mobbing targets but victims of rape, robbery, hostage-taking, war, and the Nazi camps. His last major book consisted of detailed case studies of three nurses who took their own lives after being mobbed at work (Leymann and Gustafsson 1998).

The present volume reflects my preference, in research on mobbing in academic workplaces, for the method of case study or case history: gathering as much relevant information as possible about as many instances of apparent academic mobbing as possible, then using this information to distinguish cases of mobbing from other forms of workplace dissension, and to arrive at generalizations about the origins, techniques, patterns and outcomes of mobbing episodes. My procedure has been similar to what Znaniecki (1934) and Lindesmith (1968) called "analytic induction": formulating hypotheses on the basis of the initial cases examined, then inspecting additional cases, revising the hypotheses to cover both the initial cases and the new ones, then enlarging the database further, reformulating the hypotheses yet again, and so on and on.

My procedure has been similar in some ways to what Leymann did in his clinic: he asked each research subject to tell or write an anamnesis, a complete recollection of events relevant to breakdown of his or her health. My focus, however, has been less clinical: not on breakdown of health (a common but by no means universal outcome of being mobbed), but on the antecedent condition that defines mobbing, naming social elimination from the workplace, whether evidenced by repeated illness, long-term disability, dismissal, forced retirement, voluntary withdrawal, suicide, or however else. What I have tried to gather in each mobbing case is all the evidence relevant to the eliminative fact. Further, in so far as possible, I have relied less on targets' memories of events than on letters, memos, reports, court decisions, transcripts, and other documents – evidence that is more reliable than targets' memories and that is usually abundant in academic cases, given the proliferation of written records in universities, as in other bureaucracies. This has meant a higher priority in my research on material facts – decisions taken, assessments made, meetings held, penalties imposed, appeals launched – than on the motives, feelings, attitudes, and other mental states of the people involved in a mobbing episode.

My research strategy has an important advantage over surveys of employees with Leymann's Inventory of Psychological Terrorization or similar instruments. When mobbing is measured by anonymous responses on a questionnaire, the researcher is unable to distinguish between genuine instances of self-reported mobbing and instances of respondents' misperceptions. An employee who is performing poorly may honestly report harassment, since he or she may well receive repeated unwanted negative communications from managers. Such an employee may also honestly report feelings of humiliation – the result of observing workmates' greater success and productivity. This employee may *feel* mobbed without *being* mobbed. The same goes for psychologically needy employees or those with chips on their shoulders, who may misperceive workmates' thoughtlessness or even their good deeds as signs of hostility. No good research purpose is served by lumping together the regrettable but inevitable stress felt by workers like these and the unwarranted stress felt by high achievers who are being wrongly driven from their jobs by the coordinated maneuvers of managers and/or colleagues. The method of case study, especially when informed by documentary evidence, makes it easier to distinguish authentic mobbings from fallacious ones, and it helps keep research on mobbing out of the mire of postmodern confusion between impressions and realities (for an example of harm done by an apparently false claim of being mobbed, see Martinez Jarreta *et al.* 2004). We will never understand this organizational pathology if we accept anybody's word for when it has or has not occurred; nobody's word is sufficient evidence.

To reinforce this point, I should emphasize that what led me to study at length the cases in this book was not the hurt feelings, anger and sadness of Therese Warden, Uhuru Watson, and Herbert Richardson, nor the symptoms of post-traumatic stress each of these professors exhibited to some degree. These were sequelae, not the key reality. What captured my interest was the *facts* and *circumstances* of these professors' elimination: ouster from their jobs and smearing of their names in ways that fit Leymann's, my own, and other researchers' prior definition of the concept of workplace mobbing.

A further advantage of the case study as method of research in this area is that it reveals and confronts the harsh fact in virtually all mobbing cases, that the perpetrators deny what is going on. I suspect that like most academics, the administrators who instigated the mobbings at Medaille and Toronto would agree that ganging up on a competent, hard-working professor and wrecking his or her career is a deplorable event. They would probably also agree that it nonetheless happens from time to time in universities, as people get carried away by group pressures and crowd mentalities. They might even support, following the example of many managers and legislators in Europe, the implementation of policies and laws against mobbing. But these same administrators would probably recoil with indignation from any suggestion that they themselves acted as mobbers when they effected the ouster of Warden and Watson, or Richardson. On the subject of mobbing, we academics are like judges and prosecuting attorneys on the subject of wrongful conviction: eager to condemn it in principle, but loath to admit having done it in any specific case.

Research on mobbing becomes interesting, as opposed to "purely academic," when researchers grapple with the complexities of real-life examples, identifying the target, perpetrators, chief eliminator, bystanders, rescuers, and other participants in specific cases, and detailing how these cases have played out. Again, Leymann's own research serves as an exemplar: so long as he wrote about mobbing in general terms, his work was well received, but when he identified specific cases at his clinic and in his publications, his work aroused intense opposition that led eventually to his clinic being closed. The method of case study or case history is not for Casper Milquetoasts. It is the single best method for bringing scholarly research in this area to bear on the actual conduct of life, toward the end of creating a more truthful and productive society.

### An engaged, pragmatist approach

A further aspect worth noting of this book's methodology is that none of the chapters herein was written in the first instance for specialists in research on mobbing, or as a "contribution to knowledge" in this specific field. My three papers in Part One on the

Medaille dismissals were directed first, as the accompanying letters demonstrate, to the college's trustees, administrators, faculty and students, the community in which the mobbings occurred, and secondarily to other interested parties. The AAUP report on Medaille, as also the six papers in Part Two on the Toronto dismissal, were written mainly for professors, but not in their roles as producers of specialized academic knowledge, instead as fellow citizens of the academy and of the wider society, people with not just an intellectual but a practical interest in higher education. In none of the chapters of this book will readers find a conception of an autonomous sphere of knowledge, separate from lived experience.

In its organization and substance, this book is rooted in the pragmatist tradition of scholarship set forth and exemplified by William James, John Dewey, Jane Addams, G. H. Mead, and many others, notably C. Wright Mills in a later generation. In this tradition, knowledge is understood as tied closely to action, at once shaping and being shaped by the historical conditions at hand. The object here is to develop the field of mobbing research not as an end in itself, much less as a set of formulas to be applied to or inflicted on colleges and universities for remedy and prevention of this pathology, instead as a practical dialogue back and forth between researchers in the field and our colleagues: the administrators and professors who share with us the common practical interest of making academic life worthy of public trust and students' tuition fees. The mobbing researcher is not understood here as a would-be surgeon of educational institutions, trained and eager to work *on* an anesthetized organizational patient for the sake of making it healthier. The better analogy is to a midwife, who does not impose her expertise on the patient but works *with* her patient in the furtherance of life, teaching and learning at the same time.

Dialogic research is a challenge when the subject is workplace mobbing, since the latter involves cessation of dialogue – or breakdown of communication, to use the common cliché. Conversation between mobbers and target is over. The time for talking and listening is past. The mobbers' objective is to eliminate the target, silence him or her, eject the target from respectable company with such finality that his or her claptrap will no longer be heard. On the subject of the target's elimination, dialogue ceases also among the mobbers themselves. No participant in the mob is free to comment on the target in normal human ways, with a mix of positive and negative remarks, agreements and disagreements. Once the mob has formed, all its members must parrot a refrain of unrestrained contempt for the target. Mobbing puts a chill on the normal give and take of human intercourse. It signals a breakdown of one of the basic, defining characterizations of a college or university: a place for conversation, mutual challenge, reciprocal learning, vigorous discussion and debate, a context for the meeting of minds.

Carrying out a dialogic case study of academic mobbing therefore involves attempting to resurrect dialogue, to get conversation going again, to restart the engine of reciprocal learning. Accordingly, the first audience to which the researcher offers a research report consists of participants in the mobbing itself and everybody else who has an interest in the outcome of the conflict. This in no way denies the importance of communicating research findings to one's peers in this area of research and seeking their critical feedback. It is only to insist that the subjects of the research, the administrators and professors involved in the rancorous conflict under investigation, are also the researcher's peers. Hence in my studies of both the Medaille and Toronto mobbings, I have made my research reports a kind of public intrusion of truthful analyses upon untruthful organizational processes. I have invited correction of mistakes and welcomed critical commentary, making no claim to have said anything definitive.

As described in the overviews with which Parts One and Two begin, my efforts to conduct the case studies in an open-ended, dialogic way have proceeded differently in the two contexts. I happened upon the mobbings at Medaille barely six months after Warden and Watson were dismissed, when the college community was still in very much of an uproar over them. A determined band of professors in the Buffalo area, with some AAUP support, was refusing to treat the dismissals as a *fait accompli*. Joining in that refusal, I offered successive reports of my research as evidence of the wrongness of the social eliminations that had occurred, and of the need to correct them. My first paper was published on the website created to publicize the wrongful dismissals. *New York Academe*, the magazine or newsletter of that state's branch of AAUP, printed all of one paper and parts of another. I myself sent copies of my papers to professors, administrators and trustees.

The Toronto case, by contrast, was not only far more complex but also four years in the past by the time I began to do research on it. It was seven years after Richardson was dismissed that I at last completed the comprehensive book (2005a) that details the course of his dismissal. By then, the case was cold, in the sense that controversy no longer surrounded its outcome: the academic community and the public had concluded years earlier that Richardson got what he deserved, and allowed his dismissal to recede in memory. In this context, very different from the one at Medaille, the Edwin Mellen Press nonetheless found it possible to publish my book in a creative, exceedingly fruitful, dialogic way. Part of the result is the papers in Part Two herein, along with my brief responses to each one.

The kind of social science this book represents is called by varied names: not just pragmatist or dialogic, but also action research, engaged or activist scholarship. It is not a matter of studying evidence at one's desk and then building an explanatory theory which may or may not be subsequently applied. It is a matter of building knowledge even from the start out of the interplay between thought and action, teaching and learning from the same activity, with the twin objectives of a fuller understanding of human social life, and a more civilized, reasoned way of living it.

## An Invitation

In sum, this book is a report of dialogue on mobbing in higher education. It is more than an exposition, through comparative case studies of dismissals at a little college and a big university, of what mobbing is and of a methodology for doing research on it. This book is also an invitation to all readers, regardless of what discipline they practice or institution they teach in, to join the dialogue and contribute in their respective ways to the conversation now underway. This book is not intended to be the "last word" on academic mobbing or anything else. It aims to raise as many questions as it answers, and to encourage readers to share their own experiences and insights toward making still more sense of academic mobbing, the better to prevent it from happening and to remedy cases that have already occurred.

The conclusion of this book is my paper on the Waterloo strategy for prevention of mobbing in universities. This paper offers the organizational measures suggested by the case studies herein and about a hundred more, for keeping our institutions free of this harmful, wasteful, destructive, and worst of all, untruthful pathology. Like all the papers in this book, the concluding one should be read not as a conclusive statement but above all for heuristic value.

# References

Davenport, Noa Zanolli, Ruth Distler Schwartz, and Gail Pursell Elliott, *Mobbing: Emotional Abuse in the American Workplace.* Ames, IA: New Society.

Deming, Mark, 2005. Review of *Mi Piace Lavorare – Mobbing,* in the *New York Times All Movie Guide,* available on the web.

Leymann, Heinz, 1987. "Suicide and Conditions at the Workplace," *Arbete, människa, miljö* 3, pp. 155-160. In Swedish, discussed in his "The Content and Development of Mobbing at Work," *European Journal of Work and Organizational Psychology* 5 (1996): 165-184.

Leymann, Heinz, 1988. *No Other Way Out.* Stockholm: Wahlström & Widstrand. In Swedish, English translation by Sue Baxter.

Leymann, Heinz, 1989. *När livet slår till.* Stockholm: Natur & Kultur. In Swedish, English translation by Sue Baxter.

Leymann, Heinz, 1990. "Mobbing and Psychological Terror at Workplaces," *Violence and Victims* 5: 119-126.

Leymann, Heinz, 1992. *Adult Mobbing at Swedish Workplaces: a Nationwide Study with 2,438 Interviews.* Stockholm: Trosa.

Leymann, Heinz, and Annelie Gustafsson, 1996. "Mobbing at Work and the Development of Post-traumatic Stress Disorders," *European Journal of Work and Organizational Psychology* 5: 251-75.

Leymann, Heinz, and Annelie Gustafsson, 1998. *The Suicide Factory: About Nurses' High Risks in the Labour Market.* English version, WHO and ILO, Geneva.

Lindesmith, Alfred, 1968. *Addiction and Opiates.* Chicago: Aldine.

Lorenz, Konrad, 1967. *On Aggression.* London: Methuen.

Martin, Brian, 2005. "The Richardson Dismissal as an Academic Boomerang," in *Essays in Response*, appendix to K. Westhues, *The Envy of Excellence* (Lewiston, NY: Edwin Mellen), pp. 70-83.

Martinez Jarreta, Begoña, Javier García-Campayo, Santiago Gascón, and Miguel Bolea, 2004. "Medico-legal implications of mobbing: A false accusation of psychological harassment at the workplace," *Forensic Science International* 2 (Dec.), Supplement, S17-18.

Shallcross, Linda, 2003. "The Workplace Mobbing Syndrome: Response and Prevention in the Public Sector," paper presented at the conference on workplace bullying. Brisbane, Queensland.

Westhues, Kenneth, 1998. *Eliminating Professors: a Guide to the Dismissal Process.* Lewiston, NY: Edwin Mellen.

Westhues, Kenneth, 1999. "A Test of the Biopolitics Hypothesis," *Sexuality and Culture* 3, pp. 69-99.

Westhues, Kenneth, 2001ff. *WAMI – The Waterloo Anti-Mobbing Instruments.* Handout for workshops and lectures, Waterloo, ON.

Westhues, Kenneth, 2002. "At the Mercy of the Mob," *Occupational Health and Safety Canada* 18 (December): 30-36.

Westhues, Kenneth, ed., 2004. *Workplace Mobbing in Academe: Reports from Twenty Universities.* Lewiston, NY: Edwin Mellen.

Westhues, Kenneth, 2005a. *The Envy of Excellence: Administrative Mobbing of High-Achieving Professors.* Lewiston, NY: Edwin Mellen. Includes ten essays in response. The preliminary edition in 2003 was entitled *Administrative Mobbing at the University of Toronto.* A trade edition in 2005, without the ten essays but with an introduction by Herbert Richardson, is entitled *The Pope versus the Professor: Benedict XVI and the Legitimation of Mobbing.*

Westhues, Kenneth, ed., 2005b. *Winning, Losing, Moving On: How Professionals Dean With Workplace Harassment and Mobbing.* Lewiston, NY: Edwin Mellen.

Zapf, Dieter, 1999. "Mobbing in Organisationen: Überblick zum Stand der Forschung," *Zeitschrift für Arbeits- und Organisationspsychologie* 43: 1-25.

Znaniecki, Florian, 1934. *The Method of Sociology.* New York: Farrar and Rinehart.

# Part One

# The Warden/Watson Dismissals

# at Medaille College

# Chapter One

# Overview: the Medaille Project

This part of the book consists of four papers on the mobbing of Therese Warden and Uhuru Watson at Medaille College: the three I wrote in 2002-2003, plus the report in 2004 by AAUP's Committee on Academic Freedom & Tenure. Sociologist Robert K. Moore of St. Joseph's University in Pennsylvania and historian Sandi Cooper of the College of Staten Island investigated the Medaille conflict for AAUP and wrote the initial draft of the report.

These papers are, in the main, self-explanatory. The first of my papers includes an account of how I learned of and got involved in the Medaille conflict on my visit to the college for a conference in September of 2002. Similarly, the AAUP Report describes that organization's involvement in the conflict between January of 2002, when Warden and Watson appealed to it for help, and the nationwide publication of its report two years later in *Academe*.

To make best use of these papers for developing a sociology of academic mobbing, readers may want to study them with three critical questions in mind: about the substance and method of my analysis, how my analysis differs from AAUP's, and how the larger political context impinged on the Medaille conflict.

## The Question of What I Said and Did

The first question is whether my three papers reflect a useful and legitimate way of practicing sociology. Should my first impulse have been to write up the Medaille conflict for a professional journal and send it out for peer review? Was my mixing of the roles of researcher and activist appropriate? If this is an acceptable way of conducting research on mobbing, why not also research on community power structures, adolescent subcultures, communications media, and other topics? My answers to these questions are implicit in what I did and how I did it. Most professors of sociology do not work this way. What should one make of this difference?

If my approach was legitimate, the next question is how I could have done a better job. What improvements in the content of my papers and in what I did with them might have hastened rectification of Warden's and Watson's dismissals? For these two decent and capable professors, there were eighteen long, depressing months of uncertainty between October of 2002, when my first paper was circulated, and May of 2004, when the college redressed the harm done to them. What kind of more insightful and adroit scholarly intervention on my part could have shortened this period?

From the moment I learned of the Medaille conflict (first from personal conversations, then from documents on the website of the New York AAUP), my first priority was to let the Medaille community know that their trouble had a name, that it fit a pattern, and that it had been studied scientifically. If you knew something about a rare and dread disease and then came across an agitated person in great pain who exhibits all the symptoms, your first thought would be inform the person that this syndrome has been scientifically identified and studied. Diagnosis is the first step toward cure. Hence my first paper. My motives were not all altruistic. I saw the Medaille conflict as a chance to learn. Besides, I was ashamed to have taken part in a college-sponsored conference on academic freedom that seemed to lend legitimacy to the recent wrongful dismissals. I felt a need to correct any false impression of where I stood on the matter.

The Medaille administration and board of trustees stonewalled my first paper, while Warden's and Watson's defenders welcomed it, inviting me to give a further paper at their conference, "The Crisis in Academic Freedom," the following March. I did so, seizing the opportunity to try to incite some kind of administrative response. But President Bascuas and the trustees stonewalled further. Hence my third paper that July, its further analysis tailored to the specific objective of goading the college's trustees into discussing the conflict. Again I received no response from those with authority to correct the mobbings, but word got back to me that my intrusions had outraged Bascuas. From this news I surmised that my work might be having the intended effect of reopening dialogue, fomenting discussion of the dismissals in the governing board to which he was responsible.

I do not know and will likely never learn to what extent, if any, my papers raised doubts among the trustees about the dismissals and led them to question Bascuas about them. There was turnover of more than half the trustees from 2002-03 to 2003-04. The reported chair-elect was among those who left the board. I promptly searched the web for the addresses of all the new boardmembers and wrote to each one, acquainting him or her with my research on the mobbings.

Did any of this make a difference in achieving or speeding the settlements made with Warden and Watson in 2004? I cannot say. I would like to think so, but conceivably, the only practical effects of my papers were to bolster Warden's and Watson's spirits and to encourage the AAUP in its actions on their behalf. Clearly, the threat of censure by the national AAUP was the decisive factor in forcing the college to face up to the wrongness of the dismissals and rectify them.

## My Analysis versus AAUP's

This leads to the second question readers can usefully ponder as they read these next four chapters: in what intellectual and practical ways did my analysis differ from AAUP's analysis?

In terms of adequacy of explanation, as my second paper suggests, the mobbing conceptualization seems to me to excel an analysis centered on violations of academic freedom. The latter is but one of the essential values of a college or university. Others are truthfulness, openness to evidence, respect for good work in teaching and research, fairness in evaluation, tolerance of others' viewpoints, and receptiveness to dialogue and debate. The attack on Warden and Watson flouted all these values, as mobbing usually does. What was at stake was not just tenured positions but good names and self-respect. Further, the events pointed to a kind of social contagion, the grievance tribunal's ugly echo of the dean's and acting president's sentiments, and collective passion to humiliate the two targets and crow over their defeat. For all these reasons, a diagnosis of mobbing is more precise and adequate, I argue, than a diagnosis of violation of academic freedom and tenure. Readers, of course, may disagree.

More specifically, perhaps because its conceptual frame has little room for the reality of eliminative lust, AAUP's analysis takes the accusations of wrongdoing by Warden and Watson, namely the alleged breach of confidentiality, more seriously than my papers do. The AAUP Report seems eager to concede any smidgen of possible truth in accusations that I summarily dismiss as drivel. In a further presentation in September of 2004 to the dissident professors in Buffalo (formally organized by then as the Coalition of Faculty Associations of Western New York), I juxtaposed on an overhead the concluding two sentences of the AAUP Report and the sentences I would like to have seen. AAUP's conclusion:

> In light of the available evidence, the charges against Professors Warden and Watson, even if sustained, were not of sufficient gravity to warrant dismissal and certainly did not justify taking the extreme action of dismissal without terminal salary on grounds of turpitude. Those actions were grossly disproportionate to the seriousness of the alleged offenses.

The conclusion I would have preferred:

> The charges against Professors Warden and Watson are false, unsupported by the available evidence. Even if the charges had been true, they would not have warranted dismissal. To assert that these professors are guilty of turpitude is so far from the truth as to suggest incompetence to serve on a college faculty.

The exuberance of the audience's response to this criticism of the AAUP Report astounded me.

Nonetheless, like that audience, I was grateful for AAUP's condemnation of the dismissals and for an analysis of the conflict that was empirically sound, even if limited. I happily made common cause with AAUP toward obtaining redress for Warden and Watson. When the *Buffalo News* ran a story on the college's near-censure by AAUP, I placed a follow-up letter in that newspaper, trying to ratchet up the pressure on Bascuas to set things right:

> The national body found Medaille College fully deserving of censure, one of just two institutions in the United States singled out for such disgrace this year. AAUP nonetheless

voted to defer this severest form of condemnation in Medaille's case until next year. The reason for deferral is that the college administration appears likely to resolve soon the two outstanding cases of wrongful dismissal of tenured professors, and to make revisions to its faculty handbook.

AAUP tries to serve the best interests of colleges and universities, and of the students who enroll in them. It is reluctant to torpedo an institution's reputation if its administration is actively trying to correct outrageous wrongs. AAUP decided to give Medaille President Joseph Bascuas one last chance. The college's friends should hope he seizes it. (June 28, 2004)

Any intellectual difference between my diagnosis of the Medaille conflict and AAUP's diagnosis pales, of course, beside the practical difference: that my words had to stand entirely on their own merits as the work of one sociologist from a foreign country, while AAUP's words were backed by the resources of a large, respected, national organization. Mobbing cases are no exception to the rule that the power of words depends mainly on who says them. It was AAUP's intervention, not mine, that was essential to the redress Warden and Watson obtained. Still, when words resonate closely with hearers' and readers' lived experience, that resonance by itself gives words power. I do not regret the energy I put into the Medaille project. I claim only a little credit for the outcome, but I take a lot of delight in it – despite Warden receiving only money instead of reinstatement, and despite the continuing grave problems in Medaille's administration. The college's reparation to Warden and Watson went farther than in 95 percent of the mobbing cases I have studied.

## Mobbing and the Culture War

The third and final question to keep in mind in this part of the book is how much the dynamics of the Medaille conflict reflected the larger culture war in today's America. Acting President John Donohue had a friendly relation with Stephen Balch, the founder and president of the National Association of Scholars, a powerful conservative organization that defends classic academic values against the postmodernism, relativism, and political correctness of the left. Balch was on the Medaille board of trustees. In that capacity he supported the direction in which Donohue would have taken the college had Donohue's candidacy for president been successful. Also in his capacity as a Medaille trustee, Balch arranged for the conference there on academic freedom in September of 2002, the event that struck me as a symbolic blessing of the wrongful dismissals – which Balch angrily defended against my and others' questioning. Of the other speakers at the conference whose support I enlisted for Warden's and Watson's defense, only one (historian Alan Kors, co-founder of the admirable Foundation for Individual Rights in Education, FIRE) showed any sympathy at all.

It would be a mistake, however, to generalize from the Medaille cases that academic mobbing is a rightist phenomenon. My first book on this subject, *Eliminating Professors* (1998), is mainly about professors mobbed by politically correct colleagues. The dozens of cases analyzed in *The Envy of Excellence* (2005) and *Workplace Mobbing in Academe* (2004) include some perpetrated by zealots on the right, others by zealots on the left, and still others by professors and administrators whose zealotry had a purely local focus. In the Toronto case analyzed in Part Two of this book, Herbert Richardson was attacked by a coalition composed of orthodox Catholics, secular postmoderns, and others unidentified with any political ideology.

Nor can one fairly conclude that Balch's National Association of Scholars condones mobbing. Like most political organizations, it condones only those mobbings that target people on the opposing side. Given how we clashed over the Medaille dismissals (Balch left its board the next year), I was glad to be allied with Balch in denouncing a string of dismissals at Virginia State University, where one of the main targets has been Jean Cobbs, a conservative female African-American sociologist (see Carey Stronach's analysis of these cases in *Workplace Mobbing in Academe*). I was honored to be introduced by Cobbs in October of 2004, for a talk in Charlottesville before the Virginia branch of the National Association of Scholars. In the VSU cases, moreover, AAUP has been on the same side as NAS: it formally censured the VSU administration in June of 2005.

One of the virtues of the mobbing research is that it cuts across political ideologies, recognizing the harm done by fanatic ganging up on a target, whether the perpetrators come from rightfield, leftfield, or any other field.

# Chapter Two

# The Initial Paper, October 2002:

# The Mobbings at Medaille College

Since mid-2001, an uncommon but severe organizational pathology has infected Medaille College, an institution serving 2,000 students in Buffalo, New York. Dozens, perhaps hundreds, of individuals at the college have been harmed. Two tenured senior professors, Therese Warden and Uhuru Watson, have all but lost their professional lives.

The harm is needless, serving no purpose but to weaken the college and jeopardize its future. The purpose of this paper is to identify, analyze, and explain, on the basis of publicly available documentation, the precise social ill that has laid the college low. Section 1 summarizes organizational research conducted and disseminated in Europe over the past two decades, but as yet little known in North America. Sections 2-4 apply the research to the Medaille evidence.

The trustees, alumni, administrators, faculty, staff, and students of Medaille are educated men and women with the best interests of the college at heart. Section 5 of this paper invites them all to apply this analysis critically and constructively toward restoring the college to organizational health, lest the lives of two professors be wrongly ruined, and lest a cloud of disgrace hang over the college's future for as long as it may survive. The workplace ill of which Medaille is a textbook case is not beyond remedy. The college may emerge from this episode with renewed vitality, proving true what Nietzsche said, that what doesn't kill you makes you stronger. So favorable an outcome is unlikely without reasoned, well-informed discussion in all of the college's constituencies.

Finally, Section 6 shows the larger significance of Medaille's troubles, by recounting the extraordinary circumstance in which I learned of them and undertook the investigation reported here.

## 1. Workplace Mobbing: the Concept

In the early 1980s, the late Swedish psychologist, Heinz Leymann, precisely identified and labeled the distinct workplace ill that occurred at Medaille College in 2001-02. He described it with an English word, *mobbing*, by which he meant "ganging up on someone," "psychic terror,"

> hostile and unethical communication, which is directed in a systematic way by one or a few individuals mainly towards one individual who, due to mobbing, is pushed into a helpless and defenceless position, being held there by means of continuing mobbing activities.... (1996, p. 168; see also 1990)

Leymann took the word *mobbing* from earlier research by ethologist Konrad Lorenz, who had documented "ganging up" among birds. This phenomenon is routine, for instance, in broods of chickens, where a "pecking order" is readily observable. The bird at the bottom commonly dies from the cumulative effect of being shunned, kept from food and water, and physically pecked by the rest.

A similar phenomenon among human adolescents, usually called *swarming* or *collective bullying*, is regularly in the news. Sometimes gradually over many months, sometimes suddenly, teenagers coalesce into a mob that torments, tortures, humiliates, sometimes even murders, one of their number.

Leymann's contribution was to document and study the same phenomenon among adults, even in highly professionalized, rule-bound, ostensibly civilized workplaces. The tactics differ. Workplace mobbing is normally carried out politely and nonviolently. The participants are so convinced of the rightness of their exclusionary campaign that they usually leave ample written records, proudly signing their names to extreme deprecations and defamations, without noticing how thin or nonexistent is the supporting evidence. The object of the process is the same as among chickens or teenagers: crushing the target's identity and eliminating him or her totally from respectable company.

By most researchers' estimates, between two and five percent of adults are mobbed sometime during their working lives. A Swedish study found that about twelve percent of people who commit suicide have recently been mobbed at work (Leymann 1987).

While original in its precision and elaboration, Leymann's discovery echoed time-honored insights into human nature. Asked to comment on the anticommunist witch hunts of the McCarthy era, Harry Truman said:

> You read your history and you'll see that from time to time people in every country have seemed to lose their good sense, got hysterical, and got off the beam. I don't know what gets into people. (in Miller 1973, p. 447)

A century earlier, in *The House of Seven Gables*, Nathaniel Hawthorne drew this lesson from the execution by hanging of a man innocent of crime:

> that the influential classes, and those who take upon themselves to be leaders of the people, are fully liable to all the passionate error that has ever characterized the maddest mob. (1851, ch. 12)

Awareness that fair-minded, reasonable adults sometimes "lose their heads" and wrongly mob a fellow human is older still. René Girard of Stanford University has devoted much of his life to studying the impulse to scapegoat in ancient myths. He calls it the "persecutory unconscious." Girard argues that the Judaeo-Christian myths were unique in calling the urge to scapegoat wrong and in asserting individual dignity in the face of collective persecution, thereby laying the legal and cultural foundation for human rights in Western civilization (see 1986, 2001).

My own research over the past decade (see 1998, 2001; see also Davenport *et al.* 1999, Mathias 2000) has applied Leymann's concept of *workplace mobbing* to academe. I have analyzed by now about a hundred cases in North America, Europe, and Australia, of this hugely destructive snowballing contagion among administrators and professors in colleges and universities. The process runs its course in much the same way as Leymann found in nonacademic settings: first informal ostracization and petty harassment, then some real or imagined incident that is seized upon to justify stigmatization and formal sanctions, leading to termination of the target's academic life, sometimes through formal dismissal (as in the Medaille cases), sometimes through forced retirement, suicide, mental breakdown, or stress-induced cardiovascular disease.

For grasping the mind-boggling character, so bizarre as to be almost comical, of mobbing in the academic workplace, I recommend not only the scholarly literature cited above but also three recent novels. In *The Human Stain* (2000), Philip Roth spins the compelling story of a college ex-dean run out of his job on trumped-up charges of racism. In *Blue Angel* (2000), Francine Prose describes with marvelous humor a spirited campaign to oust an English professor for sexual harassment. In *Never Fade Away* (2002), William Hart recounts how and why an ESL instructor who cared too much for his students gets the boot. Also recommended is *The First Stone* (1997), novelist Helen Garner's nonfiction account of the forced departure of a college master at the University of Melbourne, Australia.

## 2. Workplace Mobbing at Medaille

On February 8, 2002, John Donohue, acting president of Medaille College, formally dismissed from the faculty Therese Warden, professor of human services, on grounds of turpitude, a term whose meaning (to quote my dictionary) is "shameful character; baseness; wickedness."

On April 26, 2002, on almost identical grounds, Donohue dismissed Uhuru Watson, associate professor of social sciences.

From a narrowly legal viewpoint, the key fact in both cases was termination of employment. From the viewpoint of mobbing research, the key fact was not just termination but the stated grounds for it: corrupt personal identity. Warden and Watson were not just dropped from the payroll. They were officially designated as shameful, wicked human beings. Dangerous ones, too, since earlier they had both been suspended with pay and forbidden to come on campus, a penalty allowed by the Medaille College *Faculty Handbook* only if the professor's "continuance directly constitutes an immediate physical or psychological danger...."

A hallmark of workplace mobbing is the personal degradation of the target, the placing upon his or her deepest self the stigma of despicability. This rarely occurs in cases of firing for demonstrated cause. A president has no need to wound personally a professor who has embezzled college funds or failed for weeks to show up for class. The offense is clear. So is the penalty. Invective and disparagement are clues that a clear offense may not be in evidence.

In Warden's and Watson's cases, formal vilification did not stop with Donohue's letters. In the interval between suspension and termination, both professors sought redress in accordance with the *Faculty Handbook*, by appealing to the college's five-member Grievance Committee.

Its decision in Warden's case came on May 21, 2002, three months after she had been dismissed. The committee brushed aside her distress at being accused of turpitude:

> While the committee would like to delve into the definition of turpitude, unfortunately, it is not within the purview of the Grievance Committee since it is limited to matters of procedure by *The Handbook*.

The committee agreed with Warden that she should not have been suspended, and went on to justify the terminal penalty that had replaced the suspension with pay:

> Additionally, the options available to the administration in cases of turpitude are to either ignore the violation or to terminate the faculty member.
>
> *Recommendation*: While we find in favor of Dr. Warden regarding this issue, the fact that the College has dismissed her renders a recommendation moot.

The committee not only dismissed Warden's claim of unprofessional treatment, but rubbed in the stigma already imposed by the acting president:

> As her colleagues, the Grievance Committee is extremely dissatisfied with the behavior of Dr. Therese Warden in regard to the events from which these grievances are derived as well as her actions since the time of her dismissal which we believe have brought discredit to us all.

Finally, after some paragraphs of praise for tenure, shared governance, due process, professionalism, democracy, freedom, the pursuit of truth, and other high ideals, the committee recommended rituals of groveling and humiliation as a possible alternative to dismissal:

> The Acting President can reinstate Dr. Therese Warden, but only upon the mutual agreement of the parties that the following conditions precedent be met:
>
> The parties agree to a written letter of censure by the Grievance Committee to be placed in Dr. Warden's personnel file.
>
> Dr. Warden is prohibited from serving on any confidential committees for five years.
>
> The Promotion and Tenure Committee conduct an annual review for three years of Dr. Warden, which include the area of collegiality especially as it relates to new faculty.
>
> Finally, that Dr. Warden write a letter of apology to the Medaille College community that will be read at a faculty meeting.

More starkly even than Donohue's letters, the Grievance Committee's decision attests the stupendous social force that had been unleashed at Medaille: fanatic resolve to break a professor's professional back, to crush her under collective weight. Coerced public confession has long been outlawed in Western jurisprudence, yet the Committee would coerce from Warden a public apology, a statement of confession plus remorse, if Donohue should deign to receive it.

The Grievance Committee's decision in Warden's case deserves to be read in its entirety. Except for those caught up in Medaille's pathology, readers cannot help but be aghast at the contradiction of which the committee seemed oblivious, between the high ideals espoused and the low conclusions reached.

The same goes for the committee's shorter, three-page report one month earlier, on April 22, 2002, in Watson's case. Watson was at that point only suspended, not yet terminated. The committee judged that suspension was contrary to the *Faculty Handbook*: "The options available to the administration in cases like this are to either ignore the violation or to terminate the faculty member."

In its conclusion, the committee recommended that "the Acting President shall pursue one of the two options described in the Handbook (and as noted above) for cases of this nature," but then immediately contradicted itself by recommending a different alternative to termination: not to ignore the violation but to enforce rituals of humiliation:

Dr. Watson will:

Acknowledge as true, in a manner to be determined in consultation with the Acting President, the facts of the investigation conducted by the Acting Academic Dean;

Authorize the full disclosure of the Grievance Committee's facts and findings regarding the unauthorized distribution of confidential minutes of the Promotion and Tenure Committee at a full faculty meeting.

Apologize in private to the Acting Academic Dean and the Acting President for his conduct during the investigation.

Withdraw any present lawsuits and do not initiate future lawsuits with regard to these matters.

The first of these items, that Watson should be required to "acknowledge as true" ideas with which he obviously disagreed, is especially extreme in a workplace founded upon intellectual freedom. It is an explicit effort at mind control, recalling the voice of tyranny in Orwell's *Nineteen Eighty-Four*:

You are here because you have failed in humility, in self-discipline. You would not make the act of submission which is the price of sanity. You preferred to be a lunatic, a minority of one. Only the disciplined mind can see reality....

(1990, p. 261; first published 1949)

The Grievance Committee's reports in Warden's and Watson's cases highlight a key defining attribute of workplace mobbing, one that distinguishes this pathology from the related and better known pathology of bullying (see Namie & Namie 2000). In the latter, the target is up against a single domineering workmate or manager. In the Medaille cases, although Donohue was the dominant figure, Warden and Watson faced a united front of Donohue and his subordinates: Joseph Savarese, the acting dean who had recommended the dismissals to Donohue in a memorandum of December 10, 2001, the five-member Grievance Committee that joined the eliminative campaign a few months later, plus all those other administrators, professors, trustees, students, and secretaries who gossiped behind the scenes and stood idly by as the campaign progressed. The technical term for the latter is *bystanders*. The peculiarly devastating quality of workplace mobbing consists in the appearance of unanimity, that "everybody who counts knows you are rotten and wants you out of here." As the Grievance Committee declared in the final sentence of its decision on Watson: "These recommendations are offered with the unanimous approval of the Grievance Committee members."

For understanding workplace mobbing, a talmudic principle often quoted by the late French philosopher, Emmanuel Lévinas, is apt: "If everyone is in agreement to condemn someone accused, release him for he must be innocent" (quoted in Girard 2001, p. 118).

## 3. The Course of Events

That so many capable scholars could have been caught up in an irrational movement for inflicting permanent harm on two innocent professors is a hard idea to contemplate, so great is our respect for institutions of higher learning as temples of reason and sobriety. Surely Warden and Watson must have done *something* wrong.

In these as in most mobbing cases, elimination was officially rationalized by reference to a critical incident, an alleged instance of grave misconduct ordinarily involving violation of written policies and procedures. To the outside observer of the Medaille conflict, however, the clearest violation was committed not by Warden, Watson, or any other of the punished professors, but earlier, by acting dean Savarese and acting president Donohue.

On June 8, 2001, these two senior administrators convened the college's Promotion and Tenure Committee for the purpose of securing its support for ousting Michael Lillis from his position as chair of business. Savarese presided at the meeting. Attending as a guest, Donohue sought and obtained the committee's support for his determination that Lillis should be replaced.

This meeting violated college procedure and academic custom, since the issue it dealt with was not promotion of anyone to higher rank nor the award of tenure to anyone. Lillis's position as a tenured associate professor was not at issue. The issue was whether he should hold, in addition to his faculty position, the administrative position of department chair. This issue fell outside the committee's mandate. Procedures for appointment of department chairs, as set down in the *Faculty Handbook*, assigned no role whatsoever to the Promotion and Tenure Committee.

As one of the five members of this committee, Uhuru Watson noticed the violation of procedure. He was concerned in particular that Lillis had been the subject of negative comments at the meeting without having opportunity to respond – a standard requirement of the rules of natural justice. In the weeks that followed, Watson registered his concerns with Saverese, other committee members, and the Medaille College Faculty Council.

Thereby Watson acted in a way that is probably the statistically most common root of workplace mobbing: he exposed the wrongness of a decision made by his administrative superiors. He showed them up, implicitly put them to shame (see Wyatt and Hare 1997). They retaliated in kind by shaming Watson, accusing him of having violated the confidentiality of the disputed meeting, and judging this offense to warrant his being humiliated and fired. In colloquial terms, they "went after" him.

In October, 2001, a copy of the minutes of the disputed committee meeting of the previous June 8, appeared in the mailbox of Therese Warden, co-president of the Medaille chapter of the American Association of University Professors (AAUP), well-known on the campus as a high achiever and nonpartisan advocate of due process. The documentation does not indicate who placed the minutes there. Savarese later claimed it was Watson, and on this basis recommended his dismissal, though Watson did not admit to the charge.

Puzzled by the document and its mysterious arrival in her mailbox, Warden reported the matter to Savarese, who advised her to contact Donohue about it, which she did. She also gave copies of the document to Randy Brown, her co-president of the Medaille AAUP, and to mathematics/science professor Elizabeth Lucyszyn, a member of the Faculty Council. Savarese soon asked all three professors – Warden, Brown, and Lucyszyn – to return their copies of the minutes to him, which they did.

Then, however, Savarese and Donohue "went after" Warden, Brown, and Lucyszyn for the "egregious unethical behavior" of briefly possessing a document that, although not labeled confidential, could be considered so. Savarese recommended, and Donohue concurred, that Warden should be dismissed altogether for passing the document to Brown and Lucyszyn, that Brown (a junior, untenured professor) should be censured and his contract not be renewed, and that Lucyszyn should be censured and removed from her position as chair of the mathematics/science department.

If there were more evidence than that just described of misconduct on the part of Watson, Warden, and the others who were punished, it would be my scholarly duty to report it, but I have found none. The plain fact is that the administrators had no case. In civil proceedings, it could be called a *nonsuit*, or in criminal proceedings, *false arrest*. On the other hand, the evidence seems clear that Savarese and Donohue convened the Promotion and Tenure Committee for a purpose outside its jurisdiction, and that Watson and Warden sought to rectify this policy violation through appropriate channels of college governance. Savarese and Donohue displayed poor administrative skills in convening the Promotion and Tenure Committee meeting of June 8, but nobody involved in the conflict over it committed any grave ethical offense or deserved any kind of punishment.

The conclusion that the two seasoned admnistrators, Savarese and Donohue, in Truman's words, "lost their good sense" on this occasion, is reinforced by a glance at Watson's and Warden's decade-long records of successful work at Medaille. Watson enjoyed such high collegial regard as to have been elected not just to the Promotion and Tenure Committee but to the presidential search committee then underway.

For her part, Warden co-founded the AAUP chapter at Medaille in 1993. As chair of her department since 1995, she had developed successful new certificate programs. On her return from a sabbatical leave during the fall of 2000, Medaille had celebrated her innovative work in community mental health with a lengthy faculty profile and photo in its newspaper, *Horizon* (spring 2001).

## 4. Origin of the Medaille Pathology

Because the documentation reviewed for this analysis begins only in 2001, I lack data on the mobbings' informal stages that probably began years earlier. Watson has spoken publicly of an institutional culture of intimidation. If his and Warden's cases follow the pattern of others in my research, a study of social relations at the college in the 1990s would reveal professional jealousies, factional rivalries, and nefarious coalitions that led to the purge of 2002.

One cardinal fact stands out, however, as weakening the college's immunity to severe pathology: the death in February of 2001, of Kevin Sullivan, Medaille's president for the previous fourteen years, and chair of its board of trustees for seven years before that. In no period of an organization's history is good order more likely to break down than in the interval between sudden loss of a longstanding leader and appointment of a new one. That was precisely the period Medaille found itself in when Watson and Warden were mobbed.

A week after Sullivan's death, Medaille's board appointed Donohue, an accomplished anthropologist then serving as Medaille's vice-president and dean, as acting president, and began a national search for Sullivan's successor. Donohue in turn appointed Savarese, the chair of veterinary technology, as acting dean.

Donohue wanted the Medaille presidency for the longer term. The search committee welcomed his candidacy and included him among the twelve semifinalists selected in December of 2001, then among the three finalists announced in February of 2002.

Donohue must have known his success in the competition depended utterly on his managing the campus well as interim president. He needed to "keep the lid on," keep things under control, not let the college's affairs "go up for grabs" – these being the baseline expectations of any college board.

One can also plausibly assume that when Watson challenged his way of dealing with Lillis's administrative appointment, Donohue felt a greater need than he might otherwise have felt to "come down hard" and "show who is boss." His own vulnerability, one suspects, led to rash, unwarranted incursions on professors' jobs.

Such an explanation of how the college caught the mobbing bug is admittedly speculative, and could only be confirmed by personal interviews with those involved, but such, at least, is the direction in which the documentary evidence points.

On February 19, 2002, as Donohue was preparing for his formal interview for the presidency, a reporter from the *Buffalo News* phoned him for his side of the story of Warden's dismissal, Watson's suspension, and Brown's and Lucyszyn's penalties. Mobbing targets often go public and appeal for outside help; it is their only recourse against the circled wagons of their own institution.

Predictably, Donohue was not pleased. Workplace mobbing is more likely to succeed under cover of secrecy and confidentiality. In a memo to the college community that same day, he said he told the reporter

> the matter in question is an internal personnel issue that is, by nature, confidential. I am not at liberty to discuss it. I noted that Medaille College prides itself on its equitable and appropriate treatment of all its employees.

Donohue wrote in conclusion:

> It's unfortunate that some individuals felt the need to publicize an internal disagreement of this type before letting the processes we have established for review take place. While I am sure that there are people who feel very strongly on either side of the issue, I am equally sure that the procedures and processes in place at the College apply to us all.
>
> Finally, at a time when so many positive things are happening at the College, it's a shame that a few individuals have generated this type of publicity. In their zeal to act, they have hurt us all.

The story in *Buffalo News* appeared on February 20, 2002, and a longer report in *The Chronicle of Higher Education* came out on March 7. Neither article editorialized. Both were factual and clear. Thereby they exposed to the college's two main social environments, its home city and the national academic community, how far out of hand things had gotten in the year since Sullivan's death.

Soon thereafter, the Board of Trustees announced the appointment of Joseph Bascuas, a vice-president of the Argosy Education Group, as Medaille's next president. He took office in July, 2002. Donohue was named vice-president for special programs, but his name no longer appears on the college website.

## 5. What Will Happen Next

Responding to a series of pleas from Jonathan Knight, Associate Secretary of AAUP, Bascuas said in early August that he was reviewing Warden's and Watson's dismissals. That review is apparently ongoing as of October 2002, since no results have been announced.

According to research on how mobbings in general play out, the statistically most probable action Bascuas will take is none at all. He may remain silent or issue a do-nothing statement about moving ahead and letting bygones be bygones.

Leymann reported "that we have never found a single case where the employer, as the other party, could find himself at fault and give the employee some redress for wrongs suffered" (1990, p. 124). Similarly, John Polya wrote as follows about academic mobbings in Australia:

> One of the most frightening observations in several cases is how new staff and new administrators, not involved in the original witch hunt, join to defend the old errors and injustices. The only explanation for such behavior is that the pressures on certain academics, or perhaps their basic psychodynamics, demand a release of tensions on a convenient scapegoat; it may also be that, by showing a willingness to victimise a scapegoat, they ingratiate themselves with local power elites. (1986, pp. 48f)

When a college or university has officially imprinted on a professor the stigma of turpitude and drummed the person out, it commonly displays extreme reluctance to reverse itself and admit a mistake – even, as Polya pointed out, after leadership has passed to newcomers. It is often as if a new leader contracts on arrival the strain of mobbing virus that has infected the campus, and transmits it further instead of healing it.

Donohue may be gone from the Medaille campus, but those who joined with him in mobbing Warden, Watson, and the others are still there. Subtly or explicitly, most of them can be expected to urge Bascuas not to "reopen old wounds" but to turn his attention to new projects.

In fact, the wounds are fresh, raw, and festering. If Bascuas digs in his heels behind wrong decisions made before he arrived, he will then have to mount an expensive defense against Warden's and Watson's legal claims. Court proceedings may drag on for five or more years. By American labor law, no court is likely to order Warden's or Watson's reinstatement to the faculty, but an award of financial compensation could put a large dent in the college's resources.

Meanwhile, AAUP is likely to shame the institution, publishing Medaille's name worldwide on the list of colleges and universities under formal censure. Public-affairs journalists may shame the college further with exposés on TV and in the press. Medaille's position as a private college in a harshly competitive institutional environment will probably become more precarious than it is now.

In the meanwhile, the fight to regain their positions and good names will consume the time, energy, money, and possibly the health, of Warden and Watson. They will feel intense stress, not just from bearing institutional stigma but from knowing how much the prospects of getting it legally lifted depend on lawyers' procedural maneuvers and on other vagaries of the justice system. If they win monetary damages in the end, they will not likely see much actual money, on account of their own legal expenses. In any case, as many mobbing targets before them have observed, money cannot compensate for the loss of years of productive life.

In this internecine but statistically probable scenario, nobody wins, no matter what verdict is ultimately handed down or what out-of-court settlement is eventually reached.. All parties, even the lawyers, will in the end feel sick over the waste of resources that could otherwise have gone toward producing knowledge and educating youth – by Warden, Watson, Bascuas, and the college itself.

Even if probable, so destructive a scenario is not inevitable. Several cases reported in my book (1998, pp. 165-170) illustrate the more constructive outcome that may occur also at Medaille, if the leaders of its various constituencies act promptly toward correcting past mistakes and toward making the college whole again.

Neither Leymann nor I have done research on workplace mobbing as a mere academic exercise, but instead with confidence that once managers and workers are informed of it, once we all face up to and understand how wrongly we sometimes behave at work, we thereby become able to prevent and remedy the resultant harm. The present paper provides the information and understanding for the mobbing cases at Medaille College. It can thus be an instrument for restoring the college to health.

What is needed at Medaille now is open, free, blunt, honest, well-informed discussion among all those who care about the school and share an interest in its survival and success: administrators, trustees, faculty, alumni, staff, students, as well as AAUP officials and colleagues in neighboring institutions. Warden and Watson should be invited back on campus to join in the discussion, out of which a solution will emerge that is fair to all sides and serves the college well. The forgiveness, reconciliation, and hope that have been achieved elsewhere are possible at Medaille College, if only people risk exchanging reasoned views.

The initiative should not be left to Bascuas alone. As an administratively skilled outsider, new to the office of president, his role is above all to listen to the varied voices raised, then to draw the discussion to a constructive conclusion. No friend of the college should deprive Bascuas of honest input, lest his presidency be doomed to failure at the start.

The outcome of the mobbings at Medaille will be a test of Bascuas's administrative skills, as it will also be a test of Leymann's and my confidence that an understanding of mobbing enables its prevention and remedy.

## 6. Origin of this Analysis

The outcome will be a test of yet something else: whether the National Association of Scholars (NAS) stands for the classic goals of liberal education or merely for a right-wing agenda just as oppressive as the leftist orthodoxies NAS was founded to oppose. This is the larger significance of the Medaille conflict, as the story of how and why I got involved makes clear.

The analysis set down in this paper began with a question asked by a member of the audience on Friday evening, September 20, 2002, at the opening session of a conference at Medaille College on "Academic Freedom and Intellectual Pluralism: U.S. and Canadian Perspectives." I was in the audience, too. It was my first time on the Medaille campus. I was there to present a paper the next day in memory of Richard Henshel, a sociology professor at the University of Western Ontario who died in 1997.

Henshel had left most of his estate to NAS. I, along with the others to whom Henshel had entrusted execution of his will, had proposed to Stephen Balch, founder and president of NAS, that part of the bequest be spent on an academic conference in Henshel's memory. Balch had graciously agreed, and arranged for the conference to be held at Medaille, where he holds a seat on the Board of Trustees. Now at last, the conference was underway.

The program for the event was remarkable for having brought together the leaders of four major campaigns against political correctness and postmodern fanaticism in higher education. Alan C.

Kors, co-author of *The Shadow University* and co-president of the Foundation for Individual Rights in Education (FIRE), had just given the opening address, "The Betrayal of Liberty and Dignity on America's Campuses." Balch had introduced him.

In the audience was Clive Seligman, president of the Society for Academic Freedom and Scholarship (SAFS), the Canadian counterpart to NAS, who would speak the next day on "The Diversity Debate at Canadian Universities." Other prominent opponents of political correctness were also present: conservative philosopher Barry Smith of SUNY Buffalo (the conference organizer), SUNY trustee Candace de Russy, libertarian economist Walter Block of Loyola, New Orleans, and Stanley Rothman of Smith College, chair of NAS's board of advisors.

The most famous of the conference speakers had not yet arrived: neocon provocateur David Horowitz, president of the Center for the Study of Popular Culture (CSPC), who caused a stir in 2001 with paid ads against slavery reparations in the few campus newspapers willing to accept the ads. Horowitz's panel presentation the next day was entitled, "Universities as a Political Base for the Anti-American Left."

It was when the floor was opened for discussion after Kors's talk that John Schedel, a communications professor at Medaille, asked the question to which this paper is in some respects a response. I could tell Schedel was angry but also scared, in the way that one about to ask an embarrassing question often is.

In light of what Kors had just said about liberty and free speech, Schedel asked, what was Kors's opinion about the purge of tenured faculty last spring at this very college? Murmurs of "no" and "be quiet" traveled the assembly as Schedel spoke, but calmly and respectfully, he made his point.

"I don't know about these cases," Kors replied from the podium.

Balch rose quickly to his feet. He said he could not speak officially for the Board of Trustees, but that he knew these cases were not about academic freedom, instead the professors' violation of confidentiality.

Schedel sat down, and discussion turned to generalities.

Weeks earlier, I had seen the article about Medaille in the *Chronicle of Higher Education*: "Actions Against 4 Professors at Medaille College Raise Concern Over Academic Freedom." That was all I knew. Later that balmy night, on the steps of the administration building, Schedel began to fill me in. He described himself as a conservative, a scholar 180 degrees opposite to Warden and Watson on many issues, but nonetheless convinced that they in no way deserved the loss of their jobs and good names.

The more details Schedel gave me, and the more documents I read in subsequent weeks, the more troubled I became about the conference and my part in it. Why was a celebration of academic freedom being held at a college whose administration had just a few months earlier breached academic freedom so flagrantly? Why, when Schedel asked precisely the question that most needed to be asked, did Balch so quickly leap to defend the dismissals? Might the practical effect of our conference be to legitimate the recent mobbings? Might it be an instance of Newspeak, wherein freedom means slavery and ignorance means strength (Orwell 1990, p. 29)?

Two discoveries as I proceeded with research heightened my concerns. One was that ours was actually the second Medaille conference on academic freedom held in 2002. The first one, which I have watched on videotape, was sponsored by the AAUP on February 22. That conference had held the dismissals up to reasoned, critical scrutiny, in light of the standard values of academic and civilized life. Warden and Watson were on hand and allowed to speak. The practical thrust was toward constructive resolution of the conflict. That first conference was originally scheduled to be held in the Alumni Room of the Main Building of Medaille College, but was then apparently forced to move off campus, to nearby Daemen College.

The second worrisome discovery was Balch's column in the *NAS Update* of Winter, 2001-02. It was entitled "Let's Roll" – the famous phrase of the heroic passengers on United Airlines Flight 93 on September 11, 2001, who mobbed terrorist hijackers in a circumstance where mobbing was fully justified. Balch seemed in that column to call for similar aggressive action on American campuses. "If the intellectual climate of the more politicized domains of scholarship is ever to change," he wrote, "the sorts of people inhabiting them must change as well." Might the Medaille administrators have taken their cue from Balch's rhetoric? Might the panic that followed the September 11 attacks help explain how these administrators mistook two decent professors for wicked, dangerous undesirables who should be sacked?

I have no firm answers to these questions. NAS, FIRE, SAFS, and CSPC have earned my admiration and respect as needed counterweights to the forces of political correctness on American and Canadian campuses. Many if not most of the academic mobbings I have studied in recent years have been rooted in well-intentioned but fanatic and misguided campaigns to purify campuses absolutely of leftist bugbears like sexism, racism, classism, and homophobia.

The Medaille conference, however, left me wondering what the reformist organizations actually stand for. Is it academic freedom or conservative orthodoxy? Is it the curtailment of mobbing or merely a shift from left to right in the direction from which it comes?

Buffalo's magnificent Albright-Knox Art Gallery was the setting for the closing event of our conference on Saturday evening, September 21. After dinner, David Horowitz gave a rousing speech about his battles with the left. I asked him afterwards whether, by his rhetoric and name-calling, he is not as extremist and divisive as the people he opposes. I cited the research Stanley Rothman had presented earlier that day, and Clive Seligman's studies of the social psychology of value-systems, suggesting that humans are not easily divided into polar political opposites, that unless overcome by panic, people's actual behavior tends to be issue- and context-specific.

Horowitz answered politely and thoughtfully. He said my attitude was civilized, but that it was just this attitude that had permitted American campuses to be taken over by the anti-American left.

Horowitz has a point. Yet it is also true that unless his organization (CSPC) and similar ones like NAS, FIRE, and SAFS promote a genuine pluralism in our institutions, reciprocal tolerance of diverse viewpoints and reasoned debate among them, they are as bad as fanatic movements on the left and do not deserve support. What part, if any, the speakers at September's conference at Medaille College play in resolving the college's troubles will be one test, one indication of what the agendas of their respective organizations really are.

Finally, to end on a personal note, this paper springs from my commitment to be true to the late Richard Henshel's will. He would have understood and respected John Schedel's question on the opening night of the Medaille conference. Henshel often asked the same kind of question. Part of what being a professor meant to him was rising in a room full of like-minded people and asking a question that rattled their cage. It was to ensure that academic life continues to have room for such behavior that he left his money to NAS. What lies behind this paper is the sentiment Robert Service wrote in "The Cremation of Sam McGee":

> A pal's last need is a thing to heed
> And I swore that I would not fail.

## List of References

Davenport, Noa, *et al., Mobbing: Emotional Abuse in the American Workplace*. Ames, IA: Civil Society Publishing.

Garner, Helen, 1997. *The First Stone*. New York: Free Press.

Girard, René, 1986. *The Scapegoat*. Baltimore: Johns Hopkins University Press.

Girard, René, 2001. *I See Satan Fall Like Lightning*. Maryknoll, NY: Orbis.

Hart, William, *Never Fade Away*. Santa Barbara, CA: Fithian.

Hawthorne, Nathaniel, 1851. *The House of Seven Gables*.

Leymann, Heinz, 1987. "Självmord till följd av förh☐llanden i arbetsmiljön," *Arbete, människa, miljö* 3, pp. 155-169 [as summarized in Leymann 1990].

Leymann, Heinz, 1990. "Mobbing and Psychological Terror at Workplaces," *Violence and Victims* 5 (2), pp. 119-126.

Leymann, Heinz, 1996. "The Content and Development of Mobbing at Work," *European Journal of Work and Organizational Psychology* 5 (2), pp. 165-184.

Mathias, Philip, 2000. "Professors Meet Their Waterloo," *National Post*, March 11.

Miller, Merle, 1973. *Plain Speaking: an Oral Biography of Harry S. Truman*. New York: Berkley Medallion.

Namie, Gary, and Ruth Namie, 2000. *The Bully at Work*. Amazon (USA), Chapters (Canada), or by mail from Devon, UK: Roundhouse Publishing.

Orwell, George, 1997. *Nineteen Eighty-Four*. London: Penguin. First published 1949.

Polya, John, 1986. "Commentary" on C. Manwell and C. M. A. Baker, "'Not Merely Malice: the University of Tasmania versus Professor Orr," pp. 48f in B. Martin *et al.,* eds., *Intellectual Suppression.* London: Angus & Robertson.

Prose, Francine, 2000. *Blue Angel.* New York: HarperCollins.

Roth, Philip, 2000. *The Human Stain.* Boston: Houghton Mifflin.

Westhues, Kenneth, 1998. *Eliminating Professors: a Guide to the Dismissal Process.* Lewiston, NY: Edwin Mellen Press.

Westhues, Kenneth, 2001. "'The Difficult Professor,'a Pernicious Concept," with additional commentaries by N. Davenpor, H. Hammerly, H. Klatt, and J. Mueller, CAUT Legal Conference, Ottawa.

Wyatt, Judith, and Chauncey Hare, 1997. *Work Abuse: How to Recognize and Survive It.* Rochester, VT: Schenkman.

## Documents Related to the Medaille Conflict

*(Most of these are available online, as of fall 2002, at the New York State AAUP website,www.nysc-aaup.org)*

AAUP Chapter at St. Bonaventure University (J. W. Moor, S. Nuttall, J. A. White), 2002. Statement of support for Dr. T.Warden and colleagues at Medaille College, April 16.

AAUP Chapters in Western New York, 2002. Poster announcing symposium, "Crisis! The State of Academic Freedom at Medaille College and in Western New York," to be held at Medaille College, February 22.

AAUP (New York), 2002. Minutes of spring meeting on Long Island, including reports of actions taken toward resolving conflict at Medaille College.

AAUP (New York), 2002. Videotape of symposium on academic freedom held at Daemen College, February 22.

AAUP (Medaille College Chapter), 2002. *The Voice of Academic Freedom Speaking to the Crisis at Medaille College,* "The Facts Regarding the P & T Committee Document," spring.

Auer, Holly, 2002. "Professor Fired after Questioning Panel's Policy," *Buffalo News,* February 20.

Balch, Stephen, 2001-02. "Let's Roll," Column in *NAS Update*, winter.

Brace, Jim, Kim Carr, John Elmore, Robert Johnson, and Ross Runfola (Medaille College Grievance Committee), 2002. Memorandum to Dr. John Donohue stating recommendations on the grievances of Dr. Uhuru Watson, April 22.

Brace, Jim, Kim Carr, John Elmore, Robert Johnson, and Ross Runfola (Medaille College Grievance Committee), 2002. Memoranduum to Dr. John Donohue stating recommendations on the grievances of Dr. Therese Warden, May 21.

Buermann, Barry, and Terry Warden, 1993. Memorandum to Medaille College faculty concerning establishment of AAUP chapter on campus.

Donohue, John, 2002. Letter to Therese Warden suspending her from teaching and forbidding her to come on campus, January 10.

Donohue, John, 2002. Memorandum to Medaille Community about upcoming *Buffalo News* article, February 19.

Drury, Tracey, 2002. "Medaille names John Donohue to acting president," *Buffalo Business First*, February 26.

Drury, Tracey, 2002. "Medaille narrowing search for new president," *Buffalo Business First*, March 7.

Faculty Association of Niagara County Community College, 2002. Resolution supporting AAUP efforts toward "balance of governance" at Medaille College, February 26.

*Horizon*, 2001. Medaille College newspaper including feature on Dr. Terry Warden and retrospective on the late president Kevin Sullivan, spring.

*Horizon*, 2002. Medaille College newspaper reporting news since appointment of Joseph Bascuas as president, summer.

Kellogg, Alex P., 2002. "Actions Against 4 Professors at Medaille College Raise Concern Over Academic Freedom," *Chronicle of Higher Education*, March 7.

Knight, Jonathan (associate secretary, national office of AAUP), 2002. Letters to Dr. John Donohue requesting reinstatement of Professors Warden and Watson, February 8, March 7.

Knight, Jonathan (associate secretary, national office of AAUP), 2002. Letter to Dr. Joseph Bascuas requesting reinstatement of Professors Warden and Watson, July 15.

Savarese, Joseph E., 2001. Memorandum to John Donohue recommending dismissals and punishments.

UUP (United University Professors), 2002. Report of delegates' support for Medaille College faculty in struggle for academic freedom, *The Voice*, March.

Warden, Therese, 2002. Memoranda to Dr. John Donohue requesting meetings for informal resolution of conflict, January 2 and 12.

## Chapter Three

# The Second Paper, March 2003:

# The Medaille Mobbings, Part Two[1]

Snowdrops and crocuses to everyone involved in making the documents on last year's purge at Medaille College public and accessible on the web. British novelist Arnold Bennett is famous for saying, "The price of justice is eternal publicity." But even prior to justice, eternal publicity is the price of knowledge.

By my paper last October, I hoped to join and advance the conversation already underway among professors in Western New York, about the Medaille purge. Thank you for letting me in. This paper is intended to clarify last fall's analysis, in respectful and grateful response to colleagues' feedback. My objective is as before: to understand what happened, to capture it in words so far as possible, since thorough understanding is prerequisite to practical remedy.

All agree that Warden's and Watson's dismissals breached the formal and the unspoken covenants in place at Medaille, as elsewhere, for the conduct of academic life. Even perpetrator Joseph Savarese, the Medaille dean, admitted this a full year ago at a meeting with MBA students. "AAUP will censure Medaille," he is reported to

---

[1] Presentation at the symposium, "The Crisis in Academic Freedom," held at Daemen College, Buffalo, New York, under sponsorship of the Coalition of Faculty Associations of Western New York, 8 March 2003.

have said, "and it won't make any difference to accreditation or faculty recruitment." The other key perpetrator, John Donohue, was reported to have said at about the same time, in his interview for the Medaille presidency, "Shared governance is a very good idea but too much work is involved in it."

These two Medaille administrators, the ones most directly responsible for the dismissals, behaved like Farmer Jones in the rural community I grew up in. Jones used to listen in secretly on the party line to the conversations of Farmer Smith, his neighbor down the road. Jones knew this violated the rules for party lines but he did it anyway, and Smith knew he did it, having often heard the click on the line when Jones picked up his receiver to listen in. Angrily one day, in the midst of a conversation he wanted to keep private, Smith shouted into the telephone, "Jones, you hang up right now." Caught off guard, Jones blurted out his reply over the wire: "Make me."

In effect, this is what the Medaille administration has said: "Make me. So what if the firings violated the rules of academe? What are you going to do about it?"

For us now to belabor the point that these tenured professors should not have been fired is to spin our wheels and dig ourselves into a mental rut. To advance our understanding, we have to ask and answer questions like these: why did Savarese and Donohue so flagrantly violate the covenants of their college community, why have their violations not by now been rectified, and why has the new president, Joseph Bascuas, violated these covenants further by refusing to discuss issues so undeniable and so undeniably vital to the college's future?

I sent Bascuas last fall eight polite emails requesting information and keeping him abreast of my ongoing inquiry. He did not reply to even one. He declined invitations to dialogue with AAUP officials on grounds that the issues are in litigation. His position is silly. If the issues come to court, the first thing a judge will probably say is, "Would the parties please sit down and try to talk things out?" What we have at Medaille is incompetent, bizarre administrative behavior, a breakdown of academic order. To correct it, we must first make sense of it.

The best way I know is by recourse to the research literature on workplace mobbing. The essence of a mob action is brash repudiation of existing rules, policies, understandings, and covenants. In

Hobbesian terms, it is an escape from the order gained by social contract, a context-specific reversion to a state of nature wherein the powerful destroy the weak and questions about justice are not raised. In Kantian terms, it is a defiance of the categorical imperative: "No matter that academic life would crumble if little cabals of administrators could dismiss tenured professors on a whim, in this case we'll just do it." In our day, with the accumulated wisdom of Hobbes, Kant, and the other architects of civilized life embodied now in institutions of law and politics as well as custom, mobbers cannot afford to be overtly irrational. They sign their names to memoranda that seem at first glance to be reasoned, routine. Yet their claimed rationality in the mobbing context is like that of John Claggart, the man who led the mobbing of Billy Budd, as Melville described him: "Though the man's even temper and discreet bearing would seem to intimate a mind peculiarly subject to the law of reason, not the less in heart he would seem to riot in complete exemption from that law, having apparently little to do with reason further than to employ it as an ambidexter instrument for effecting the irrational."

Western society today, its academic sector not least, is so suffused with rationality, so laden with bureaucratic procedures like Medaille's hierarchy of authority, Faculty Handbook, and dispute-resolution mechanism, that we find it hard to wrap our minds around the idea that Warden's and Watson's dismissals were instances of mobbing. The term seems too wild, too savage, too out of character for holders of doctorates. That destructive, spiteful, irrational ganging up can happen among children (as in *Lord of the Flies*), teenagers (what is called swarming or wilding), religious sectarians (as in the Amish ritual of shunning), and uneducated folk (as in your everyday lynch mob), is commonly acknowledged. That it can happen in a nonviolent way among titled holders of high positions of authority in a temple of reason like Medaille College, is harder to see.

## Workplace Mobbing vs. Academic Freedom

It is easier to treat the purge at Medaille as a violation of academic freedom, this being a sacred value in academic life, much as the Bill of Rights is in American civic life. What prompted my own involvement in this conflict was the Orwellian contradiction I perceived (with John Schedel's help) between the purge and shortly thereafter, a college-sponsored conference celebrating academic freedom. Most of the questioning of Warden's and Watson's dismissals by AAUP chapters and similar bodies, as well as by articles in *Buffalo News* and *Chronicle of Higher Education*, has been from the standpoint of academic freedom. The title of today's symposium reflects the same view.

Yet this focus is a little off. Ben Singer, emeritus sociologist at Western Ontario, suggested to me that these dismissals had more to do with vocational than academic freedom, that they resulted from an administrative hassle that could have occurred in any organizational setting. These cases, Singer pointed out, are not like that of Western Ontario psychologist Philippe Rushton, whom the provincial premier wanted fired in 1989, on grounds that Rushton's research was "offensive to the way Ontario thinks." The Medaille administrators did not fire Warden and Watson for their thinking or teaching or writing, at least not officially, instead for a breach of confidentiality. The 1940 AAUP statement on academic freedom does not read as if designed for such cases.

One can argue in response to Singer that the stated reason for the dismissals was a smokescreen, that the real reason was to shut these professors up. Such an argument keeps the cases within the conceptual frame of academic freedom, makes them easier for AAUP to deal with and less threatening to our own image of academic life. If Savarese's and Donohue's agenda was to prevent certain ideas from being taught at Medaille, and if in pursuit of this agenda they fabricated a case against two proponents of these ideas, their behavior may have been wrong but it remains intelligible in rational terms.

The evidence, however, persuades me to admit Singer's point. What happened to Warden and Watson bears close resemblance to what I have seen happen, in my research, to nurses, police officers, factory workers, school teachers, and secretaries, among others. This resemblance is lost in the conceptual frame of *academic* freedom. Should we say that false accusation, humiliation and elimination are acceptable when inflicted on nonacademic workers, reprehensible only when inflicted on professors? Of course not. No worker, whether on a college faculty or not, deserves to be treated the way Warden and Watson have been treated at Medaille. The infringement in their cases, nicely captured by the word *turpitude*, was not just of their freedom to teach but of their good names and livelihoods, their dignity as citizens. Academic freedom is the icing on the cake of rights professors need to do their jobs. Warden and Watson lost more than the icing. They lost the whole cake.

To admit that the firings did not infringe precisely *academic* freedom does not excuse them. If breach of committee confidentiality were an offense punishable by dismissal, most workplaces would have to close for lack of personnel. Savarese wrote to Donohue that Watson "disseminated" the confidential minutes to Warden. This is linguistically impossible. The word *disseminate* means "scatter widely" or "spread abroad." You cannot do it to one other person. The most Watson could have done was *pass on* the minutes to Warden, but the evidence places even this in doubt. Fact is, *nobody* disseminated those minutes: they are not even now scattered widely or spread abroad. Besides, since college policy gave the PT Committee no authority on administrative appointments, the meeting that Watson allegedly gave Warden the minutes of was not a meeting of the PT Committee, but of the members of that committee, along with Donohue, convened by Savarese for a purpose outside its jurisdiction. To an illegitimate meeting, no rule of confidentiality applies.

York University historian Michiel Horn, author of the standard history of academic freedom in Canada, reacted to my paper by kindly sending me his take on what happened. An insecure administrator, Horn wrote, seems to have turned a legitimate criticism of his actions into evidence of disloyalty, and muddied the waters to such an extent that his offense against due process was lost from sight. Horn got it right. The grounds on which Warden and Watson were fired are drivel.

Granted that inspecting the Medaille purge from the angles of academic freedom, tenure, confidentiality, governance, and corporatization yields some insight, the more adequate focus, in my view, less abstract and closer to the data, is on the relation among identifiable men and women, acquaintances, co-workers, even friends – John Donohue, Therese Warden, Joseph Savarese, Uhuru Watson, Stephen Balch, Robert Stevenson, William Collins, Michael Lillis, Jim Brace, Beth Lucyszyn, Randy Brown, and others – whose lives intersected at Medaille last year in a way that did none of them good and a few of them great harm.

Nebraska novelist Willa Cather once wrote: "Isn't it queer: there are only two or three human stories, and they go on repeating themselves as fiercely as if they had never happened before; like the larks in this country, they have been singing the same five notes for thousands of years."

Sure, there were unprecedented predisposing conditions at Medaille that gave rise to the ritual degradations: the recent death of longtime president Kevin Sullivan, the inexperience of Donohue and Savarese in their jobs, the mood of panic in the wake of the September 11 attacks, disputes about the college's mission and program priorities. But these conditions merely set the stage for reenactment of an ancient story, one in that handful of stories Cather referred to: ganging up on a fellow human, humiliating, scapegoating, and eliminating him or her. It was this note, sung in our species since time immemorial, that was blared last year at Medaille as fiercely as if for the first time.

René Girard, the Stanford classicist whose work deserves its wide respect, recounts the story set down by Philostratus two millennia ago, about when Apollonius of Tyana was called to Ephesus to heal that community of the ills plaguing it. Apollonius surveyed the assembled Ephesians, singled out one of them, and said to the rest, "There's your problem. He is an enemy of the gods. Stone him." The Ephesians were shocked. The fellow did not look like an enemy and was begging for mercy. Apollonius egged them on, and they began to throw stones at the man. As soon as he was hit and felled, the stone-throwers saw that he was really a demon, and so they pelted him so thoroughly a cairn of stones arose around the slain man. Apollonius then bade them remove the stones, and when they did, they found no man at all but an oversize dog, pounded to a pulp and vomiting foam. Their community having been cured, the Ephesians praised their savior Apollonius and erected on the spot a statue to the god Hercules.

We begin to understand the story that unfolded at Medaille last year when we notice how it repeats the story of Apollonius and the Ephesians two thousand years earlier–essentially the same story as of the trials and eliminations of Socrates, Jesus, and Joan of Arc, and of lynchings in nineteenth-century America. Not with respect to violence. There is no criminal offense with which any of those who joined in eliminating Warden and Watson can rightly be charged.

"The phenomenon in question," Girard writes, "doesn't usually lead any longer to acts of physical violence, but it does lead to a 'psychological violence' that is easy to camouflage. Those who are accused of participating in hostile transference never fail to protest their good faith, in all sincerity." We should take today's mobbers at their word, grant the good intentions they typically claim, and repeat the prayer that is another in the handful of basic human stories: "Father, forgive them, because they do not know what they are doing."

## Workplace mobbing vs. Intentional Harm

Some researchers of workplace mobbing, so I was reminded by comments on my earlier paper in our internet discussion forum, disagree with me about how conscious and purposeful the mobbers are. Jan Gregersen, a respected colleague at Akershus University College in Norway, sent me a quote from a leading Norwegian psychiatrist, known there as a hunter of psychos in organizations. "All researches," this psychiatrist says, "point in the same direction: those who participate in mobbing know what they do and that their actions are wrong. All talk about 'hysteria,' 'brainwashing,' etc. is nonsense."

The psychiatrist overstates. My research, about a hundred case studies by now, points in a different direction: that mobbers vary in how much and what kind of thought they give to their eliminative actions. Perhaps a few have malicious intent. Most do not. I doubt that Savarese, despite knowing that his actions contravened AAUP principles, intended to behave cruelly toward Warden, Watson, and the others. Mob leaders are typically caught up in a headlong quest to reach some lofty goal. To them, the people they run over along the way look like roadkill in the rearview mirror of a speeding car, fast receding from sight and mind. Most of the mob followers, typically farther down in the organizational hierarchy, take their cue from the higher authorities and interpret their eliminative actions as just doing their jobs. The members of the Medaille grievance committee probably reflect this pattern.

Participation in a mob action, I should emphasize, is self-reinforcing: the more stones you throw at the target, the more clearly you see, as the Ephesians did, that the target deserves to be stoned. Belgian researcher Frederic Caufrier referred me to a classic by

Charles MacKay, first published in 1841, that I had not read until now, but that illuminates the purge at Medaille even by its title: *Extraordinary Popular Delusions and the Madness of Crowds.*

A useful analysis of the Medaille mobbings, as of other evils, an analysis that might facilitate remedy, attends less to the motives and mental states of the mobbers than to the actual events and their consequences. Since no one can know for sure what goes on inside another's head, the question of whether Donohue or Savarese or anybody else was acting in good faith or bad faith, is ultimately moot. It is plain as day, on the other hand, that Warden and Watson did nothing to warrant punishment, that Savarese and Donohue sacked them and deemed them turpitudinous, and that the grievance committee, board of trustees, and many individual professors, staff, and students acquiesced. This is the behavioral reality, the nub of the issue, and it matters far more than what, if anything, was going on in the mind of any one of those involved.

## Workplace mobbing vs. Bullying

I want also to distance my analysis from the assumption implicit in some research in this area, especially where the term *bullying* is preferred to *mobbing*, that the real problem in cases like these at Medaille is an identifiably defective individual person, a psychopath or bully, who makes everybody else misbehave – the bad apple in the barrel. The bottom line, from such a viewpoint, is that it was all Donohue's fault, or Savarese's, or the fault of some trustee behind the scenes. Research on bullying turns the tables, shifting the stigma of infamy from the person who was destroyed to the ringleader among the destroyers. The implicit solution is to humiliate and destroy that ringleader. From such a viewpoint, what the people of Ephesus should have done is turn on Apollonius and stone him, for having incited them to stone an innocent man. Once beaten to a pulp, Apollonius would have been the one looking like an oversize dead dog foaming at the mouth, the *real* demon.

The most important social psychological research finding I know, replicated in dozens of studies, is Fundamental Attribution Error, the common tendency to attribute what people do too much to their personal qualities and too little to the situations they are in. Nothing in the evidence of the Medaille purge persuades me that John

Donohue or Joseph Savarese or anybody else deserves a label – like *bully* – that would exclude him from respectable company. An analysis of the purge is weakened, not strengthened, by impugning Donohue's overall character or competence. There is no need to dispute even one accolade on the long list of them placed on Savarese in a recent Medaille press release. The relevant truth is simply this: that certain decisions Donohue and Savarese made as interim administrators at Medaille in 2001-2002, their decisions to smear and eliminate colleagues no less worthy than they, decisions plenty of other people chimed in on, were hideously harmful and wrong.

## Toward Remedy

Why were those decisions not corrected a year ago, when their wrongness was proclaimed in blunt faculty statements from area colleges? During his interview for the Medaille presidency at that time, Joseph Bascuas was asked what he would do to remedy the conflict. "I am a very good communicator," Bascuas was reported to have answered, and he said he would "talk to all parties involved and do some healing."

Why has Bascuas not followed through? So far as I know, he has not talked to Warden or Watson, nor healed anything. Generally, when a mobbing has reached the stage of institutional defilement and official elimination of the target, as in the Medaille cases, remedy and healing must await a change of institutional leadership. A mob leader's identity is typically so heavily invested in the elimination, that he or she cannot admit a mistake and correct the harm, even at the cost of having to leave office. At Medaille, however, leadership changed already last summer. As a newcomer to campus, Bascuas has no personal stake in defending the wrong decisions of his predecessor. One is led to suspect, though all the evidence is not yet in, that the main leader of the mob that got Warden and Watson may not have been Donohue or Savarese, but an individual or cabal on the board of trustees, who now threatens to pull the plug on Bascuas's presidency if the latter sets things straight. Bascuas is thus left looking foolish and ineffectual, while the conflict drags on and the college languishes.

In this sorry circumstance, that Warden and Watson should seek redress in the courts is as understandable and predictable as that they should appeal for help to AAUP. Yet the most the courts will do is take some of the college's money away, and give it to the professors who were wrongly dropped from the payroll. The most AAUP will do is take some of the college's reputation away, and give it to the professors who were wrongly smeared. These are poor and partial solutions to grievous harm.

The better, more genuine  solution is to continue doing what we are doing today, except in ever-widening circles of the Medaille community and its constituencies: to keep talking until what Daniel Yankelovich calls *The Magic of Dialogue* brings remedy. From Iowa, Noa Davenport, co-author of *Mobbing: Emotional Abuse in the American Workplace*, sent Bascuas an email after she read my earlier paper. "What is important," she told him, "is the space for everyone to speak and for everyone to be heard. It is my conviction that you could make a major contribution by calling all parties together for a deep conversation."

So far as I know, Bascuas did not reply to Davenport's email. Nor, except possibly among themselves, have the Medaille trustees yet joined the conversation about the purge. Of the four national organizations whose presidents spoke at last September's conference at Medaille on academic freedom, only one – FIRE, the Foundation for Individual Rights in Education – has so far begun to investigate the dismissals.

Nobody promised us a rose garden. Mobbing is hard grain; mills grind it slowly. From reasoned conversation, if we continue to engage in it, insist on it, and broaden it, will eventually come a story almost as old as scapegoating but happier, the story powerfully told in Beeban Kidron's film, *Swept from the Sea*, based on Conrad's short story, "Amy Foster," the story of repentance, forgiveness, reconciliation, redemption and hope, a story that will involve offering Warden and Watson reinstatement to the Medaille faculty, and the college's acknowledgment of its mistake in firing and degrading them.

The jurors in Salem, Massachusetts, who convicted 150 fellow citizens of witchcraft in 1692, can be remembered with shame for their reenactment on that occasion of the old, wintry, eliminative story. They can also be remembered with honor for changing their story five years later to one that shows what grandeur our species is capable of, a story that bursts like spring with the promise of renewal of life:

> We do therefor hereby signify to all in general (and to the surviving sufferers in especial) our deep sense of and sorrow for our errors in acting on such evidence to the condemning of any person, and do hereby declare that we justly fear we were sadly deluded and mistaken, ... and do therefore humbly beg forgiveness.... And we also pray that we may be considered candidly and aright by the living sufferers as being then under the power of a strong and general delusion, utterly unacquainted with and not experienced in matters of that nature.

To acquaint us all with matters of that nature is the purpose of both my earlier paper and this one. We humans, even those of us with "Dr." before our names, are not entirely rational beings. Under conditions of stress and ambiguity, we sometimes fly off the handle, as if evil spirits had got hold of our relations with one another. This downside of the human condition deserves the most careful study, toward finding ways to correct and prevent the resultant harm.

## Endnotes

The author welcomes feedback by post or to kwesthue@watarts.uwaterloo.ca

For responses to my initial paper, "The Mobbings at Medaille College in 2002," I am grateful to Jan Gregersen (Akershus University College, Norway), Frederic Caufrier (Free University Brussels), Noa Davenport (Ames, Iowa), Michiel Horn (York University, Toronto), Stephen Balch (NAS), Benjamin D. Singer (University of Western Ontario), Therese Warden (Medaille), John Schedel (Medaille), John K. Wilson (Chicago, collegefreedom.org), Jeanine Plottel (NY AAUP executive director), John Diehl (editor, *NY Academe*), Clive Seligman (SAFS, Western Ontario), and Heinz Klatt (King's College, Western Ontario). Responsibility for the present paper, as for the earlier one, rests entirely with me.

References in this paper are mostly to classics like Melville's and Cather's novels, and to documentation on the Medaille purge available on the website of the New York Conference of the AAUP (http://www.nysc-aaup.org/), where the paper to which this one is a sequel is also published. The quotations from Savarese, Donohue, and Bascuas are taken from "Ground Zero Bistro" (http://riccistreet.net/). The story of Apollonius and the Ephesians is in R. Girard, *I See Satan Fall Like Lightning* (Orbis 2001). For a lucid summary of research on Fundamental Attribution Error, see Malcolm Gladwell, *The Tipping Point* (Little, Brown, 2000).

# Chapter Four

# The Third Paper, July 2003:

# The Medaille Crisis in Mid-2003

**Cover Letter to Trustees and Administrators, 11 July 2003**

Trustees and Senior Administrators
    Dr. Joseph Bascuas, President
    Dr. Mike Mitchell, Vice-President
    Dr. Joseph Savarese, Dean
    Mr. William Stevenson, Board Chair
    Dr. Nicholas Trbovich, Board Vice-chair
    Ms. Susan Warren Russ, Board Vice-chair
    Mr. William M. Collins, Board Treasurer
    Dr. Stephen H. Balch, Trustee
    Mr. Stuart H. Angert, Trustee
    Ms. Patricia D. Barry, Board Secretary
    Dr. Donna M. Fernandes, Trustee
    Ms. Jean Taggart Fonzi, Trustee
    Mr. Andrés Garcia, Board Asst. Secretary
    Ms. Arlene F. Kaukus, Trustee
    Mr. Michael Keating, Trustee
    Mr. Hal P. Kingsley, Trustee
    Honorable Joseph G. Makowski, Trustee

Mr. Michael K. Walsh, Trustee
Ms. Wanda E. Zygmuntowicz, Trustee
Medaille College
Buffalo, New York 14214

Dear

As part of my continuing study of conflict in the academic
workplace, and in a further effort to be helpful to the College for
which you are responsible, I have written an update or sequel to
my earlier papers, this one entitled "The Medaille Crisis in Mid-
2003." Especially because I refer to you by name in this paper, I
am sending you a copy herewith in advance of publishing it. If you
should find any factual errors, please let me know promptly either
by post or email (kwesthue@uwaterloo.ca) and I will correct them.

Be sure of my respect and thanks for your work on behalf of
higher education and scholarship, and of my hope that even these
tentative results of social scientific research may assist you, the
faculty, staff, and students in resolving current problems fairly and
constructively. Best wishes for summer.

Sincerely yours,
Kenneth Westhues

## Cover Letter to New Trustees, 22 October 2003

New members of the Board of Trustees
Dr. Elizabeth Altmaier
Mr. Christopher Jacobs
Mr. Dominick F. Antonelli
Honorable Joseph S. Mattina
Mr. Tom Donahoe
Dr. Kathleen C. Owens
Mr. David L. Edmunds
Mr. William H. Pearce, Jr.
Dr. Juanita K. Hunter
Mr. Joseph E. Wolfson
Medaille College
Buffalo, New York 14214

Dear

Congratulations on your recent election to the Medaille Board of Trustees, and thank you for assuming this responsibility at this critical juncture in the college's history. I have been studying the Medaille crisis for about a year, as part of my ongoing research on mobbing and other forms of conflict in academic workplaces.

As President Bascuas will have informed you, the AAUP has condemned the college administration in its recent report, and will probably soon place Medaille under official censure. This is AAUP's severest form of condemnation, imposed over the past decade on about 20 of the 4,000 colleges and universities in the United States.

The gravity of the Medaille crisis can be grasped by analogy to its sister institution in western New York, St. Bonaventure University, whose administration was condemned and censured by AAUP in 1996. In that case, the St. Bona Board of Trustees put on a brave face and pretended nothing was amiss, allowing the crisis to fester until it erupted in scandal last spring. By then it was too late for constructive resolution. The St. Bona board fired President Robert Wickenheiser and other administrators in March. The board chair, Buffalo banker William Swan, hanged himself on August 20, leaving a note of remorse for the St. Bona meltdown.

To help avert so tragic an outcome in the Medaille case, I have sought to facilitate a constructive resolution of the conflict by apprising all concerned of the results of my research. Most of my analyses, along with others', are available on the New York AAUP website: http://www.nysc-aaup.org/medaille.html Enclosed herewith is a copy of my most recent paper, which I sent to all members of the 2002-03 Board of Trustees last July.

It is a common pattern in college and university governance that as the board of trustees increases in size, fewer of its members know what is actually going on. Key decisions are made by a small circle of administrators and board officers, the remaining trustees lending their names blindly for legitimacy. The danger of this happening this year at Medaille is the more serious, given that the six officers have, on average, seven years experience on the board, during which they oversaw the decisions that define the present crisis, while the remaining eighteen trustees have, on average, one year of experience on the board.

I urge you not to let a betrayal of trustee responsibility happen in the Medaille case, instead to be persistent in asking questions and informing yourself from as many points of view as possible about how the college got itself into its present predicament, and how it intends to get out of this predicament and move ahead.

Experience with other institutions in crisis leads me also to remind you that in accepting a position on the Medaille board, you assume responsibility not only for the college's assets, its financial and moral capital, but also for its liabilities, its financial and moral debts. "Starting with a clean slate" is out of the question. Medaille's slate, like that of any institution, is already covered by its history, which cannot be erased but only corrected, enlarged, and improved upon.

Finally, I need to make a correction in the paper enclosed. In a telephone conversation with former trustee Susan Warren Russ, who has left the board this year after 14 years of service, she told me the Junior League of Buffalo was mistaken in publicly identifying her last year as "president-elect" of the Medaille Board of Trustees.

Again, thanks and respect to you for your work on behalf of higher education in general, Medaille College in particular.

> Sincerely yours,
> Kenneth Westhues

copies:   President Joseph Bascuas
              Board Chair William Stevenson
              Dr. Therese Warden
              Dr. Uhuru Watson
              Dr. Jeanine Plottel, Executive Director, New York
              AAUP

*Respectfully dedicated to all the professors at Medaille who, in a trying circumstance, have kept faith with their scholarly vocations and resisted the wrongful exclusion of Therese Warden and Uhuru Watson from their community.*

*And with thanks to Bill Pauly for teaching me the poem, "Outwitted," by Edwin Markham:*

*He drew a circle that shut me out—*
*Heretic, rebel, a thing to flout.*
*But Love and I had the wit to win:*
*We drew a circle that took him in!*


To the researcher of workplace conflict, the interesting question at Medaille College is no longer why two veteran tenured professors, Therese Warden and Uhuru Watson, were wrongly dismissed in early 2002. The question in mid-2003 is why the college has not by now offered them reinstatement and remedied in so far as possible the damage to their livelihoods, reputations, careers – their very lives. The present paper sheds light on this question. It updates and extends the analysis in my two earlier papers on this conflict, "The Mobbings at Medaille College in 2002," and "The Medaille Mobbings: Part Two."

## Deepening Crisis in 2002-2003

In choosing a new president in the spring of 2002, the Board of Trustees at Medaille understandably passed over insider John Donohue, who as acting president had fired the two professors for "turpitude," without any evidence of wrongdoing on their part. The trustees instead appointed outsider Joseph Bascuas, who had described himself during his interview as "a very good communicator" and who had promised to "talk to all parties and do some healing."

Yet during his first year in office, Bascuas stonewalled all efforts by AAUP officials and others from both inside and outside the college to negotiate a resolution of the conflict. It was as if someone muzzled Bascuas and tied his hands, forced him to go back on his word as the price of being Medaille's president.

Already by the time he took office in July of 2002, concerned professors at Medaille, faculty associations at neighboring institutions, the New York State AAUP, and the national AAUP had all come to Warden's and Watson's defence and pleaded with the College to set things right. The outrageousness of the dismissals had been exposed in articles in *Buffalo News*, *New York Academe*, and *The Chronicle of Higher Education*.

During the 2002-03 academic year, the extent of the harm requiring remedy was revealed to be greater than first thought. When Donohue suspended Warden in January of 2002, a month before dismissing her, he forbade her to enter the campus. She thus lost access to the files in her office – records of courses taught, research, and community projects, as well as social research data awaiting analysis. In the fall of 2002, after Bascuas had taken over, Warden wrote to him requesting shipment of these materials to her home. Bascuas sent a shipment, Warden received it, but it contained almost nothing. It thus appears that after banning Warden from coming to campus, the college may actually have destroyed the research data, records, and other personal property in her office.

Also during the 2002-03 academic year, Bascuas and the College trustees got a series of pointed additional reminders of the need to correct the offence against truth and decency that the dismissals of Warden and Watson constituted.

On February 28, 2003, AAUP investigators Robert Moore of Saint Joseph's University in Philadelphia, and Sandi Cooper of CUNY Staten Island, travelled to Buffalo for a formal inquiry into the Medaille troubles. Notified by AAUP in advance of their visit, Bascuas refused to talk to them. Their report may well result in AAUP's placement of the college under official censure.

On March 8, 2003, the Coalition of Faculty Associations of Western New York, whose organization was triggered by Warden's and Watson's dismissals, held a full-day conference at Daemen College on "The Crisis in Academic Freedom." Reported in detail on the web and in *New York Academe*, the conference showed the significance of the Medaille dismissals for the future of higher education in America.

On March 23, 2003, the Foundation for Individual Rights in Education (FIRE) formally asked the College to reconsider the dismissals, and expressed hope "that Medaille will be able to come to a fair and equitable resolution of this matter." FIRE offered its assistance.

Given Bascuas's rebuff to the local, regional, state and national bodies that have urged rectification of obvious wrongs, it is not surprising that he and the trustees have snubbed me as well. My intended contribution toward resolving the conflict has been to put an accurate name on what happened (*workplace mobbing*) and to share with all parties results of research on this uncommon but devastating organizational process. Hoping to reduce the heat by shedding light, I sent copies by post of my initial paper, on October 29, 2002, to all the administrators and trustees as well as to Warden, Watson, and other professors. Bascuas did not reply. One trustee, Stephen Balch, replied, but with personal invective.

Having been invited to speak at the conference at Daemen College on March 8, 2003, I contacted beforehand board chair Robert Stevenson and several other trustees whose email addresses I was able to locate, and urged them to attend the conference as a first step toward dialogue and constructive resolution of the conflict. I drove to Buffalo on March 7 in time to stop by the college and personally deliver advance copies of my paper to Bascuas and to Joseph Savarese, the dean who had recommended Warden's and Watson's dismissals on December 10, 2001. Both administrators were elsewhere on campus. I left the copies with a secretary, along with friendly notes assuring them of my respect and my hope that they would take part in the next day's conference.

They did not, nor did any members of the Board of Trustees. The college's lawyer, Thomas Brydges, sat in on part of the conference, a presentation by Warden's lawyer, Robert Moriarty. Brydges's presence, combined with the absence of administrators and trustees, conveyed a message that instead of entering into dialogue toward correction of obvious wrongs, the college authorities planned to exacerbate the wrongs by defeating Warden and Watson in court.

On June 22, 2003, in a dramatic sign of how precarious the college's position has become, *Buffalo News* published detailed results of a confidential evaluation of Bascuas by the Medaille Faculty Council, showing that only six of 58 respondents in a survey of faculty and staff found him trustworthy. The article said comments on the survey followed a similar theme:

> Bascuas will say one thing to one group of people and something else to another group; he's not good at dealing with people; and he doesn't consult before making decisions. ...

One staffer called Bascuas "controlling, a micromanager
and very manipulative." Another said he is "a dictator and
treats his colleagues like second-class citizens."

And a third said he "overall is not presidential material."
Obviously, the college is in crisis, much or most of it traceable to the
president's and trustees' unwillingness to solve the big problem
Donohue left as his legacy.

## Inadequate Answers to the Pressing Question

The question is why such intransigence. In many academic
mobbings, the issues and evidence are complex, but the dismissals at
Medaille were transparently unjustified. In the wake of longtime
president Kevin Sullivan's sudden death, and in the context of post-
9/11 hype across America, two inexperienced temporary
administrators, Donohue and Savarese, made a panicked response to a
reminder of their own procedural mistakes, summarily fired two
tenured colleagues, and imposed lesser discipline on several more. It
was a rash, indefensible blunder of a kind that happens in
organizations under stress. There is nothing to do but take back the
wrong decisions, mend fences, and get back to work.

If Donohue were still president, the intransigence would be
understandable. It is a well established finding in mobbing research
that the "chief eliminator," the administrator who has led the
eliminative campaign, has typically demonized the target so
completely as to be unable to redress the harm. Often, it is
psychologically impossible for the chief eliminator to "take it back,"
however right and essential to the organization's welfare this may be.

But Donohue left the college in the summer of 2002, shortly after
Bascuas took over. In a number of academic mobbing cases I have
studied, the harm was remedied and the conflict quickly resolved
once new leadership was in place. Why has this not occurred at
Medaille?

The debilitating deadlock is not for want of education or general
intelligence. Bascuas and Savarese have Ph.D.'s. So do trustees
Nicholas Trbovich, Donna Fernandes, and Stephen Balch. Other
trustees have advanced professional degrees. All are college
graduates. These are not people whose failure to rectify obvious
wrongs can be explained or excused by dullwittedness or low IQ.

Few of the administrators or trustees appear to be expert in conflict resolution, but lack of knowledge in this specific area is no excuse either. My initial paper on the mobbing research, sent to every administrator and trustee more than eight months ago, provided a more than adequate overview of the relevant scholarship, applied in detail to the Medaille situation. Besides, though specialized expertise may facilitate solutions to workplace conflicts, it is hardly prerequisite. The majority of conflicts in the majority of workplaces are routinely solved by good judgment and common sense.

Nor can the intransigence of Bascuas and the other administrators and trustees be accounted for in moral terms, as if they were simply "bad characters." On the contrary, they are respected leaders with long lists of achievements in varied circles of academic and civic life. I doubt that any of them has been convicted of a crime. The college over which they preside is a place that cultivates not only knowledge but morality. In the winter, 2003, issue of *Horizon*, college librarian Yvonne Cleveland described the importance of teaching morality in Medaille's business program:

> When we make ethics a priority, then our students will carry what they learn into the workplace, thus making their organizations better, one person at a time.

## Toward an Adequate Answer

For explaining the college's refusal so far to rectify the wrongful dismissals and restore decency to its system of governance, the most promising focus is not on personal qualities of any administrators, trustees, or professors, but on factional politics among them. The most plausible hypothesis is that in the wake of Kevin Sullivan's death in February, 2001, control of the college was seized by a loose network of six to twelve individuals, mostly members of the Board of Trustees. The key figures in this network backed Donohue as acting president, and acquiesced in his dismissal of Warden and Watson. Now, even with Donohue gone, they fear losing face and losing control if the wrongness of the firings is admitted and Warden and Watson are restored to the Medaille faculty.

This network or elite is not formally organized, though it acts through formal bodies like the Board of Trustees and is nourished by other places of meeting on and off campus. It is not a conspiracy, in the sense that its members consciously act in concert for nefarious purposes. It is an ever-evolving faction or cabal with mutual doing of favors and pats on the back, and with a blind spot for resolving the single main issue hanging over the campus and clouding its future. Members of this network chat easily and intelligently about many things, but probably in the context of an unstated norm that Warden's and Watson's dismissals are not to be discussed.

Who belongs to this network? What kind of ties bind its members? What common educational priorities and aspirations for Medaille, however unfocussed or vague, do they share? Who are the leaders and on what basis do they have power? Is the network tight or loose, cohesive or fragile, stable or shifting? In answers to questions like these lies the key to understanding the current impasse at Medaille, the key also to overcoming the impasse and getting the college back on track.

Definitive answers to these questions would require weeks of interviewing. Tentative answers can be obtained by adroit searching of the web and then reflecting on information found there in light of documentary evidence about the Medaille conflict and general knowledge of how academic institutions work. The following paragraphs give such tentative answers, suggesting promising directions for further inquiry, and illustrating, as a side benefit, the enormous potential of electronically available information for social research.

To understand Bascuas's intransigence, one has to look beyond Bascuas, at who – so to speak – pulls his strings. Nothing in his record portrays him as an academic visionary, ideologue, or charismatic leader, a person who inspires commitment to some larger purpose. On the contrary, he is a career administrator who steadily worked his way up in academic bureaucracies. The move to Medaille was the next wrung on the ladder. The *News* article on June 22, 2003, reported a telling comment from Bascuas in his own defence, in the face of massive discontent by faculty and staff:

> The college became something different before I got here, and I do not intend to take it in any other direction except for the direction that was set for the college and that I inherited.

Bascuas arrived in Buffalo as an unknown outsider with no power base of his own either on campus or in the local community. In such a circumstance, general organizational principles would predict that as a career administrator, he would be intensely loyal to the network or elite that managed his appointment, and loath to do anything that might displease it.

This network, so far as I can tell from the web, is defined by interests more than values or principles. The members do not seem to be joined by commitment to some mission, whether liberal or conservative, religious or secular, political or educational. They have full-time jobs elsewhere. Medaille is just one of their many voluntary involvements or hobbies – a toy that is fun to own, even without agreeing on how to play with it. They just want to "grow the college," as board chair Robert Stevenson put it in the recent article in *Buffalo News*. The current construction program is probably best understood as reflecting a lack of shared values: we don't know what else to do, so let's put up new buildings.

To judge from the web, Stevenson is less central to the controlling network than his formal position would suggest. As the scion of a venerable, century-old, family-owned manufacturing concern, he probably lacks the entrepreneurial, go-for-the-jugular spirit required in today's cultural elites. His main function may be to lend the actual network the legitimacy of old Buffalo money. He was not in the photo taken at the groundbreaking ceremony on April 7, 2003, featured in the spring issue of *Horizon*. Pictured with Bascuas were two other trustees, vice-chair Nicholas Trbovich, founder and president of the high-tech firm, Servotronics, and treasurer William Collins, president of Buffalo's largest public-relations firm. The smart money would guess either of these men throws more weight than Stevenson.

Such a bet is confirmed by the fact that Collins chaired the presidential search committee that chose Bascuas. The other trustees on that committee were Trbovich (an exceptionally major donor to the college), Susan Warren Russ, and Arlene Kaukus.

In the *News* article of June 22, 2003, two trustees besides Stevenson were quoted as supporting Bascuas. Both William Collins and Susan Warren Russ endorsed him strongly and showed no sympathy for critics. "When you're faced with a situation like that," said Collins, "you have to move, and I think [Bascuas] moved quickly and he moved decisively." Said Russ: "I think the majority of trustees wanted [Bascuas to be] a systematic agent of change. But that means you ruffle feathers and tick people off." Neither Collins nor Russ gave any indication of the content or goal of the change toward which Bascuas has allegedly moved decisively.

In the betting on who actually leads Medaille's ruling network, the smartest money would probably settle on Russ, vice-chair of the Medaille board, described in 2002 by the Junior League of Buffalo as the board's "president-elect." Building networks is Russ's profession and livelihood. She is Executive Director of Leadership Buffalo, an organization whose mission has been described in *Buffalo Business First* as "to unite existing and emerging leaders from diverse backgrounds and perspectives in order to increase their knowledge and understanding of community issues, broaden their vision and enhance their ability to lead."

One of the programs of Leadership Buffalo is First Impressions, a series of five evening sessions, dinner included, to introduce newly relocated senior executives to the Buffalo Niagara Region – at a cost of $2700 per executive. Bascuas was enrolled for the fall of 2002. Medaille trustees Donna Fernandes, CEO of the Buffalo Zoo, and Hal Kingsley, Sales Director at RoncoNet, were enrolled in 2001. Kingsley went on to serve with Susan Russ the next year on the Board of Directors of Leadership Buffalo, for which RoncoNet has done web design. Fernandes's organization is among those listed by Leadership Buffalo as working with its Community Facilitation Team. The list also includes several programs of the United Way, whose president, Arlene F. Kaukus, was on Bascuas's selection committee. Yet another Medaille trustee, Wanda Zygmuntowicz, partner and chief operating officer of the management consulting firm, Customericity, took the First Impressions program in 2000.

At least six Medaille trustees are shown as graduates of Leadership Buffalo's elite training program: Supreme Court Judge Joseph Makowski in 1988; the United Way's Arlene Kaukus in 1990 (she has also served on the Leadership Buffalo board); Patricia D. Barry, senior vice-president of First Niagara Bank, in 1995; Jean Taggart Fonzi, alumnus, in 1998; Michael Keating, division manager of Wegman's Food Markets, also in 1998; and Stuart H. Angert, CEO of the automotive finance firm Remarketing Services of America, in 2002. Nicholas Trbovich's son, also named Nicholas, is a 1991 graduate. Medaille trustee Andres Garcia, vice-president of Kaleida Health, has served as guest speaker in Leadership Buffalo programs.

It appears that at least 13 of the 17 members of the Medaille Board of Trustees have ties to the organization whose executive director is the Medaille Board's president-elect.

Web searches have yielded one notable connection of Leadership Buffalo to a member of the Medaille faculty. Ross Runfola, lawyer, poet, and Medaille professor, graduated in the Leadership Buffalo Class of 1999. In 2002, Runfola was one of the five members of the grievance committee at Medaille that approved Warden's and Watson's dismissals and reinforced their humiliation. On April 29, 2003, Runfola received the "Hero Award" from the United Way of Buffalo and Erie County, the organization Kaukus heads. The United Way gave $1000 to Medaille in recognition of Runfola's work. He dedicated the award to his parents, for having taught him "that we have a responsibility to work for the good of others." Runfola was recognized in Medaille's *Horizon* (spring 2003) for having donated $5,000 to the college's capital campaign; other donors included Joseph Savarese ($25,000), Robert Stevenson ($5,000), and Susan Russ ($1,500). Kaukus, meanwhile, was commencement speaker at the Medaille graduation ceremony on May 16.

More precise identification of the network currently in control of Medaille and of its remarkably compliant president must await first-hand research. If the conflict continues to escalate, as reflected in the *News* article of June 22, dissenting trustees and administrators may themselves expose the network to public view. For now, from sources on the web, one can safely guess that central to the network are the following trustees: Susan Warren Russ, William Collins, Arlene Kaukus, possibly Nicholas Trbovich, with Robert Stevenson in a supporting role. Around these central figures are probably a half dozen trustees whose silence gives consent, and a handful of favored professors like Runfola.

## Promising Leads

Even more tentatively, information on the web leads the outside researcher to wonder what cleavages exist on the Medaille Board of Trustees. The board is remarkable for its relative homogeneity, all but one or two of its members being identifiably part of the Buffalo civic elite. Still, the apparently key members of the college's ruling network (Russ, Collins, Kaukus), as well as Kingsley, Angert, Barry,

Walsh, and Zygmuntowicz, work in newer occupations where image and contacts count for more than tangible goods (like the products of Stevenson's and Trbovich's companies, the inhabitants of Fernandes's zoo, or the groceries in Keating's supermarkets). The ruling network appears to reflect postmodern culture, wherein power is pursued more purely for its own sake than in the older culture of modernity. I lack at this point evidence by which to say if the board is divided along these lines.

With progressive concentration of capital in global corporations, family businesses have become rare in America, and so has the rugged individualism that a simpler, more decentralized economy once allowed. Yet three of the Medaille trustees (Stevenson, Trbovich, and Walsh) are personally and occupationally rooted in successful family businesses. How do their priorities mesh with those of less pedigreed, less independent trustees? At this point I cannot say.

The clearest anomaly on the Medaille Board is Stephen Balch – educator, activist, president of an academic organization, with no ties or roots in the Buffalo community. His position on the board has to be exceptional. Is he seen as a sage from Princeton whose opinions carry more weight than those of the average trustee? Or is he the "odd man out" whose seat on the board is seen as a regrettable historical accident? The data by which to answer these questions have yet to be brought to light.

Two further promising leads for understanding the Medaille impasse are worth mentioning, though nothing conclusive can yet be said. First is the extent of dependence of the college's ruling network on the advice of lawyers – college attorney Thomas Brydges, trustee Judge Joseph Makowski, professor Ross Runfola, along with any trustees' spouses and friends who practice law. The understandable bias of most lawyers is toward solving workplace conflicts in the way they know best: through the courts. Further, in the adversarial structure of the justice system, it is a lawyer's professional duty to advise a client so as to achieve victory. The result is that fair resolution of mobbing cases is sometimes delayed for years by lawyers' insistent advice to busy presidents and trustees, "Just leave it to me, quit worrying, don't talk, do as I say, you can win this." Brydges's silent presence at the Daemen College conference in March, 2003, leads me to suspect that excessive deference to legal advice, the condition of being "overlawyered," helps explain why the Medaille conflict was not resolved many months ago, but this is only suspicion on the basis of limited evidence.

The other tentative lead concerns interlocking directorates and other networks joining those who control Buffalo's small liberal-arts colleges. Four informational tidbits from the web have twigged this lead. First is that Thomas Brydges, while serving as counsel to Medaille College, is also a member of the Daemen College Board of Trustees. Second is that Justice Joseph Makowski, a Medaille trustee, was appointed in 2001 to the Canisius College Board of Regents. Third is that John Donohue, despite a disastrous year as acting president of Medaille, was almost immediately appointed academic vice-president of D'Youville College. Fourth is a variety of lesser connections (alumnus, donor, advisor) between Medaille trustees and the college's sister institutions in the local area. It may be that the network controlling Medaille is part of a larger, looser network consolidating its control of Buffalo's colleges and universities, but I have too little evidence to say.

## The New VP: Obstacle or Aid?

As of July 1, 2003, a new player entered Medaille's politics: Mike Mitchell, chemist, midwesterner, long-time professor and administrator at Bethany College in Lindsborg, Kansas. His post at Medaille is the newly created number-two spot of academic vice-president. The Medaille press release quoted his understatement, "I will have plenty of chances to use both my people-working and problem-solving skills."

It was clear from the advertisement for the position that the idea for it and the choice of who would fill it rested mainly with Bascuas. The chair of the search committee, over which Bascuas appeared to have veto power, was psychology professor Judith Horowitz.

Odds are that Mitchell will prove to be a further obstacle to correcting the wrongs done to Therese Warden and Uhuru Watson. Indeed, the creation of the post of vice-president, separate from that of dean, is probably best understood as a device (unpopular presidents at many institutions have used it) to shield Bascuas from questions about the dismissals and other sources of faculty discontent – a way to get critics "off his back." Bascuas all but admitted this in the spring, 2003, issue of *Horizon*, observing that the new vice-president "will free me to pay more attention to other issues – especially external relations and fundraising." As a newcomer to Buffalo and the East with no local power base, Mitchell will depend on Bascuas for guidance. If anyone asks him about the purge of faculty, he can say honestly, "That's water under the bridge. It happened before I arrived. It's in the hands of the lawyers. I want to look ahead."

The creation of the vice-presidency and Mitchell's appointment to it can be seen as exemplifying the techniques by which organizations (or more precisely, the networks controlling them) steel themselves against correction of the harm they have done.

On the other hand, Mitchell may turn out to have a mind of his own and a vulnerability to conscience and principle. Or he may have ambition enough to curry favor with the regnant network of trustees and go after the job of his faltering boss. Crisis situations, as the Medaille story already illustrates, sometimes bring out surprising sides of individuals. Sooner or later, reasons will surface for why Mitchell, a Missouri native who has taught at a college in rural Kansas for thirty years, suddenly pulls up stakes and moves to Buffalo, New York.

## Conclusion

It is one thing for a car crash to occur, whoever may have been at fault. It is another thing, far worse, to leave broken bodies in the wreckage, without trying to make them whole again. Similarly, it is bad enough for a workplace to suffer the mobbing of one or more of its members, but another thing, far worse, to let the suffering continue without remedy. This paper is my best effort, on the basis of the information and research available, to suggest why the harm and suffering occasioned by the mobbing of Therese Warden and Uhuru Watson at Medaille College have been allowed to continue for more than a year without remedy. I welcome feedback on the explanation I have offered, just as on my two earlier papers about this conflict.

My objective is not just to produce an explanation but to produce one that facilitates remedy, and not just for Warden and Watson but for all concerned. Unless Bascuas is a psychopath, which he is not, it must be torture for him to go to campus every day, knowing that 80 percent of staff and faculty respondents have a low opinion of his leadership, and that *Buffalo News* has informed the whole city of this fact. Mitchell cannot help but feel something akin to terror as the reality of what he has gotten himself into sinks in. No friend of the college can enjoy the bad press about it, the opprobrium AAUP and FIRE have placed on it, or the real prospect that in the competitive environment of higher education, this little college is in the process of destroying itself. Resolving the conflict is to everybody's advantage.

# Chapter Five

# January-February 2004:

# AAUP Report on the Dismissals at Medaille College[1]

## Committee A, AAUP[2]

### I: Introduction

This report concerns events that occurred from June 2001 to April 2002 at Medaille College, a private, nonsectarian, coeducational

---

[1] Reprinted with the permission of AAUP from *Academe* (Jan.-Feb. 2004).

[2] The text of this report was written in the first instance by the members of the investigating committee. In accordance with Association practice, the text was then edited by the Association's staff, and, as revised, with the concurrence of the investigating committee, was submitted to Committee A on Academic Freedom and Tenure. With the approval of Committee A, the report was subsequently sent to the faculty members at whose request the inquiry was conducted, to the administration of Medaille College, and to other persons concerned in the report. In light of the responses received, and with the editorial assistance of the staff, this final report has been prepared for publication.

institution, located in Buffalo, with branch campuses in Amherst and Rochester, New York. Founded in 1875 and initially accredited in 1951 by the Middle States Association of Colleges and Schools, the college today awards associate's, bachelor's, and master's degrees, the latter in business administration and education. The college has approximately seventy full-time faculty members and enrolls some 1,750 students, most of whom commute to campus.

The governing board of Medaille College is composed of seventeen members, and its current chair is Mr. Robert L. Stevenson. Dr. John J. Donohue served as acting college president during most of the events discussed in this report. He had previously served the college as dean and then concurrently as dean and vice president for academic affairs before being named acting president in February 2001 after the death of President Kevin I. Sullivan. Dr. Donohue was one of three finalists for the regular position replacing President Sullivan. Following the selection of Dr. Joseph W. Bascuas as president of Medaille College effective July 1, 2002, Dr. Donohue left to become vice president for academic affairs at D'Youville College in Buffalo. Dr. Joseph E. Savarese was acting dean at Medaille College throughout the period of concern in this report.

The cases to be discussed deal with actions taken by the administration and the governing board of Medaille College against Professor Therese Dillon Warden, a tenured member of the Department of Human Services, and Professor Uhuru Watson, a tenured member of the Department of Social Sciences, culminating in their dismissals for cause.

Professor Warden earned a BA in nursing education from St. John's University in New York in 1964. She received an MS in social science from the State University of New York at Buffalo in 1978, and a PhD in cultural anthropology from the same institution 1985. She joined the Department of Human Services at Medaille College in 1986 and was promoted to the rank of associate professor with tenure in 1993. Professor Warden was active in campus governance and also served as president of the local AAUP chapter. In her earlier years at the college, she was instrumental in developing academic programs that resulted in substantial increases in enrollment, notably among minority students.

Professor Watson received a BA in political science and sociology from Kent State University in 1969 and an MA in political science from the State University of New York at Buffalo in 1972. He earned a PhD in political science from SUNY, Buffalo, in 1980. He began teaching at Medaille College as assistant professor in the Department of Social Sciences in 1979, was promoted to the rank of associate professor in 1983, and was granted tenure in 1987, the first African American to gain a tenured appointment at the college.

## II. Events of June 2001-April 2002

This section describes the background to the cases discussed in this report and the specific events of interest from June 2001 to November 2001 and from November 2001 to April 2002.

### 1. Background to the Cases

Before and during his term as acting president, Dr. Donohue undertook steps to move the college in a new direction. He espoused a model for initiating change based on his research on and practice of martial arts, explaining his approach to reaching decisions in a speech before the Rotary Club of Buffalo on January 3, 2001.

He described his own academic specialization in East Asian culture, and stated that his preferred model for making strategic changes was to be found in the writings of Miyamoto Mushashi, a seventeenth-century samurai warrior. He revealed that he had incorporated Mushashi's writing in the MBA curriculum at Medaille College, and that students respond positively to the "ease with which this four-hundred-year-old guide for swordsmen can be adapted to a variety of circumstances requiring strategic visions today." Summing up his views, he observed:

> In a competitive educational marketplace, academics today are increasingly challenged to develop new and innovative programs. This growing dynamic, almost entrepreneurial, approach to program development seems, in many ways, to be diametrically opposed to academic culture: one of cautious, gradual change whose custodians have intense personal and professional investment in the status quo.... This is uneasy territory where ideas, resources, and personalities meet.

The president sought to strengthen the traditional liberal arts program at the college by using career-oriented programs, such as business, as funding sources. During his earlier years as dean of the college, Dr. Donohue became embroiled in several controversies with members of the business department, including its chair. In 2000, controversies arose over grade changes initiated by Dr. Donohue and the administration's charge against a faculty member, whose grades were changed, with violating campus policies about class meetings. Also controversial was the administration's decision, said by faculty members to have been reached without meaningful consultation with the business faculty, to contract with the University of Phoenix to establish an MBA program at off-campus sites.

It is evident to the undersigned investigating committee that serious antagonism existed between the business department and Dr. Donohue before he was named acting president of the college in February 2001.

## 2. June-August 2001

On June 8, 2001, Medaille College's five-person promotion and tenure committee met to discuss several personnel matters. Professor Watson was one of four faculty members serving on the committee. Dean Savarese was its fifth member. Dr. Donohue, as acting president, attended the June meeting at the invitation of the committee. The secretary to the office of the president prepared the minutes of the meeting, which were distributed to the faculty members on the committee in early August.

According to the minutes, the purpose of the meeting "was to communicate to Dr. Donohue concerns of the Promotion and Tenure Committee about the Business Department and its department chair." The members of the committee and President Donohue candidly and critically discussed at length the work of the department chair. The minutes record that Professor Watson "asked if Dr. Donohue, as Acting President, would convey in a formal fashion the very thoughtful deliberations and concerns of the Committee." The minutes further record that Dr. Donohue stated that "some level of action needs to be taken" concerning the department chair and that he saw a "new person coming in." The minutes report that "Dr. Donohue polled individually the P&T Committee. The group concurred with this proposal." The meeting ended with Dr. Donohue's remarking, "Whether people discuss [the situation of the business department chair] or not, what takes place in the P&T meeting(s) is confidential; members cannot breach it. The same applies to [the president]."

In a memorandum dated June 20, Dr. Donohue stated to the business department chair that he had decided not to renew his administrative appointment. "This action," the president asserted, "is taken with the approval of both the P&T Committee and your immediate supervisor." A week later, in a memorandum of June 27 addressed to the members of the promotion and tenure committee, the chair sharply questioned not only the substance of the committee's reported action but also the committee's authority. The college's *Handbook of the Teaching Faculty*, the memorandum stated, does not provide for the promotion and tenure committee to make recommendations about the appointments of chairs. The memorandum concluded: "Your actions represent a flagrant disregard for the rights of faculty and are in clear violation of the duties assigned to you."

After receiving the June 27 memorandum, as well as a personal note from the department chair expressing disappointment that he had carried out his responsibilities "in such an inappropriate manner," Professor Watson wrote to the other members of the promotion and tenure committee on July 26. He pointed out that the committee is "not involved in the president's institutional and exclusive responsibility to decide, announce, name, and appoint Department Chairpersons at Medaille College"; that Dr. Donohue's memorandum of June 20, with its reference to the promotion and tenure committee, was apparently unprecedented; and that the committee should meet as soon as possible to clarify these matters.

In a separate memorandum to Dean Savarese on August 3, Professor Watson revisited issues he had raised in his July 26 memorandum, but also singled out the dean and Dr. Donohue for criticism. This August 3 memorandum concluded: "I could loathe both of you for ensnarling me in your 'administrative web spinning.'"

Responding to Professor Watson's concerns, Dr. Donohue wrote to the promotion and tenure committee on August 3 and encouraged the committee to meet. He expressed a willingness to issue a new memorandum to the department chair stating that he alone had "made the final determination." The committee met on August 17 and called on Dr. Donohue to issue a clarifying memorandum, which he did on September 6. "For the record," he wrote to the department chair, "let me explicitly state I alone made the decision in regard to your appointment. The P&T Committee made no recommendation to this effect, nor did it 'approve' this action."

Meanwhile, on August 21, Professor Watson had notified Dean Savarese that he was resigning from the promotion and tenure committee, effective immediately, because he believed that his integrity "vis-à-vis the frank comments that must be made about faculty colleagues on this Committee has been profoundly compromised, and I no longer have confidence and trust in the current P&T membership to address errors and mistakes in a timely fashion and to adhere to the . . . Handbook provisions and sections."

### 3. November 2001-April 2002

No further developments arose concerning the promotion and tenure committee until early November 2001, when the administration began an inquiry into an alleged "breach of confidentiality" of the committee's minutes for the June 8 meeting. The inquiry focused on Professor Warden, who had served on the college's five-person Faculty Council during the 2000-01 academic year, and on Professor Watson. Two other faculty members were also implicated: a tenured professor who was a current member of the Faculty Council and chair of an academic department, and a nontenured faculty member who was serving as president of the AAUP chapter.

In a December 10 memorandum to Dr. Donohue, Dean Savarese, "after a lengthy investigation" conducted by him and the college's director of human resources, concluded that Professor Watson "appears to have initially disseminated the confidential minutes" to Professor Warden. Professor Watson, the dean wrote, "has not admitted this, [but] there is a reasonable body of evidence to suggest that he is the likely suspect."

The dean recommended that Professor Watson be dismissed. The dean stated that Professor Warden had "admitted that she received the minutes," duplicated them, and shared and discussed their content with two other faculty members. He recommended that Professor Warden also be dismissed. As for the other tenured professor, the dean recommended that she be removed as chairperson and censured because, although she had not given the minutes to anyone else, she had discussed them with Professor Warden, did not notify the dean "of the situation," and failed to notify colleagues on the Faculty Council "of her personal involvement" in the matter. The nontenured faculty member's alleged wrongdoing was to have received the minutes from Professor Warden and discussed them with her. Dean Savarese recommended that this individual be censured and not reappointed.

Dr. Donohue asked and received from the senior professor her resignation as department chair. (She was subsequently reappointed to the position by President Bascuas.) The nontenured professor left Medaille College of his own volition at the end of the academic year – he had not been issued notice of nonreappointment – and is now teaching elsewhere.

In letters dated January 10, 2002, Dr. Donohue notified Professors Warden and Watson, respectively, that their conduct as reported by Dean Savarese was grounds for dismissal, that he was prepared to review additional evidence before reaching a final decision, and that, pending a final determination, each was relieved of teaching obligations, effective immediately, with full pay and benefits. Neither professor was to come onto the campus without prior approval of the president or the dean.

The letters stated, as grounds for the action, the following: "Your conduct constitutes grounds for dismissal under Section 7.2. of the *Handbook of Teaching Faculty* for turpitude and for active and voluntary participation in activities deliberately and specifically designed to bring discredit to the college."[3] In addition, Dr. Donohue charged Professor Watson with insubordination – "an independent basis for the recommended discipline" – on grounds that he "refused

---

[3] The college's faculty handbook defines turpitude as a "felony conviction or obvious and repeated misconduct in [the faculty member's] performance of academic duties." The handbook, in accordance with the 1940 *Statement of Principles on Academic Freedom and Tenure,* states further: "Faculty on continuous appointment who are dismissed for reasons not involving turpitude shall receive their salaries for at least a year from the date of notification of dismissal whether or not they are continued in their duties at the institution." The 1940 *Statement of Principles* was issued jointly by the AAUP and the Association of American Colleges and Universities.

to fully cooperate" with Dean Savarese's investigation, and that he cancelled a meeting with the president "without an adequate explanation."

Replying on January 12, Professor Warden stated that she was "shocked" by the president's letter, that she would be pleased to meet him before he reached a final decision on her case, and that she had done nothing to warrant suspension let alone dismissal from Medaille College. Professor Warden concluded, "The Handbook states that 'this manner of proceeding [contesting an action] is in accord with the 1940 AAUP document on academic freedom and tenure.' If that is so, then I request that you make no final decision, even after you and I meet, before a committee of faculty peers passes on it."

Writing on January 15, Professor Watson addressed each of the charges against him, denied that he had circulated the minutes, and denied knowledge of "anyone circulating the minutes." He concluded, "I await word of when my scheduled meeting with you regarding this matter is to take place."

Dr. Donohue met with Professor Warden on January 24. In a subsequent letter, dated February 5, the president informed Professor Warden that their meeting "confirms the substance of the investigation's findings. As a result, it is my decision to dismiss you from your faculty position at the College, effective 8 February 2002." Because, according to the president, Professor Warden's conduct constituted turpitude, he discontinued her salary as of that date.

Professor Warden reports that, along with losing her faculty position and her salary, she learned later in the summer that Dr. Donohue had moved into her office in order to make way for newly appointed President Bascuas and that nearly all the papers she kept in the office – lesson plans, evaluations of students, and irreplaceable data for applied research projects – had disappeared.

In his February 5 letter, Dr. Donohue informed Professor Warden that she could file a grievance under the relevant provisions of the faculty handbook. She did so on that same day with respect to the suspension, dismissal, and charge of turpitude. In her complaint to the five-person grievance committee, an elected faculty body, Professor Warden stated that in late October she discovered that the minutes for the promotion and tenure committee meeting had been placed anonymously in her campus mailbox, and that she photocopied them and gave the copies to the two other faculty members.[4] She stated further that, within two weeks of receiving the minutes, she met, at her initiative, with Dean Savarese to inform him of what she had received and that he proposed that she speak with Dr. Donohue, whom she then called.

According to Professor Warden's account of her conversation with the president, she identified the two individuals to whom she had given copies of the minutes and told the president that she had asked them not to distribute the minutes to anyone else. She declared that her conduct was not blame- worthy and asked to be reinstated to her tenured faculty position.

On February 5, the president also wrote to Professor Watson, who, on January 29, had filed a grievance concerning his suspension. The president reiterated the charges and asked that Professor Watson meet with him before February 8. "If you continue to refuse to meet with me," the president stated, "your employment will be terminated effective Monday, February 11, 2002." There followed correspondence between Professor Watson's attorney and the administration, and Professor Watson and his attorney met with Dr. Donohue on February 21. The president issued his decision on April 26, informing Professor Watson that he was dismissed effective that date. Salary payment also ceased as of April 26.

Professor Warden, accompanied by her attorney, appeared before the grievance committee on March 21 and April 30. Professor Watson, also accompanied by an attorney, met with the grievance committee on February 26 and April 16. The grievance committee heard testimony from Dean Savarese on April 17 and from Dr. Donohue on April 18. Neither Professor Warden nor Professor Watson (nor their respective attorneys) was present when the dean and the president gave their testimony. Neither the dean nor the president attended the meetings of the grievance committee when Professors Warden and Watson testified.

Four days before the president dismissed Professor Watson on April 26, the faculty committee that had convened to hear his grievance concerning his suspension issued its report. The same committee had separately taken up Professor Warden's grievances,

---

[4] One member of the grievance committee had served on the promotion and tenure committee when it discussed the status of the business department chair in June 2001.

and on May 21 it issued a report on her case, which is discussed below. The grievance committee in Professor Watson's case, citing the provision in the faculty handbook concerning suspension ("suspension of a faculty member from contractual duties will be made by the President only if his or her continuance directly constitutes an immediate physical or psychological danger to himself or herself, to others, or to the college"), concluded that Dr. Donohue suspended Professor Watson without adhering to the college's "specific procedures" for such action.

The committee's report went on to offer a series of alternative steps. The administration could "ignore the violation" – apparently a reference to the charges against Professor Watson – or dismiss him. In the event that the administration moved to dismiss, the grievance committee recommended, "in lieu of this option," that Professor Watson "acknowledge as true" the "facts of the investigation" conducted by Dean Savarese; that he "authorize the full disclosure" of the grievance committee's report and the results of the dean's investigation "at a full faculty meeting"; that he "apologize in private" to the dean and to Dr. Donohue "for his conduct during the investigation"; and that he "withdraw any present lawsuits" and not "initiate future lawsuits with regard to these matters."

Following the president's dismissal of him on April 26, Professor Watson, in a May 9 letter from his attorney to the chair of the grievance committee, requested a hearing on his dismissal. He disputed the allegations against him, and he also disputed the administration's position that the allegations, "if true, support the conclusion that they amount to turpitude or activity designed to bring discredit to the College." The letter expressed the "expectation" that the grievance committee "will conduct a full, fair and impartial hearing," and that, consistent with the faculty handbook, there will be opportunity to "question and/or confront within reasonable limits" all adverse witnesses.

The grievance committee's May 21 report in Professor Warden's case concluded, as had the committee's report of April 22 in Professor Watson's case, that her suspension was inconsistent with the faculty handbook. With respect to dismissal, the committee was "extremely dissatisfied" with Professor Warden's conduct "as well as her action since the time of her dismissal which we believe [has] brought discredit to us all" – the latter presumably a reference to her meeting with faculty members on other campuses to discuss her case.

With respect to the charge of turpitude, the committee declined "to delve" into the matter because it was "not within its purview . . . since [the committee] is limited to matters of procedure." Lastly, the committee recommended, "in lieu" of dismissal, that the administration "reinstate" Professor Warden under several conditions: that she agree that the grievance committee could place a "letter of censure" in her personnel file; that she be "prohibited from serving on any confidential committees for five years"; that she agree to undergo an annual review for three years to be carried out by the promotion and tenure committee; and that she would write a "letter of apology to the Medaille College community that will be read at a faculty meeting." Professor Warden found none of these recommendations acceptable.

As stated above, the committee had also received a grievance from Professor Watson with regard to his dismissal. In addition to filing the internal grievance, Professor Watson submitted a complaint to the New York State Division of Human Rights, alleging discrimination on the basis of race. Responding to the complaint on May 15, counsel for the college stated that Professor Watson's intramural grievance "will allow the [Grievance] Committee to directly address the issue of whether the Complainant's discharge was for requisite cause." In a letter to Professor Watson dated June 3, the chair of the grievance committee stated that "[i]t is our determination that the issues raised in your grievance are substantive matters. The Grievance Committee is limited to procedural matters only." The committee therefore declined to hold a hearing on Professor Watson's dismissal. The letter went on, "Additionally, when you distributed a packet of information to the Medaille College faculty on or about May 16, 2002, you took your petition outside the ordinary grievance procedure and compromised the Grievance Committee since any decision rendered would have at least the appearance of impropriety."

Professors Warden and Watson sought the assistance of the Association with respect to the disciplinary actions against them in January 2002, and its staff wrote to Dr. Donohue on February 8, 2002, and again on March 7 to convey the AAUP's concern that the actions that had been taken against the two professors to that point presented issues of tenure and academic due process. The chair of the

New York State AAUP Conference's Committee A on Academic Freedom and Tenure wrote on March 1 to Dr. Donohue to express the same concerns.

The president did not reply to the staff's letters. But in a March 8 letter to the New York State AAUP officer, the president stated that it would be "inappropriate" for him to discuss the "employment situation" of the two professors, that the college's faculty handbook "contains a process whereby a faculty grievance committee may review and conduct a hearing with respect to . . . employment decisions," and that "[a]ny information that you have been given that these individuals have been denied access to this process is inaccurate."

The Association's staff wrote again to the administration on July 15, urging newly appointed President Bascuas to allow Professors Warden and Watson to return to their faculty positions pending any further consideration of their cases consistent with the college's official policies and Association-supported standards. Replying on August 2, the president stated that he had been directed by the chair of the board of trustees to review the cases. "However," he wrote, "my review will be limited to ascertaining whether or not the appropriate process as outlined in the faculty handbook was followed in each instance and will not be a de novo review of the facts." The president stated that he anticipated concluding his review in late August or September.

In a letter of November 4, President Bascuas informed the staff that he had completed his review, that he had provided the chair of the board with an oral report, and that he had found that "the process followed in each instance did not deviate materially from the process outlined in our Faculty Handbook and the grievants were given a fair hearing by their colleagues."

In mid-December, with the issues of Association concern not having been resolved, the AAUP's general secretary authorized an investigation into the cases of Professors Warden and Watson, and President Bascuas was so informed. As noted previously, Professor Watson had filed a complaint with the New York State Division of Human Rights. Professor Warden has initiated a civil action in New York State's Supreme Court.

In a letter dated January 28, 2003, President Bascuas informed the Association's staff that the college, "acting on the advice of legal counsel, . . . declines to participate in any way in the investigation you propose." The chair of the undersigned investigating committee wrote to President Bascuas on February 21, expressing the committee's "desire to learn more about the administrative perspective" on the two dismissal cases and providing information about where the committee could be reached while it was in Buffalo. The president did not reply. The investigating committee chair wrote similarly to Dr. Donohue, but received no reply from him.

The committee visited Buffalo on February 27 and 28, 2003, where it interviewed Professor Warden, Professor Watson, and an additional ten current and former Medaille College faculty members, including individuals who had served on the grievance committee. The committee regrets that the current Medaille College administration and Dr. Donohue chose not to cooperate with the investigation, but it believes that it has sufficient information for the findings and conclusions which follow.

### III. Issues and Findings

This section describes the suspensions of Professors Warden and Watson and the procedural and substantive issues relevant to their dismissals.

### *1. The Suspensions*

As recounted earlier in this report, the Medaille College *Handbook of the Teaching Faculty* states that "[u]pon the recommendation of the academic dean, suspension of a faculty member from contractual duties will be made by the president only if his or her continuance directly constitutes an immediate physical or psychological danger to himself or herself, to others, or to the college." Regulation 5(c)(1) of the Association's *Recommended Institutional Regulations on Academic Freedom and Tenure* states that a faculty member "will be suspended . . . only if immediate harm to the faculty member or others is threatened by continuance."[5] The regulation further provides

---

[5] This regulation is consistent with the 1958 *Statement on Procedural Standards in Faculty Dismissal Proceedings*, which, like the 1940 *Statement of Principles*, was issued jointly by the AAUP and the Association of American Colleges and Universities.

that, before suspending a faculty member, the administration will consult with a faculty committee concerning the "propriety, the length, and the other conditions of the suspension."

Professors Warden and Watson were suspended from their faculty duties on January 10, 2002, and then remained on suspension until their dismissals on February 8 and April 26, respectively. Dr. Donohue gave no reason for suspending either professor. The principal charges against Professors Warden and Watson focused on their alleged mishandling of a faculty committee's minutes for a meeting that took place in June 2001. The suspensions were imposed nearly seven months later, and some two months after the administration began its inquiry into alleged "breaches of confidentiality." In the investigating committee's judgment, nothing in the alleged misconduct of Professors Warden and Watson remotely constituted "an immediate physical or psychological danger to [themselves], to others, or to the college," and a repetition of the alleged misconduct was not prevented by denying them further access to their classes or to the campus. Moreover, the administration did not consult with any faculty body about its intended actions. The investigating committee finds that the Medaille College administration suspended Professors Warden and Watson from their academic responsibilities in disregard of the college's own stated policy and of Association-supported standards of academic due process.

## 2. The Dismissals: Procedural Issues

The 1940 Statement of Principles and the 1958 *Statement on Procedural Standards in Faculty Dismissal Proceedings* provide that a faculty member is entitled, before dismissal, to a hearing on the charges before an independent faculty body. The procedures in a dismissal case set forth in Regulations 5 and 6 of the AAUP's *Recommended Institutional Regulations* require preliminary discussions between the faculty member and administrative officers "looking toward a mutual settlement" and "informal inquiry by the duly elected faculty committee" (a separate body from the one that holds the hearing of record), which may recommend that proceedings should be undertaken "without its opinion being binding upon the president."

During the hearing, the burden of proof "shall be satisfied only by clear and convincing evidence in the record considered as a whole." The faculty member "will have the right to confront and cross-examine all witnesses" and "a verbatim record of the hearing or hearings will be taken and a typewritten copy will be made available to the faculty member without cost." Should the president reject the report of the hearing body, "the president will state the reason for doing so, in writing, to the hearing committee and to the faculty member, and provide an opportunity for response before transmitting the case to the governing board."

The Medaille College faculty handbook states that a faculty member who is notified of dismissal and "wishes to contest the action" can "initiate the grievance procedure of this handbook; this manner of proceeding is in accord with the recommended procedure in the 1940 AAUP document on academic freedom and tenure." The grievance committee has the "full and complete authority" to "assure the right of each party and advisor to question and/or confront within reasonable limits all witnesses who testify" and "to keep an adequate record of the hearing." The handbook further provides that "[i]n any case in which the president decides against the recommendation of the Grievance Committee, he or she will meet with the committee to explain the decision."

To allow a faculty member a hearing on dismissal only by initiating a grievance after he or she has been dismissed is fundamentally at odds with academic due process as provided in the 1940 *Statement of Principles*. In a dismissal proceeding that is in accord with the 1940 *Statement*, the accused faculty member is afforded the opportunity to present his or her position to a faculty hearing body before dismissal can occur.

One consequence of the administration's judging and penalizing Professors Warden and Watson without having first subjected these cases to the test of academic due process is that the two professors in effect had to prove why they should not have been dismissed. A telling illustration of this problem occurred when Professor Warden and her attorney met with the grievance committee on March 21, 2002. According to a transcript of the meeting prepared by Professor Warden from electronic tapes provided to her by the committee, the following exchange took place between her attorney and two members of the committee:

*Attorney:* There is something very radically wrong [with] what is going on. As you know, I think the most important grievance filed by Dr. Warden deals with the lack of due process. We should be looking for at this point a hearing before an appropriate faculty committee. The burden of proof is on Medaille in respect to what has been done to Dr. Warden.

*First Committee Member*: You are saying the burden may be on you?

*Attorney:* To justify the grievances. I'm saying that I don't think that is proper.

*Second Committee Member*: As the Handbook outlines procedures [the] onus is on the faculty member to clearly articulate how circumstances, how experiences violated the Faculty Handbook. Whatever way we go about getting a clear understanding is not as important as how we arrive at clarity.

This inherent defect in the Medaille College faculty regulations was compounded by severe flaws in the proceedings that took place before the grievance committee.

Under Association-supported standards of academic due process, the subject faculty member has the right to confront and cross-examine witnesses in a dismissal proceeding. As noted above, the Medaille College faculty regulations require the grievance committee to ensure that each party will "question and/or confront . . . all witnesses who testify." Professors Warden and Watson each appeared before the grievance committee with only their respective attorneys present, and they were not present when Dean Savarese and President Donohue testified against them. They were thus denied the opportunity to confront and cross-examine witnesses whose testimony was plainly central to their cases.

In Professor Warden's case, the grievance committee stated that it was "extremely dissatisfied" with her conduct but recommended reinstatement if she agreed to several punitive conditions, all of which she rejected. Despite having concluded that Professor Warden's conduct in the matter of the promotion and tenure committee minutes was blameworthy, the committee declined "to delve" into the charge of moral turpitude on grounds that its purview was "limited to matters of procedure."

The investigating committee does not find the grievance committee's position tenable. Nothing in the Medaille College faculty handbook limited the jurisdiction of the grievance committee to "matters of procedure"; indeed, as noted above, the grievance committee is identified in the handbook as the faculty body that is to consider the substance of the charges in a dismissal case. Moreover, the grievance committee had addressed the substance of the dismissal charges against Professor Warden; its unwillingness to address the even more serious charge that her conduct was morally turpitudinous was, in the judgment of the investigating committee, an abuse of its responsibilities.

In Professor Watson's case, the grievance committee asserted that it declined to hold a hearing on his dismissal because the issues he had raised were substantive and the committee was "limited to procedural matters only." The committee's position in Professor Watson's case was in striking contrast to its willingness to render a judgment on the substance of the dismissal charges against Professor Warden.

The committee's refusal to consider the dismissal of Professor Watson also stands in contrast to the judgment it reached in its report on his suspension. In that instance, the committee recommended, "in lieu" of dismissal, that Professor Watson "acknowledge as true" the charges against him and that, among other measures, he apologize for his conduct and authorize the "full disclosure" of the committee's report. The committee had plainly concluded that Professor Watson was guilty of misconduct, but it denied him the opportunity to be heard in his defense that the alleged misconduct was not sufficiently grave to warrant the severe sanction of dismissal and the even more severe sanction of dismissal on grounds of moral turpitude.

Moreover, the evidence used against Professor Warden and Professor Watson was expanded beyond the events concerning the possession and distribution of the promotion and tenure committee minutes. In its report of May 21, 2002, the grievance committee reproved Professor Warden for "her actions since the time of her dismissal which we believe have brought discredit to us all." The investigating committee understands those actions to have been her seeking the assistance of the AAUP and her meeting with faculty members on other campuses to discuss her case. With respect to Professor Watson's case, the chair of the grievance committee, writing on June 3 to inform him that the committee did not intend to consider his dismissal, questioned his having distributed information about his case to faculty members at Medaille College after he had been dismissed. According to the committee chair, when Professor Watson "took" his petition "outside the ordinary grievance procedure," he "compromised the Grievance Committee since any decision rendered would have at least the appearance of impropriety."

The grievance committee seems to have assumed that what Professors Warden and Watson did after they had been dismissed constituted additional instances of inappropriate conduct bearing upon their fitness as faculty members at Medaille College. There was no opportunity for the two professors to rebut such an assumption.

Beyond the defects in the actual hearing procedures, the administration did not meet with the grievance committee to explain why it had decided to override the committee's recommendation in each case to impose severe sanctions "in lieu" of dismissal. The Medaille College faculty handbook required this step, as does Regulation 5 of the AAUP's *Recommended Institutional Regulations*.

Overall, the investigating committee finds that the procedures attending the dismissals of Professors Warden and Watson were inimical to basic requirements of academic due process. Indeed, the committee finds the failures to have been so severe as to raise serious doubts regarding the adequacy of procedural safeguards for any faculty member at Medaille College who faces dismissal or other serious sanctions.

### 3. The Dismissals: Substantive Issues

The 1940 *Statement of Principles* refers to "dismissal for cause" of faculty members. Regulation 5 of the Association's *Recommended Institutional Regulations* provides that adequate cause for dismissal "will be related, directly and substantially, to the fitness of faculty members in their professional capacities as teachers or researchers." It further provides that "the burden of proof that adequate cause exists rests with the institution, and shall be satisfied only by clear and convincing evidence in the record considered as a whole."

The Medaille College faculty handbook states that "[t]ermination for cause of a continuous appointment . . . may be made only for the gravest reasons: obvious abuses of academic freedom, consistent failure or inability to discharge responsibilities, turpitude (i.e., felony conviction or obvious and repeated misconduct in his or her performance of academic duties), or active and voluntary participation in any activity deliberately and specifically designed to bring discredit to the college."

Dr. Donohue charged Professor Warden with having "knowingly copied and distributed" confidential minutes of the promotion and tenure committee to persons unauthorized to receive them "in violation of established practice and policy." He charged Professor Watson with having distributed the minutes to persons unauthorized to receive them, also in violation of established practice and policy. Professor Watson was further charged with insubordination for not "fully" cooperating in two meetings with Dean Savarese in his investigation of the matter and for canceling a meeting with the president "without an adequate explanation." In each case, President Donohue stated that the alleged misconduct with regard to the minutes of the promotion and tenure committee amounted to "voluntary participation in activities deliberately and specifically designed to bring discredit to the college," and that the purported misconduct constituted turpitude as defined in the faculty handbook.

Questions raised by these dismissal letters include, first, whether Medaille College had an established practice and policy concerning the confidentiality of the minutes for the promotion and tenure committee. Second, if such a practice and policy existed, did Professor Warden or Professor Watson violate it? Third, if either did, was her or his conduct sufficiently grave to warrant dismissal? And, fourth, was the conduct of Professors Warden or Watson so blameworthy as to constitute turpitude? Finally, there is the charge of insubordination against Professor Watson.

From what the investigating committee has been able to determine, the official policies of Medaille College contain no provision regarding the confidentiality of the minutes of any faculty committee. Whether and to what extent the minutes of a particular faculty committee at Medaille College have, in practice, been considered confidential no doubt has varied with the committee and the issue before it. With respect to the promotion and tenure committee, the minutes for its meeting of June 8, 2001, stated that "what takes place in the P&T meeting(s) is confidential; members cannot breach it." The investigating committee has no reason to believe that this statement represented a departure from the committee's past practices, or to believe that the minutes for the committee's meeting of June 8, 2001, were not considered confidential by the members of the promotion and tenure committee, including Professor Watson.

Professor Watson, in his meetings with Dean Savarese, as the latter was conducting an inquiry into the breach of confidentiality, and in his statements to the grievance committee, denied that he had shared the committee's minutes with a person not authorized to receive them. In his memorandum of December 10, 2001, to Dr. Donohue, the dean acknowledged Professor Watson's denial but went on to say that there was "a reasonable body of evidence to suggest that he is the likely suspect."

That "body of evidence" was not identified in the memorandum; in Dr. Donohue's letter of January 10, 2002, suspending Professor Watson; in the grievance committee's report of April 22, which refers to Professor Watson's "violation" of confidentiality; or in the president's letter of April 26 dismissing Professor Watson. Perhaps Dean Savarese or Dr. Donohoe, in their meetings with the grievance committee, offered evidence in support of their claim that Professor Watson was the "likely suspect," but Professor Watson was given no opportunity to question the dean or the president and to respond to their testimony.

Whatever their view of Professor Watson's conduct as a member of the promotion and tenure committee, however, the grievance committee and the administration, by their reported comments and actions, indicated scant appreciation of the importance of academic due process in resolving the disputed facts. Even if there were "clear and convincing evidence" that Professor Watson wrongly gave the committee's minutes to Professor Warden, the question remains whether doing so warranted his dismissal from the faculty of the college.

A dismissal is a grave action and should be undertaken, as stated in the Medaille College faculty handbook, "only for the gravest reasons." The administration presented the charge against Professor Watson (as well as against Professor Warden) in such a way as to satisfy the standards set forth in the faculty handbook for dismissing a tenured faculty member. It accused him of engaging in an "activity deliberately and specifically designed to bring discredit to the college."

In the investigating committee's judgment, however, Dr. Donohue failed to demonstrate that the charge against Professor Watson reached the level of gravity envisioned in the handbook. The president asserted that Professor Watson wrongfully shared the minutes with Professor Warden, but the investigating committee is aware of no evidence in support of the administration's contention that he "deliberately" and "specifically" intended by this action "to bring discredit to the college." Nor does evidence exist that the administration gave consideration to Professor Watson's "record as a whole" in reaching its decision to dismiss him. The investigating committee believes that Professor Watson's dismissal was grossly disproportionate to the gravity of the alleged offense.

As to the charge that Professor Watson refused to cooperate fully with Dean Savarese, and that he canceled a meeting with Dr. Donohue "without an adequate explanation," the available evidence indicates that Professor Watson was angered by the inquiries directed at him, and that his initial discussions with the administration were marred by considerable tension on both sides.

Professor Watson's meeting with Dean Savarese on November 30, 2002, is illustrative. According to Professor Watson's account of what happened, he was "confronted" by the dean while en route to his class, and the dean "insisted" that he meet with him "right at that moment." Professor Watson did not want to meet at that time "because of the proximity to my class," but he agreed to "[t]his unscheduled and coerced meeting."

The investigating committee observes that Professor Watson was not charged with having failed to cooperate with the dean, but rather with not having cooperated "fully." Nor was he charged with having failed to provide any explanation to the president, but with not having offered an "adequate" one. Apart from the question whether and to what extent a faculty member's conduct might properly be considered insubordinate, the charge of insubordination in this case was too insubstantial, in the judgment of the investigating committee, to warrant dismissal or any sanction at all.

With regard to Professor Warden, she acknowledged that she had received the minutes of the promotion and tenure committee, although in her meeting with the grievance committee in April 2002 she questioned the official status of the minutes. "They were a draft of something," she stated. "They did not say confidential on them. I have seen other documents that say that. These did not."

She had earlier told the grievance committee that what she read "was clearly disturbing, for . . . [they] did not reflect the legitimate process and functions of that committee." She copied the minutes and gave the copies to a member of the college's Faculty Council and to the president of the local AAUP chapter, two individuals she considered "representatives of governance bodies on campus." She reports that she asked these two faculty members not to give the minutes to anyone else, and that she notified Dean Savarese and Dr. Donohue of what she had done.

Professor Warden believed that the minutes revealed that the promotion and tenure committee had not functioned properly in an important personnel matter, and that this problem needed to be called to the attention of two faculty leaders. Professor Warden's assessment of the seriousness of the matter and what to do about it was based on her long service in faculty governance at Medaille College.

Faculty committee documents that are clearly marked confidential must remain so. If they do not, confidentiality for committee documents would have no meaning. The investigating committee recognizes that Professor Warden could reasonably conclude from the document she had received that the unusual problems experienced by the promotion and tenure committee called for an unusual response. The question remains, however, whether Professor Warden's conduct exceeded the limits of legitimate action. An evaluation of her conduct involves questions of degree and intent. The investigating committee believes that even if the administration's charges against Professor Warden were sustained, they could not justify the actions it took against her.

Professor Warden gave copies of the minutes to the two faculty members and to no one else. She additionally sought to limit any further distribution by asking the two individuals to keep the minutes in confidence, and there is no evidence that they failed to honor her request. She spoke with Dean Savarese and Dr. Donohue and told them what steps she had taken. In sum, the available evidence indicates that Professor Warden, having found the committee's minutes in her campus mailbox, intended by her actions to deal responsibly with what she saw as a serious issue of governance.

One might still conclude that Professor Warden should have done no more than give the minutes to the administration. If the course she actually pursued was a mistake, however, the investigating committee believes that her conduct did not warrant the conclusion that she was no longer fit to serve as a tenured professor at the institution. As in Professor Watson's case, the committee believes that the dismissal of Professor Warden was grossly disproportionate to the seriousness of the offense.

The investigating committee thus finds no substantial evidence in the cases of Professors Warden and Watson to justify the sanction of dismissal, and certainly, the committee finds no evidence to justify the even more severe sanction of dismissal because of moral turpitude.

The 1940 *Statement of Principles* provides that tenured faculty members who are dismissed for cause will receive at least one year's salary "whether or not they are continued in their duties at the institution" unless there has been a finding of moral turpitude. Interpretive Comment 9 on the 1940 *Statement* states that moral turpitude refers to conduct that is "so utterly blameworthy as to make it inappropriate to require the offering of a year's teaching or pay. The standard is not that the moral sensibilities of persons in the particular community have been affronted. The standard is behavior that would evoke condemnation by the academic community generally." The Medaille College faculty handbook provides for terminal salary for a dismissed tenured faculty member consistent with the provisions of the 1940 *Statement*. The handbook, as noted earlier, defines turpitude as a "felony conviction or obvious and repeated misconduct."

Professor Warden received notice of dismissal on February 5 effective February 8, 2002, and her salary ceased on that date. Professor Watson received notice of dismissal on April 26, which date also saw the cessation of his salary. The administration justified the immediate cessation of salary on grounds that the faculty members' conduct amounted to turpitude. The grievance committee did not recommend dismissal in either case, and the investigating committee is unaware of any other evidence that the administration's position concerning turpitude reflected a consensus of the particular community constituting Medaille College, let alone the academic community generally.

Dr. Donohue may have been offended by what he considered to be the misconduct of Professors Warden and Watson, but his hostility toward them, in this investigating committee's judgment, should not have been cause for charging them with turpitude and dismissing them from the faculty of Medaille College. The harm inflicted on Professors Warden and Watson by dismissing them was compounded in Professor Warden's case by the unexplained disappearance of nearly all the research records, evaluations of students, and other files that were in her campus office.

The investigating committee remains uncertain about the reasons for the drastic actions taken by the administration of Medaille College against Professors Warden and Watson. Did the allegation of turpitude result only from the incident concerning the minutes of the promotion and tenure committee (and in Professor Watson's case, from alleged insubordination), or from some additional circumstance? The investigating committee cannot provide the answer. Dr. Donohue did not respond to any of the staff's letters, and neither he nor President Bascuas was willing to meet with the committee.

The investigating committee does find that the administration's action in dismissing the two professors for conduct it claimed to be turpitudinous, without having demonstrated the validity of its claim in a proceeding in which the professors could be heard in their own defense, warrants condemnation in the strongest terms.

## V. Conclusions

1. The administration of Medaille College suspended Professor Therese Dillon Warden and Professor Uhuru Watson from their academic responsibilities and barred them from the campus without evidence of a threat of immediate harm as required in the 1958 *Statement on Procedural Standards in Faculty Dismissal Proceedings* and the college's own official policies.

2. In subsequently dismissing Professors Warden and Watson from the faculty, the administration denied them academic due process as called for in the 1940 *Statement of Principles on Academic Freedom and Tenure*, the 1958 *Statement on Procedural Standards,* the Association's derivative *Recommended Institutional Regulations,* and the college's own policies. The faculty grievance committee contributed to these denials of due process.

3. In light of the available evidence, the charges against Professors Warden and Watson, even if sustained, were not of sufficient gravity to warrant dismissal and certainly did not justify taking the extreme action of dismissal without terminal salary on grounds of turpitude. Those actions were grossly disproportionate to the seriousness of the alleged offenses.

> *Investigating Committee:*
> Robert K. Moore (Sociology), Saint Joseph's University, *Chair*
> Sandi Cooper (History), College of Staten Island, City
>     University of New York

*Committee A on Academic Freedom and Tenure* has by vote authorized publication of this report in *Academe: Bulletin of the AAUP*. Chair: JOAN WALLACH SCOTT (History), Institute for Advanced Study. Members: JEFFREY HALPERN (Anthropology), Rider University; MARY L. HEEN (Law), University of Richmond; EVELYN BROOKS HIGGINBOTHAM (Afro-American Studies and Divinity), Harvard University; DAVID A. HOLLINGER (History), University of California, Berkeley; CANDACE C. KANT (Social Sciences), Community College of Southern Nevada; STEPHEN LEBERSTEIN (History), City College, City University of New York; ROBERT C. POST (Law), Yale University; CHRISTOPHER M. STORER (Philosophy), DeAnza College; DONALD R. WAGNER (Political Science), State University of West Georgia; MARTHA S. WEST (Law), University of California, Davis; JANE L. BUCK (Psychology), Delaware State University, *ex officio*; MARY A. BURGAN (English), AAUP Washington Office, *ex officio*; DAVID M. RABBAN (Law), University of Texas, ex officio; ERNST BENJAMIN (Political Science), Washington, D.C., *consultant;* MATTHEW W. FINKIN (Law), University of Illinois, *consultant*; ROBERT A. GORMAN (Law), University of Pennsylvania, *consultant*; LAWRENCE S. POSTON (English), University of Illinois, Chicago, *consultant*; GREGORY SCHOLTZ (English), Wartburg College, *liaison from Assembly of State Conference.*

# Part Two

# The Richardson Dismissal

# at Toronto

# Chapter Six

# Overview: the Mellen Project

The asymmetry between this chapter's title and that of the corresponding chapter in Part One points to differences between the two parts of this book. In my study of the Warden/Watson dismissals, my purpose was to teach and learn about academic mobbing and assist in its remedy, in the context of their specific college. I therefore thought of the research as my "Medaille Project." My study of the Richardson dismissal, by contrast, was more ambitious, cast from the start in a context broader than the University of Toronto. Few professors there were any longer concerned about the case. It was no longer in the news. Remedy was not likely in the short run. It made no sense to embed my research specifically in the academic home from which Richardson had moved on. I therefore infused this project with dialogic principles and methods in a different way than at Medaille. My aim was to foster awareness of mobbing in the academic world at large, to lodge the concept in the vocabularies of professors far and wide, first by producing a worthy, comprehensive book on the subject, with the Richardson dismissal as the main case-study, and then by using that book to start conversations on mobbing in a variety of specific contexts. Mellen Press shared these objectives and put resources toward achieving them. The result was what I came to think of as my "Mellen Project."

A shorthand description of how Parts One and Two herein differ is that while the Medaille dismissals and the one at Toronto are all extreme examples of academic mobbing, the one at Toronto is more extreme – at least from the vantage point of 2006. The reason is that the disgrace and social elimination inflicted on Warden and Watson in 2002 are now seen to have been temporary. Both professors have been officially restored to respectability. It is hard now to imagine how indelible their earlier stigma appeared to be. The wrongness of what was done to them seems obvious – in retrospect. The disgrace and social elimination inflicted on Richardson in 1993-94, by contrast, has remained as a stigma upon him for more than a decade. By official judgment of the University of Toronto, this professor is still a villain. On account of the weight of institutional verdicts, the wrongness of what was done to him is hard to see – also risky to suggest, since defending Richardson might arouse the same anger in Toronto administrators as defending Warden and Watson did in Medaille administrators in 2002. The Richardson elimination is thus a more extreme case, at least for now.

The present chapter describes how Mellen Press and I handled the lengthy manuscript resulting from my research. But first things first. Since many readers of this book will not have read my comprehensive book, *The Envy of Excellence* (2005), I need to include here a brief summary of the analysis detailed there of the Richardson case. Readers familiar with that book can skip or skim the section below. Readers unfamiliar with the longer account will find in the following paragraphs enough detail on the Richardson case to let them understand and respond critically to the remaining chapters herein.

## Summary of the Richardson Mobbing

Herbert Richardson's elimination from St. Michael's and Toronto began in 1986. Basic background information from the 1970s and earlier about the professor, church, and university at issue is essential to making sense of how and why this mobbing occurred later on:

- *The professor.* Born in Baltimore in 1932 to parents of modest means, Richardson earned a BA in French from Baldwin-Wallace in 1952, an MA in American Culture from Western Reserve in 1953, an STB from Boston in 1955, and a PhD from Harvard in 1962. He was ordained to the Presbyterian ministry in 1956. From study in France and Germany, he had made himself fluently multilingual. He taught at Bucknell in 1961-62, then at Harvard until 1968. His pedigree and his publications, especially *Toward an American Theology* (Harper & Row, 1967), placed him in the forefront of young American Protestant theologians, but on the conservative side. While supporting the social gospel, the civil rights and feminist movements, and most new technologies, Richardson opposed relativism, secularization, the God-is-dead movement, and Robert Bellah's concept of civil religion. Arguing strongly for institutional pluralism and tolerance, he defended the autonomy of religious faith, the validity of conversion experiences, and the right of new religions like the Moonies and Scientology to exist. He published about one book a year during his first two post-PhD decades, and held visiting appointments at Princeton, Iowa, St. Louis, Iliff, Quebec, and elsewhere. He founded a publishing company in 1973, initially for scholarly works on religion, and named the press for his maternal grandfather, Edwin Mellen.

- *The Catholic aggiornamento.* During and after the Second Vatican Council of 1962-65, the Church of Rome opened itself to the world, enacted reforms, and embraced ecumenism. In the hopeful climate of the time, St. Michael's College, the Catholic constituent of the University of Toronto, run by the Basilian Fathers, invited Richardson in 1968 to join its Institute of Christian Thought. Richardson agreed, dividing his time the first two years between Toronto and the University of Tübingen, Germany. It was a bold move both for John Kelly, the St. Michael's president, and for the young Protestant theologian. The goal was that Richardson would join in creating an ecumenical Christian theology for the modern world. St. Michael's promoted him to full professor in 1972, when he was forty years old. Richardson had a large student following at Toronto, as at Harvard. He supervised more than two dozen PhD theses, and twice that at the MA level.

- *The dual institutional structure at Toronto.* Richardson's position at Toronto was nested in the distinctly Canadian structure of large, nonsectarian universities including smaller, church-related colleges and universities as integral parts. Thus, Richardson's tenured position as a theology professor of the University of St. Michael's College meant that he was also a tenured professor in the Department of Religious Studies of the University of Toronto. His salary was paid by St. Michael's, but the cost was shared by that college and the larger university.

Richardson was thus subject to two separate administrative hierarchies: a president plus deans of arts and theology at St. Michael's, a president plus an academic vice-president, deans and vice-deans of arts and science, and a department chair on the main university campus. College administrators would consult with their university counterparts for teaching assignments and evaluations of professors with dual affiliations. Such arrangements worked amicably in the halcyon days of the 1970s, less so as time went on. With tightening of budgets and waning interest in religion, the university gradually usurped the powers of the church-related colleges.

The hopeful climate in which Richardson joined the St. Michael's faculty did not last. The longer-run outcome of the Second Vatican Council was a crumbling of Catholic institutional structures in North America. Mass attendance dwindled. Priests and nuns left the church in droves. Colleges like St. Michael's that had depended on clerical faculty foregoing full salaries found themselves in a financial pinch. The first of two big turning points was 1978, when the reformist Pope Paul VI died, the permissive Toronto Archbishop Philip Pocock resigned, and the world-affirming St. Michael's President John Kelly retired. The new pope, John Paul II, slowly pulled back from the spirit of Vatican II into a reaffirmation of orthodox Catholicism. The new Toronto Archbishop, Emmett Carter, was imperious and magisterial. The ecumenical movement began to lose steam. Church discipline tightened. At St. Michael's, the earlier openness began to wane.

Then came the huge turning point of 1986. Cardinal Joseph Ratzinger (now Pope Benedict XVI), at that time the Vatican's chief disciplinarian, made an official visit to St. Michael's and gave a major speech in Toronto's Varsity Stadium, reaffirming Catholic dogma and insisting that professors in Catholic universities adhere to it. One of Ratzinger's former students from his time as a professor at Tübingen, the Jesuit Michael Fahey, became Dean of Theology at St. Michael's that same year. Richardson was directly under Fahey's authority, since the Institute of Christian Thought to which he had initially been appointed had been abolished.

On January 7, 1987, Fahey officially informed Richardson on behalf of the St. Michael's governing board: "I want you to know that although you have served St. Michael's generously we would be prepared to accept other possibilities for your intellectual future, even your resignation to devote your full talents to publication."

The Protestant professor did not resign. There ensued six years of harassment, marginalization and isolation, as Fahey and other administrators inched him out. In March of 1989, Fahey required all theology professors at St. Michael's to sign a new set of bylaws affirming their "special responsibilities to the Roman Catholic Church." On grounds of conscience, Richardson refused. Relations between him and Fahey grew icier. On September 27, 1990, Richardson wrote to Richard Alway, the new St. Michael's president, complaining that Fahey was sending him memoranda that made

allegations and insinuations of professional neglect and misconduct. The obvious purpose of these memoranda is to compile a file to be used against me. ... You have asked me to wait so that the problem can be resolved quietly. I agreed to do so, but it is apparent that SMC is using my time of waiting to construct an adverse case against me and, so to say, redefine the issues. How else do you think a reasonable man should interpret these things?

In July of 1991, Alway proposed that Richardson cease to be a professor of theology at St. Michael's and transfer his teaching to religious studies in the larger university. Richardson was agreeable, but an organizational procedure for such transfer was lacking. Richardson's courses lost their St. Michael's designation, and he was left in a kind of no man's land.

Despite their eagerness to get rid of Richardson, the St. Michael's administrators could not fire him outright. He had been a prominent member of its faculty for a quarter century. He was tenured and within a few years of mandatory retirement at 65. It was hardly in the college's interest to be seen as persecuting a Protestant. Some alternative reason to oust him had to be found, preferably something that would justify main-campus administrators going after him. If the St. Michael's administrators were the first of the three groups that eventually coalesced for Richardson's elimination, the main-campus administrators were the second. What drew them into the campaign was a student's complaint to the Dean of Arts and Science in the fall of 1991, that Richardson had gotten angry in his evening class on October 30.

Handling such complaints from students is a routine part of administrators' jobs. They usually draw the problem to the offending professor's attention, sometimes ask him or her to meet with the complainant or apologize to the class. Sometimes an offended student is allowed to switch to another class. Many professors who are total disasters in the classroom but who are in the administration's good graces survive in their jobs for decades. Richardson was not a disaster. He was sometimes disorganized, erratic, irreverent, and challenging, but the standard student evaluations of his courses were generally positive. Many students counted him among their most respected and valued teachers.

There were probably several reasons why the main-campus dean, Martha Chandler, chose not to handle the complaint against Richardson in the normal way, instead to treat it as a "critical incident." She might have been acting on advice from the St. Michael's administrators or from Joanne McWilliam, the chair of Religious Studies, whom Richardson considered lightweight and whose appointment he had opposed (she was the ex-wife of one of his friends). McWilliam described Richardson in a memo to Chandler as "a time-bomb waiting to explode." The main-campus administrators may have had reasons of their own to go after Richardson. He was a well-known antismoking activist, while President Prichard sat on the board of a major tobacco company. His press had become large enough to compete with the university's own press. He was an unashamed upholder of classic values like Christian faith, reason, and free expression, values out of sync with the increasingly dominant ethos of relativism and postmodernism.

Whatever the reason, the main-campus administrators seized upon the student complaint to justify a far-reaching investigation of Richardson's teaching, research, writing and publishing. Richardson himself was not informed of the complaint for five months, and then only in vague, menacing terms. Meanwhile the main-campus administrators (Chair McWilliam, Dean Chandler, Vice-deans Craig Brown and Don Dewees, and their superiors) exchanged information and suspicion about Richardson with the St. Michael's administrators (President Alway, Theology Dean Fahey, and Arts Dean Joseph Boyle), and gradually formed among themselves a consensus that Richardson was abusive, dangerous, dishonest, and unfit to remain on the faculty.

The upshot was a letter from Dewees to Richardson on September 25, 1992, threatening him with severe discipline, possibly dismissal, identifying six ways in which his teaching would henceforth be monitored, and calling into question not only his teaching but his scholarship, his service to the university, and his outside activities. Richardson was by then under a physician's care for stress. In a long, respectful response to Dewees, he defended his pedagogy but also apologized for offending some students in the previous year's night class. Richardson sought a personal meeting with Dewees, whom he had not previously met, in the hope of mutual understanding and reconciliation. Instead, when they met on December 7, 1992, Dewees said Richardson should take early retirement as soon as arrangements could be made, and he confirmed this request in a letter of December 18, 1992. The time for dialogue was past.

Richardson was angry, sad, depressed, scared: devastated in all the ways a mobbing target usually is when the weight of the eliminative effort sinks in. He returned to his doctor, Robert Francis, head of a well-known Toronto clinic specializing in workplace-related ills. Francis placed Richardson on medical leave for stress, informing the university on January 7, 1993, that

> it is my opinion that it would be injurious to Professor Richardson's health to perform his teaching duties at University of Toronto at this time. The medical treatment required will also prevent him from performing these tasks for at least the next three months.

The medical leave extended from January 4 to April 19, 1993. Richardson spent most of this time away from Toronto: in a health program at Duke University in Durham, North Carolina, resting, vacationing, and traveling in connection with projects at Mellen Press. He was also tending to family responsibilities. His first marriage had ended in 1988. He had recently remarried and was the father of a one-year-old son, with a second baby on the way.

Meanwhile, for the administrators at St. Michael's and Toronto, the medical leave provided additional time to forge themselves into a coordinated two-pronged front against Richardson and build the case against him. They hired a private investigator (it is not clear who paid the bill) to track his travels and activities. During this period, they also had a stroke of extraordinary good luck, in being approached by

Robert West, leader of the third prong of what became a three-pronged attack.

West was a senior, trusted employee of Mellen Press working far from its head office in Lewiston, New York. West lived in San Francisco, where he was to develop a branch office. Richardson considered him a friend and spoke freely with him on the week-long trip to Europe the two of them made together on press business in March of 1993. Shortly thereafter, Richardson discovered that West had been using his position with Mellen to develop a competing publishing company of his own, to which he had redirected Mellen authors and manuscripts. Richardson therefore fired West.

West was angry at Richardson. As he would say later, "I wanted to get this off my chest, I wanted to vent some spleen." Beginning on April 14, 1993, West made a series of anonymous phone calls (using the name, "Mr. Shaw") to St. Michael's Arts Dean Boyle, bad-mouthing Richardson. Boyle then transmitted West's defamations to his fellow administrators. West told Boyle that Richardson was not sick but that he was using the medical leave to run his publishing company and to try to start a university in connection with it. There was some truth in this. It was a matter of casting Richardson's actual activities in a negative light. From the latter's viewpoint, Mellen was a vehicle of important scholarship, nothing to be ashamed of. Travel on its behalf was a way of *relieving* the debilitating stress of his position at Toronto.

By June 23, 1993, all the relevant Toronto administrators were on side in the decision to dismiss Richardson. On that date, Dewees sent the professor a lengthy letter – the administrative equivalent of an indictment – detailing four allegations deemed to warrant dismissal:

- *Scholarly misconduct.* Richardson was said to have claimed others' scholarship as his own, listed a nonexistent book on his vita, and misrepresented edited collections as books he had himself authored. (By the time of the tribunal hearing on Richardson's dismissal a year later, the university had backed away altogether from these allegations. They were never retracted but nothing more was heard of them.)
- *Bad teaching.* Dewees claimed Richardson frightened, harassed, abused, terrorized, and bullied students, and that his courses lacked substantive content. (In the eventual tribunal hearing, the university's lawyers disparaged Richardson's teaching at great

length, focussing mainly on his anger in the evening class of October 30, 1991. The tribunal agreed that Richardson's classroom behavior was terrible, but not so terrible as by itself to constitute gross misconduct or justify dismissal.)

- *Managing Mellen Press.* Dewees accused Richardson of failing to provide university authorities with a full statement of his work at his publishing company and the associated new university. (The tribunal upheld this allegation and ruled that it constituted gross misconduct warranting dismissal. That Richardson had been publicizing the press aggressively for twenty years and had published through it the work of numerous Toronto professors was judged to fall short of the "full statement" required.)

- *Abusing the medical leave.* Richardson's Mellen activities and travels during the medical leave were said to constitute gross misconduct and to warrant dismissal. (The tribunal upheld this allegation, faulted Robert Francis for authorizing the leave, and claimed that stress alone does not warrant a medical leave, but only illness caused by stress. The tribunal deemed Richardson in this context "a dishonest and untrustworthy employee.")

The same day Dewees sent this indictment letter to Richardson, Dean Chandler (Dewees's administrative superior) wrote to Vice-President Joan Foley, asking her to recommend to President Robert Prichard that Richardson be dismissed. Chandler added, "The effect of dismissal will be to leave Professor Richardson solely in the employment of St. Michael's College. St. Michael's College will move to dismiss him."

On June 28, 1993, Foley recommended Richardson's dismissal to Prichard, who then officially dismissed the professor on July 9. Five months later, on November 26, 1993, President Alway dismissed Richardson from St. Michael's, pending ratification by a three-person tribunal and the college's governing board.

However complex the dismissal proceedings were, they were but part of Richardson's mobbing. The main other part was the smearing of his and the press's names in public media. Robert West took the lead. Besides contacting the Toronto administrators and persuading another former Mellen employee to do the same, West contacted Jeffrey Kittay, editor of *Lingua Franca*, a magazine based in New York that was popular among academics at the time. West told Kittay he had a "hot story" about a "rogue professor" involved in "vanity academic publishing" and "selling doctorates." Kittay ran with the story, which appeared in the issue of September/October 1993. It depicted Richardson as a "one-time Moonie apologist" running a "quasi-vanity press cunningly disguised as an academic publishing house with a moniker conveniently similar to that of the better known Mellon Foundation...." Not only Richardson's good name but even that of his grandfather, Edwin Mellen, got drubbed.

Richardson promptly sued *Lingua Franca.* The suit did not come to trial until 1996, and then it was thrown out. *Lingua Franca* ceased publication in 2001. Meanwhile, the damage was done. Sales of Mellen books plummeted. All but six of Mellen's 40 employees had to be laid off. Not until 1999 did the press regain its former momentum and begin a period of stupendous growth.

In the fall of 1993, the press's very survival seemed in doubt. No sooner did the *Lingua Franca* article appear than the main Canadian media picked up the story. The *Globe and Mail,* at the time Canada's only national newspaper, headlined its front-page article on October 1, 1993: "When academe draws the line. Is tenure bulletproof? A prof shown the door...." Over the next twelve months, the *Globe* published 24 stories on the Richardson dismissal, while the *Toronto Star*, Canada's largest daily, published 19, and the *Toronto Sun* published twelve. Newspapers elsewhere in Canada picked up the story from wire services. Richardson was held up as an abusive, dishonest, generally bad man, for all of Canada to see.

Given the remarkably successful coalescence in 1993 of the three groups bent on Richardson's elimination – the entire administrative hierarchies of St. Michael's and Toronto, plus Robert West and friends – and given the extent of negative publicity about Richardson, the tribunal hearings of 1994 were anticlimatic, something of a ritual or formality. Two of the three members, Barry Brown and Robert Tully, were professors at St. Michael's and thus subject to the college administration's authority. The tribunal chair was John Evans, a prominent law professor at York University who was subsequently appointed to the Federal Court of Canada.

The contrast in duration and quantity of output between the Evans tribunal and the ones at Medaille College that upheld Warden's and Watson's dismissals is striking. The hearings in Warden's case lasted two afternoons, in Watson's just one, but in Richardson's case seventeen days between May 30 and July 22, 1994. The written decision in Warden's case took six double-spaced pages, in Watson's case three double-spaced pages, but in Richardson's case 56 single-spaced pages, not counting the boxloads of exhibits.

The bottom line at Toronto, however, was the same as in the cases at Medaille: that the professor on trial was not just guilty of specific offenses but possessed of basically bad character. My comprehensive book, *The Envy of Excellence*, includes a *prècis* of the truthful, factual, conciliatory decision the Evans tribunal could have rendered, had it not been so caught up in eliminative fury:

> Our first, basic finding is that over the past decade, the St. Michael's administration and the professor it seeks to dismiss have moved in opposite academic directions. The ecumenical institute to which Professor Richardson, a Protestant theologian, was appointed in 1968, no longer exists. The college now pursues a distinctly Catholic agenda. In 1987, the college asked Professor Richardson to leave. He has increasingly pursued his own scholarly agenda away from the college, at Mellen Press and in the wider academic community.

> Our decision must respect both the college's academic freedom and Professor Richardson's, both its autonomy and his tenure. Our decision must also recognize that dialogue between these two parties has broken down, and is unlikely to resume.

> Our second finding is that for 26 years, Professor Richardson has faithfully and innovatively satisfied his scholarly and teaching obligations to St. Michael's, the University of Toronto, the academic community at large, and the public. He has published far more than average. Up to and including 1992, he has taught and supervised a greater than average number of students, many of whom have found him to be an excellent teacher.

> He has not, by the evidence of this hearing, excelled equally in all classes or in the eyes of all students. Witnesses on both sides have testified about his outburst of anger in an evening class on October 30, 1991. When he was informed many months later of several students' complaints about that class, Professor Richardson promptly and voluntarily wrote a formal apology for this outburst,

pledging to tone down his emotional exuberance in the classroom.

Our third finding is that the growth of Mellen Press in recent years has placed steadily greater demands on Professor Richardson's time, demands likely to increase further. He has stretched himself thin, to the likely detriment of his teaching and of his own health.

In view of all the above, our decision is that St. Michael's College should accept Professor Richardson's offer to reduce his appointment to half time, effective immediately. Two years in half-time status, 1994-95 and 1995-96, along with credits already earned, should entitle him to a terminal sabbatical leave in 1996-97, by the end of which he will have turned 65, the mandatory retirement age.

Such a decision would have smoothed things over and saved face for all concerned. Such, however, is not the aim of workplace mobbing. It's aim is to rub the targeted party's face in mud. That is what the St. Michael's tribunal did to Richardson. Robert West was its star witness. The tribunal said it found West's evidence credible. In 2003, as mentioned earlier, West retracted his testimony:

> I recognize that Professor Herbert Richardson has had a distinguished career as a scholar and researcher. He has been a pioneer in the serious study of new religions as well as an innovative publisher of academic scholarship via Edwin Mellen Press.
>
> I regret the difficulties he has had with *Lingua Franca* magazine and the University of Toronto. I do not believe Herbert Richardson to be a "rogue professor" nor do I believe that the Edwin Mellen Press was organized to be a vanity operation.

The foregoing summary of the Richardson case, sufficient for present purposes, is drawn from my comprehensive book, *The Envy of Excellence* (2005), to which readers are referred for further discussion of the many ins and outs, twists and turns of the case.

### What to Do with a Big Book

The core of the Mellen project was and is the 350-page book I finished in the spring of 2003. Researching and writing it had taken four years and involved investigation of three overlapping subjects. First was the Richardson mobbing. I read and analyzed not only the mountain of documentation on his dismissal and the related attacks on him and Mellen Press, but also enough of his own scholarly work, the background of St. Michael's College, and trends in intellectual culture to let me place his mobbing in historical context. The second subject was workplace mobbing, a rich understanding of which I wanted to convey in my book. I sifted through literature on everything from adolescent swarming to the Holocaust, from attribution error to organization theory, from political correctness to Renè Girard's theory of scapegoating. The third subject was the additional cases of academic mobbing that came to my attention through personal contacts and news reports. I settled on fifty such cases for systematic comparison to Richardson's, in order to capture general insights. As coherently as I could, I pulled all three of these investigations together in the resultant book.

The question was what to do with this big book. The plan that took shape can be understood in terms of where I agree and where I disagree with Karl Marx, perhaps the most important of the founders of social science. On Marx's tomb in London's Highgate Cemetery is inscribed the famous line from his *Theses on Feuerbach* (1845): "The philosophers have only interpreted the world in various ways; the point is to change it." I share this sentiment. Marx's *praxis*, like William James's *pragmatism*, comes from the Greek word for *action*. It is what my big book was written for: not just to shed light on academic conflict, provide intellectually satisfying explanations of events, but to achieve these objectives along the way to a more ambitious one: helping change academic structures and cultures so as to prevent the waste, harm, and untruthfulness mobbing entails. In writing *The Envy of Excellence,* my intent was to produce knowledge so truthful and powerful, so congruent with current realities, that it would be used to transform these realities in beneficial ways.

My disagreement with Marx comes in the manner of trying to bring about such change. Marx sketched on paper a plan for a political and economic reality that would be better for people, more humane and decent, than the capitalist reality he observed and illuminated in the Europe of his day. He favored implementation of that plan by state authority, even by dictatorship. He would *make* people be good, whether they liked it or not. From the vantage point of our generation in this new millennium, the results of the Marxist kind of praxis have been generally disappointing. However attractive a communist society might look on paper, the reality created by well-intentioned communist governments falls short of expectations and results in much misery (Stan Weeber's chapter herein describes some of that misery in Stalinist Russia).

For the same reason as I oppose Marxist readiness to bring about new communist realities by force, I recoil from attempts to reduce the incidence of mobbing by enacting and enforcing anti-mobbing laws and policies. The use of "expertise" to persuade administrators and lawmakers to impose such policies on workplaces, even to announce "zero tolerance" for mobbing, has flourished in Europe and has begun in North America. I doubt that its effects will be positive. You cannot *make* people be good. If the effect of my comprehensive study of academic mobbing were to be merely the introduction of anti-mobbing clauses into collective agreements and policy manuals of colleges and universities, I would be disappointed, fearful that I had made things worse. In *The Envy of Excellence*, I wrote that if Toronto had had an anti-mobbing policy on the books when Richardson was mobbed, administrators there would probably have found him guilty of gross misconduct warranting dismissal for violations of that policy.

Mellen Press and I therefore devised a way of handling my book that would be consonant with values on pluralism and free expression, so as to attack the practice of mobbing at its heart. Since mobbing cuts off open, far-ranging, reasoned dialogue, we sought to publish my book about it in a way that would promote such dialogue.

Instead of releasing *The Envy of Excellence* immediately, advertising it and sending out review copies in the usual way, Mellen produced a preliminary, paperback edition, and sent complimentary copies to scholars in diverse disciplines and in institutions small and large, public and private, in North America and abroad, inviting these professors to write critical commentaries in response. The idea was that the manner of publishing the book should itself reflect and serve the values underlying it. We hoped for more than journal reviews declaring the book a worthy contribution to the literature, more than sales to academic libraries. We aimed for the book to be thrown around, its subject matter talked and argued about in the action contexts of specific disciplines and institutions.

The strategy worked, increasing exponentially the case histories of mobbing and the insights about this pathology even prior to formal publication of my book. The press accepted for publication forty of the essays submitted in response to its invitation.

It published nine of them as an appendix bound with *The Envy of Excellence*, so that readers of that book would be confronted from the start with varied and conflicting views on its subject matter, and thus be encouraged to form their own views instead of just taking my analyses at face value. Also in that appendix, and invaluable for adding an administrator's perspective on academic mobbing, is the review of the preliminary edition that appeared in the *Canadian Journal of Education* by Michael Manley-Casimir, at that time dean and acting vice-president at Brock University.

Reviewing the submitted essays, the editors at Mellen Press and I discerned that a further eighteen of them, along with a few articles of mine, could be assembled into a useful, stand-alone introduction to the field of academic mobbing, an alternative to *The Envy of Excellence* for readers preferring a variety of authors, cases, and viewpoints. I agreed to act as editor for this volume: *Workplace Mobbing in Academe: Reports from Twenty Universities* (2004).

The next phase of the Mellen Project was to gather nine of the essays that chronicled case histories of mobbing in higher education, secondary education, business and medicine into a volume entitled *Winning, Losing, Moving On: How Professionals Deal with Workplace Harassment and Mobbing* (2005). That volume includes studies of incipient mobbings that never reached full force as well as extreme cases. The first chapter, one of the ugliest of the many ugly stories submitted in response to Mellen's invitation, is by a professor who took his own life shortly after putting on paper the full account of the destruction of his career.

Now finally comes this concluding volume in the Mellen Project, for which we have reserved six essays that take widely varying viewpoints on what happened to Richardson at Toronto. The chapter immediately following this one is by James Van Patten, an education professor and specialist in the study of college and university administration. Then comes the essay by sociologist Stan Weeber, who systematically compares Richardson's dismissal to the Soviet Union's punishment of dissidents – to the likely horror of some readers who see no similarities at all.

Chapter Nine, by English professor and Christian minister Jo Baldwin, represents a major shift of gears since she approaches Richardson's dismissal not in some standard research paradigm but from the viewpoint of undisguised, unembarrassed religious faith. Chapter Ten shifts back to more conventional social science, as sociologist Anson Shupe weighs conflict theory and social exchange theory for their insight into the Toronto case study.

The perspectives brought to bear on the Richardson case by Van Patten, Weeber, Baldwin, and Shupe will be new to readers outside their respective disciplines. Not so the perspective offered by education professor Barry Birnbaum in Chapter Eleven. As was apparent in Part One of this book, academic freedom is recognized by nearly all professors as an essential value of academic life. Birnbaum looks at the Richardson case in light of this value.

The concluding chapter of this part of the book is by one of Richardson's former students, religious studies professor James Gollnick. Most of us academics have trouble seeing beyond the blinkers of our respective fields to the fullness and complexity of human life. Gollnick manages to do that, partly because of his personal ties to Richardson and partly from his own calling to religion, psychotherapy, and dream analysis.

These six very different responses to my big book reflect some of the precious intellectual diversity in higher education today, a diversity that has to be respected, safeguarded, and nourished if our institutions are to achieve their noble public purposes. To point the way toward yet further dialogue, I have responded briefly to these chapters in brief comments after each one.

Publication of essays written in response to *The Envy of Excellence* is not, of course, the end of the Mellen Project. Nor does the project end with the present volume of dialogue. The culmination of the project is and will be the entry of this series of books, and of the mobbing conceptualization in general, into the political fray of specific colleges, universities, and professors' organizations – what happened at Medaille College, as Part One describes. It is happening elsewhere, too, in far-flung institutions where the research has been brought to bear on campus conflicts: Virginia State, Southern Illinois, Guelph, Calgary, Santa Cruz, Laney College, Simon Fraser, Memorial, Irvine, Newcastle, among others. If I have done my job well enough, maybe the reader's home institution will be next.

## Chapter Seven

# Captains of Erudition:

# Use and Misuse of Administrative

# Power

## James J. Van Patten

Westhues's detailed portrayal and analysis of workplace pressures, politics, intrigues, as well as use and misuse of administrative power, is a major contribution to understanding organizational climate. His illustrations of the intense degradation and humiliation of people in the workplace are at once painful to read and yet so absorbing that it is impossible to put the book down until it has been read in its entirety. As one reads the chapters, emotions come to the surface for those of us whose academic lives involved similar experiences with administrative mobbing. The scope of the problem of mobbing in the academy is seen in the outpouring of correspondence Westhues received from dedicated faculty members who had been physically and psychologically challenged by having the deck stacked against them. While granting that some academic dismissals can be justified, the concern here is with attacks on professionals whose careers are left in shatters by a process designed to humiliate them to the point of resigning of their own accord.

The academic community is unique in many ways. Faculty give their lives to the mission of teaching, writing, professing at professional meetings. There is boundless joy in collegiality, and sadness to see it disappear with changing times and circumstances. The evolution of change in higher education from the early days of Herbert Richardson's career to the current academic scene reveals internal and external pressures on universities and colleges that have changed the focus from the Ideal of the University to a consumer-oriented, money-driven, competitive environment conducive to one-upmanship in theory and practice. In more than four decades of academic life, I have seen how academic infighting, administrative posturing, and ruthless management reek havoc on individual and organizational health. Westhues depicts the change of focus in terms of the rise of the new class of professional administrators often referred to as bureaucrats. This new managerial class multiplies policies, procedures, ethical reviews, periodic appraisals, performance evaluations, and accountability indicators, too often just to enlarge administrative power and control over professors, students and staff. In his *Higher Learning in America* (1918), Thorstein Veblen noted the bureaucratic power of "captains of erudition," a perhaps unintentional hindrance to a positive organizational climate. Veblen wrote that it would be helpful if faculty could be more involved in directing their own departments with minimal interference from administrators.

> It should be plain that no other and extraneous power, such as the executive or the governing boards, is as competent – or, indeed, competent in any degree – to take care of these matters, as are the staff (faculty) who have the work to do. (1918, p. 284)

Veblen went on to note that faculty do take care of their own affairs, but now under the inhibitory surveillance of the executive with his (or her) extraneous interests:

> ...And under the exactions of a super-imposed scheme of mechanical standardization and accountancy that accounts for nothing but its superimposition. At the same time the working force of the staff (faculty) is hampered with a load of dead timber imported into its body to administer a routine of control and accountancy exacted by the executive's need of a creditable publicity. (pp. 284f)

In *The American University* (1968), Jacques Barzun wrote that some institutions respond to observations that there are not enough top-level administrators by appointing vice-presidents freely as in a bank. Offices of public relations, alumni affairs, development (institutional enhancement or fundraising), arts, science, professional schools, affiliates, and what not other divisions, natural and artificial, have been set up as bailiwicks for those new chiefs to run (p. 118). Barzun also notes the tendency for universities to expand in all directions, each one requiring more administrators. As in a cancer, there is a tendency for new growths to metastasize. Soon programs and "centers" are all over the place, making the university resemble the God of Empedocles – "a circle whose center is everywhere and circumference nowhere" (p. 274f).

The challenge of entropy, that all living systems run down and need to be renewed, faces all organizations. New and senior faculty are under pressure to keep up with current research and literature. Attendance at professional conferences is one way to keep up, but many universities have limited budgets for travel. Faculty pay their own way or compete in the marketplace for grants to attend conferences. Other ways to keep current are to engage in networking with other professionals through websites, email, team research, and publication.

Faculty members with top credentials like Herbert Richardson are vital and precious to institutions. They are the mainstay of excellence and serve to attract top-notch students, faculty and administration. This is particularly so in theological schools. Historical, philosophical changes within the Catholic Hierarchy made Richardson's position difficult as the ecumenical movement became threatened. The openness of the Second Vatican Council gave way to pressure for Catholic universities to be brought under closer hierarchical control. This left Protestant theologians such as Herbert Richardson without the firm anchor they had in the past.

Richardson's contributions to religious studies changed over time to reflect changes in the larger society, especially surrounding gender, sex, race, ethnicity, and multiculturalism. His contributions were major and important. With infinite faith in the goodness of humanity, he was a free-thinking Protestant who assumed that all diverse members of the ecumenical academic community in which he saw himself were committed to reason and evidence, committed also to producing a Christian theology for a sociotechnic world. His vision was a prophesy of the future. The trend toward diversity has been anchored, regardless of controversy, by the Supreme Court decision in 2003, on the reverse discrimination case at the University of Michigan. Affirmative action, the use of race as a factor in admissions to achieve diversity, was upheld following the Bakke decision (1978) earlier. It continues to be an avenue for assuring access and equity to minority populations. Women's political activism through feminism has expanded opportunities for them in the workforce and education. Richardson was among the Christian theologians who seized the opportunity to participate in the egalitarian trend throughout the world.

Thus Richardson was at the cutting edge in his writings, teaching, and research. One might project that as time goes on, religious unity will become more prominent as global interdependence becomes more essential. The Internet has created a new form of communication that can at the same time enhance the quality of civilization and provide seeds of social fragmentation as anti-intellectuals spew forth their venom of hate and violence language. Monitoring the quality of the information from the Internet and a multiplicity of media outlets will be vital for the survival of civilization. Rumors, innuendo, lies, and unfounded allegations face all societies and are entertwined with religions as witness terrorism and war in our era. Many mainline religions have shown decline in membership while evangelical movements have multiplied vociferously. These factors affected the environment at St. Michael's and the University of Toronto during the time of Richardson's tenure there.

Richardson demonstrated his commitment to morality, ethics, and adherence to his basic philosophical beliefs and academic credentials when he refused to sign a memorandum of agreement that non-Catholic professors would have to satisfy the Superior-General that they are knowledgeable about Catholic teachings and willing to share, in accord with the nature of their specific discipline, the special responsibilities of the Faculty of Theology, to adhere to special responsibilities of the Church and to teach accurately its history, doctrines, tradition of ministries. Richardson responded to the administrative decree by noting that he could not agree that the magisterium of the Catholic Church has a right to determine how

Catholic theologians interpret and teach Scripture. Richardson said that was what Protestant protest was all about. As Westhues points out, Richardson had a life-long commitment to theological freedom. This is not to deny that the Catholic Church or any other denomination has a right to advocate the teaching of its doctrine in its schools at all educational levels. It is rather to underline the importance of contractual fulfillment. Richardson was hired under St. Michael's commitment to an ecumenical movement in the late 1960s. Today there is often overlapping attendance at Protestant and Catholic services especially in the academic community. Differences seem much less among our youth. The future generation is opening up new horizons, exploring new vistas, breaking old molds, and challenging fixed authoritarian traditions. Richardson was a risk-taker, willing to venture toward new horizons with his peerless credential, a Harvard Ph.D. Had he chosen to serve in Protestant theological seminaries, Richardson would not have had the challenge of philosophical changes so sweeping as to threaten his career. Even in the face of repeated mobbing, he held firm in his convictions. No matter how difficult the confrontations became, Richardson acted with compassion, dignity and outreach, strengthened by his faith in the goodness of humankind.

Herbert Richardson, as Kenneth Westhues describes, witnessed a transition in higher education from a period of stability to a one of phenomenal change. The Internet, email, superinformation global highway all threatened institutional stability. Traditional university underpinnings were rocked by technological advances. New instructional delivery systems were introduced, allowing students opportunities to take classes, enter degree programs at every educational level, from their workplaces, their homes, even abroad through websites, distance learning, Internet courses, and study on weekends and in the evening. University administrators rushed to add technology to libraries, laboratories, faculty offices, to compete with new distance learning institutions such as Phoenix University. Traditional institutions such as St. Michael's and the University of Toronto faced financial challenges. Salaries, facilities and technology costs soared while available funds to maintain the institution were often stagnant.

University administrations in the new era of technology and competitive degree programs pushed faculty and staff into getting grants, implementing seminars, hosting academic association meetings to enhance the institution's prestige and recruit students. Richardson hosted many academic conferences at his home institution and abroad. His international academic reputation brought positive contributions to St. Michael's College and the University of Toronto. Through his own experiences with increasing pressures for publication and research, he was aware of the need for publishing outlets. Faculty throughout the world are pressured to publish, and publishing opportunities are limited. It was a paradox that the university accused Richardson of being a dishonest and untrustworthy employee after he had spent his own money for years to provide colleagues with a publishing outlet, the Edwin Mellen Press. When his enterprise started to turn a well-deserved profit, he was subjected to a conflict of interest claim. Often the effort to discredit a professor involves a faceless committee of administrators and peers who issue collective verdicts. As noted in Westhues's book, the characters involved in Richardson's dismissal were reasoned scholarly types who currently hold positions of distinction in a number of fields. Decent and honorable men and women collectively humiliated Richardson with detailed charges that led to his dismissal. It is interesting that dismissal committees, however composed, fail to engage in reasoned, compassionate, humane examination of possibilities for letting a distinguished faculty member have options to protect, save, and maintain his or her dignity, integrity, self-respect and pride in past achievements. This is not to infer that there are not instances where faculty dismissal is appropriate, but ganging up on a distinguished scholar, adding further instances of infractions the longer the case lingers, and engaging in mobbing – this is incivility, the law of the jungle. In this case the unbalanced reporting by the Toronto press illustrates a continued failure of the press for accuracy in reporting. Sissela Bok in her book *Lying: Moral Choice in Public and Private Life* (1978) noted that the awareness that everything in life and experience connects, that all is a seamless web such that nothing can be said without qualifications and elaborations in infinite regress, results in a sense of lassitude stealing over the most intrepid. Bok noted the role of disinformation in media reporting. Print media often contain errors due to carelessness in editing, unintentional omissions, and failure to check sources. Individuals who are attacked in the press with unbalanced news reporting have little recourse.

Retractions are rare. In this case, the Toronto newspapers cannot be too severely faulted. They reported the information they were fed by the University of Toronto administration. On the other hand, presenting Richardson's defense in detail would have been the ethical route.

Founding the Edwin Mellen Press was a major contribution to colleagues in higher education. Richardson incorporated the latest technology into the press in order to meet faculty needs in an era of transition. By any measure, he made major and lifelong contributions to St. Michael's College and the University of Toronto.

The shift of resources and support toward technological faculty and resources often led to diminished resources for the arts and sciences. Religious studies faced a period of change as societies the world over entered an age of muckraking. The politics of personal destruction was and is seen in attacks on Presidents, corporate executives, and prominent figures in business and industry. Social fragmentation was seen in electoral disputes and attacks on individual and institutional authority.

Westhues's detailed account of the institutional pressures suggests that for the sake of good health, a faculty member should have a hobby, an outside activity, other interests than the university. Many university professors "do almost nothing, apart from eating and sleeping that does not fall into the categories of teaching, research, and administrative service. They often live in high-rise condos, alone or with similarly job-obsessed partners...Ties with relatives and community groups are few. These professors live for their work, as defined by the university" (Westhues 2004, pp. 231f). Their careers are the reason for being, but it is vital for long term success to put things into proper perspective or Aristotlean Golden Mean, a balance between extremes for long-term success.

Herbert Richardson demonstrated his sensitivity to student needs and his role in the faculty by communicating with university administrators about his sabbaticals, his intellectual journeys, his continued work to keep current in his field, and his belief that the university ought ideally to be a collegial enterprise. He typifies the gentility, comity, and civility of committed professionals with his letters to administration about how much he appreciated the college, the university, the students and the institution to which he gave a great proportion of his life.

The challenge of balancing scholarship with service to the university depends on the unique tradition of the institution. When I first started teaching in higher education, serving on committees within the college and at the university level was considered vital for promotion and tenure. Faculty worked diligently on these committees, and I soon learned that one of the rationales for administration was committee service. One could not help but stand in awe of administrators whose lives were dedicated to committee membership. Higher salaries went with this attribute in the ranking order of power and prestige. In recent years, new faculty in major research universities were cautioned against service of any kind so they could publish, acquire grants, and gain international stature in their respective fields. They were counseled to avoid committee service at least until tenure was achieved. My avoidance of committees was founded on my perception that they tilted at windmills too much. Committees would deal with an issue with intensity, sincerity, and conviction only to find that their final report would either be ignored by central administration or filed away for future reference, policy decisions on the subject having already been made.

St. Michael's and the University of Toronto appear to be have insisted on university service on a continuing basis. Throughout my university tenure I strove mightily to avoid service on committees. If there were no alternative, I worked to get a committee that met infrequently and had a small mission. Thorstein Veblen in *Higher Learning in America* put it this way:

> In the force of circumstances, chief of which is the executive office, the faculties have become deliberative bodies charged with power to talk. Their serious attention has been taken up with schemes for weighing imponderables and correlating incommensurables, with such a degree of verisimilitude as would keep the statistics and accountancy of the collective administration in countenance, and still leave some play in the joints of the system for the personal relation of the teacher and disciple. It is a nice problem in self-deception, chiefly notable for endless proliferation (1918, p. 206).

University central administration finds it helpful to involve faculty in a wide range of committees often to keep them busy tilting at windmills, while the policy decision-making power brooks no interference. Faculty work on committees often is deep-sixed at the end of the school year. Faculty look forward to a summer respite, off-campus teaching, lectureship at home or abroad or an opportunity to relax while composing articles, books and research projects. Happy to wind down from workplace pressures, they often forget their committee work and its findings. Next school year, new committees are formed to rethink new projects and suggest new topics. The cycle goes on endlessly. Committee reports are filed in libraries or administrative offices, then thrown out as new administrators come aboard, and are never read again. Senior faculty are often resented by administrators when they bring up the fact that a topic of intense committee work had already been dealt with in the past. Their knowledge is a threat to organizational power and structure, and senior faculty soon learn it is best to remain silent.

Top-down hierarchical authority is sacrosanct for major decisions. As Westhues points out, faculty contracts are drawn up in such a way that dismissal is possible for virtually any real or imaged offense. A professor's job description includes teaching students, researching, serving on college and university committees, plus a section under the heading of "everything else" (Westhues 2004, p. 231). It is that last item that can be used to build a case against a faculty member whom the administration wants to dismiss. One of the things that the Richardson case reveals, generally true in cases of academic mobbing, is the administrative effort to find as many things as possible to guarantee dismissal. That is why it is better to deal with a grievance issue as quickly as possible before the administration commences the additive process of adding insult to injury. In the Herbert Richardson case, as in others, there is a wall of incivility, indecency, and isolation built against the victim. Rumors, innuendo, often planted, lead colleagues to avoid contact with the intended victim. Planned incidents of humiliation in front of peers, students, and colleagues are not infrequent in efforts to eliminate tenured faculty. While faculty members subjected to such behavior respond in different ways, most show personality or health changes. Heart attacks, depression, and other serious health problems requiring hospitalization are often the result of the politics of personal destruction in the academy.

Perhaps such attacks, intended or not, are more devastating in the academy because prestige, competency, academic respectability, records of excellence in research and publication, are in the long run all the professor has as his or her contribution to history through work. Firings in business and industry are more common. They are devastating, too, but they seldom yield the depth of psychological despair and personal humiliation of dismissals from the academy.

The use of incompetence as grounds for dismissal is devastating especially for faculty who have excelled in service, research, publication, and commitment to models of professionalism. When picked up by school newspapers or the popular press, the devastation is complete. Lawsuits are seldom effective and often serve to keep the issue in front of the public rather than letting it die over time. The incivility of administrators sending first-class registered letters to a faculty member identifying causes for dismissal is not only destructive to the collegial environment but also sends a message of power and ruthlessness, causing others within an organization to live in an atmosphere of fear. In my experience, such actions cause disharmony within organizations and a sense of alienation. Faculty begin to distrust one another as well the administrators. Various types of behavior can be seen in a healthy versus a disruptive, dysfunctional organization. Withdrawal into offices with closed doors, intensity of work orientation, and isolation are typical responses to an organization lacking trust, fairness, openness and integrity.

One of the most heart-rending events in Westhues's analysis was the detailed letter written by Richardson identifying his decades-long contribution to St. Michael's. It was a lengthy summary of his career, record of productivity, continued work to maintain and develop his intellectual growth while adding new competencies and fields of interest, and his record of scholarship in directing dissertations to completion. The dean to whom the letter was addressed (one really wonders if the dean read the letter or merely skimmed it) responded in typical administrative style. "May I begin with special greetings for the New Year and continued success in your research and publications....I want you to know that although you have served St. Michael's generously we would be prepared to accept other possibilities for your intellectual future, even your resignation to devote your full talents to publication. In light of the new character of St. Michael's .. we would not be as destitute now if you decided in the future to put your energies elsewhere" (quoted in Westhues, 2004, pp. 165-172).

Sincere faculty messages, written from the heart, recounting past productivity and future plans, far too often meet with harsh responses. One can feel the personal destructive attack in this dean's response, which was a collective one, based on discussion among the top-level administrative staff. This is not to deny the need for administrative ruthlessness when faced with major challenges to organizational stability. It is to identify excess in response to decent individuals whose lives exemplify the best ideals of humankind.

Kenneth Westhues's *Eliminating Professors* (1998), together with his subsequent book on administrative mobbing (2004) would provide a worthy addition to the library of anyone in or interested in higher education. Westhues deserves credit for articulating the ravages on human lives of mobbing. It is an unfortunate indictment of higher education that incivility, the dog-eat-dog law of the jungle, is entrenched within the ivory tower. Perhaps arbitration and mediation ought to be incorporated into university management in order to prevent tragic incidents of mobbing. John Dewey once noted that society influences schools and schools influence the larger society. Social fragmentation, divisiveness, hate language, intolerance, prejudice, and politics of personal destruction have become part of our society within the last two decades. Humaneness is a mission for all people at all times in all places everywhere. Lives are precious and each individual is responsible within his or her sphere of influence for the dignity and respect shown to others. One would hope that each of the players in the tragedy described in Westhues's book would read it carefully. Individuals acting in concert with others, reinforcing one another's convictions of Richardson's deservedness of punishment, humiliation, and degradation, acted to the detriment of their institutions and the morale of future generations of faculty. Others in St. Michael's College saw their organization become dysfunctional and bailed out when they could. Richardson's involvement with the Unification Church and the Moonies was a reflection of his outreach to alternative forms of religion in a new age. These forms are continuing in new directions and forms. Drive-through churches, the Internet, new age communication systems, are meeting the demands of a new generation. The fulcrum of change and stability will continue to advance and retreat as our new century advances.

Westhues's final chapter, on "Human Betterment," calls for humane discourse to address unproductive, unethical mobbing in the academic community. Each of the examples throughout the book brings recollections of similar events to the minds of long- term faculty members who have served in multiple institutions of higher education. One should note in fairness that not all institutions, colleges, and departments face mobbing. Collegiality still exists in islands of tranquility, but collegiality is threatened by the pressures of consumerism, marketing, recruiting, raising funds, and acquiring grants. Many times in talking to colleagues I find painful expressions of flawed faculty morale. Feeling imprisoned in uncaring, unconcerned institutions, these colleagues say to me, "They would not care if I dropped dead. None of my books, articles, achievements means anything except to list in college and university achievements at years end." There are few certainties, few anchors, and a decreasing community of like-minded values in our new electronic villages.

The chapter on "Human Betterment" says mobbing is unnecessary harm, a lose-lose situation for the institution and the faculty members. An effective administrator would not take away anyone's dignity. Compromise, reconciliation, affirmation of human dignity are routes to problem resolution. Creative options and alternatives can turn negatives into positives. There should always be open doors to the future of human hope through reasoned, compassionate dialogue. Westhues points to a model of conflict resolution in the Oregon State Department of Environmental Quality of 2001. An "Anti-Mobbing" policy began with the statement of assurance that all DEQ employees are provided with an emotionally safe, respectful work environment, free of intimidation, hostility, harassment and other mobbing behaviors. The prohibited behaviors included threatening, intimidating, hostile acts, slander, discrediting a co-worker, acts of physical or emotional isolation, prohibiting due process, bullying, threatenings or disrespect (Westhues 2004, p. 305).

Westhues deserves commendation for this book. So does Richardson, for being able to rise above the mobbing. My memory of a compassionate administrator, chancellor Emeritus William Pearson Tolley of Syracuse University, requires me to quote from his writing:

> Education should deal with the whole [person].. Schools and colleges should minister as best they can to the needs of the whole [person]. They should try to inculcate integrity and honor. They should try to build character. They should

attempt to protect our health. They should attempt to keep us sensitive to religious and moral values. They should try to give us concern for beauty as well as truth and goodness. And finally, they are conscious of the unmet needs of the world. They should try to teach us to be good citizens and to be socially useful. (1977, p. 103).

These words apply to all who inhabit our higher education institutions. Breen in *Christianity and Humanism* (1968) notes that there is a need for Christian consecration of single-minded devotion in higher education. This consecration must include morality. Jules L. Coleman in *Markets, Morals and the Law* (1988) notes that what is collectively rational during a period of intense pressure is individually irrational from an ethical and moral standpoint. The conundrum of collective action, even when solved at one level, recurs at another. Collective mobbing is unethical when viewed from moral and ethical principles of human decency.

In an interconnected world with limited lifespan, it behooves everyone involved in workplace issues to respect, honor, and cherish all those with whom we work.

### Let There Be Peace On Earth
Let there be peace on Earth, and let it begin with me,
Let there be peace on earth,
The Peace That Was Meant To Be.

With god as our Father, Family all are we,
Let me walk with my Family, in perfect harmony

Let peace begin with me, let this be the moment now.
With every step I take, let this be my solemn vow,
To take each moment and live each moment
In peace eternally.

Let there be peace on earth and let it begin with me.

– Jill Jackson and Sy Miller (Christmas Carol modified)

## References

Bok, Sissela, 1978. *Lying: Moral Choice in Public and Private Life*. New York: Panetheon Books.

Barzun , Jacques, 1968. *The American University: How It Runs and Where It is Going*. New York: Harper Colophon Books.

Breen, Quirinus, 1968. *Christianity and Humanism*. Grand Rapids, Michigan: Willaim B. Eerdmans Publishing Company.

Coleman, Jules L., 1988. *Markets, Morals and the Law*. Cambridge: Cambridge University Press.

Tolley, William Pearson, 1977. *The Adventure of Learning*. Syracuse: Syracuse University Press.

Veblen, Thorstein, 1946. *The Higher Learning In America*. New York: Hill and Wang. (Originally published in 1918).

Westhues, Kenneth, 1998. *Eliminating Professors: A Guide to the Dismissal Process*. Lewiston, NY: Edwin Mellen Press.

Westhues, Kenneth, 2004. *Administrative Mobbing at the University of Toronto*. Lewiston, NY: Edwin Mellen Press.

# Response

Nostalgia for an earlier academic time pervades Van Patten's essay. He is sad to see the "boundless joy in collegiality" disappear and the shift of organizational climate toward a "consumer-oriented, money-driven, competitive environment conducive to one-upmanship." I share his nostalgia. The third quarter of the twentieth century inflicted plagues like McCarthyism on academic life, but fewer plagues than the final quarter of the century or the present day.

Jane Jacobs dwells at length on the degeneration of academic life in her bleak book, *Dark Age Ahead* (Random House, 2004). For her, the displacement of education by credentialing undermines higher education. She laments above all the abandonment of science.

A university is essentially an assemblage of people seeking truth. Many institutions' mottoes include that very word. *Truth* is the defining academic goal: to come up with verbal and numerical formulations that square with natural and historical realities better than current formulations do. A university does not grow food, make clothes, build houses, or manufacture useful commodities. It cannot justify its existence the way the police or civil service does, by the necessary enforcement and administration of public order. The university is where people step back from everyday mundane concerns and look at things, study them, try to penetrate their mysteries by disciplines of reason and evidence, write articles and books about them, and teach what is learned to the coming generation and the citizenry at large.

From this it follows, as Van Patten correctly suggests, that a university should be controlled primarily by people for whom truth-seeking is a vocation, a consuming passion, indeed an obsession – the scientists and scholars who constitute its faculty. A university cannot be better than its professors. Their control should not be absolute. Students, being subject to faculty authority, deserve countervailing power. Outside interests – economic, political, and cultural – must also have some say in how a university is run (on governing boards, for instance), since it draws resources from the larger society and provides in return some knowledge of practical relevance. Still, professors are a university's *sine qua non*. They alone can say: we *are* the university.

The academic climate becomes poisonous and mobbings commonly occur when the university is hijacked for purposes other than seeking truth.

In the Richardson case, the main hijacker was the Catholic Church: college administrators more loyal to the Vatican than to the necessarily ecumenical project of seeking truth. The college's Catholic character did not require such a priority. Richardson's books show a Calvinist theologian's deep respect for Catholic tradition. He maintains even now that had it been up to his colleagues on the St. Michael's faculty, he would not have been dismissed. For Fahey and Alway, however, eagerness for dialogue with Catholic scholars was not enough. Richardson had to put the church's magisterium before and above his search for truth. He said no. Hence he had to go.

In public and nonsectarian universities, a common hijacker is big business. Today as in the past, many professors are mobbed because their truth-seeking conflicts with the interests of large corporations that control research funds, philanthropy, and governing boards. This is not new, as Van Patten points out. His quotations from Thorstein Veblen's classic analysis of the intrusion of the interests of capital on a university's purposes are appropriate and apt. My colleague at Waterloo, John Goyder, has lately drawn my attention to another book from the same time period that chronicles in compelling detail the persecution of professors whose scholarship somehow went against the regnant economic powers: Upton Sinclair's *The Goose-Step: a Study of American Education* (1922).

In recent decades, the economic undermining of academic purpose that Van Patten, Jacobs, I, and many others are concerned about has gone farther than occasional intrusion of corporate power on academic decision-making. It is instead the penetration of the market mentality into academic culture, so that education is reduced to a commodity useful for securing employment, students are seen as consumers, professors as service-providers, and administrators as corporate executives. In this mentality, research is understood as new-product development, patentable ideas for commercial spin-offs. My home university probably embodies this mentality more than any other in North America. The University of Waterloo opened an office on Wall Street in 2005, and our president was honored to ring the opening bell of the New York Stock Exchange. For the majority of students here, even in the arts and social sciences, the meaning of a degree is which jobs it qualifies the holder for, and at what rate of remuneration.

What I would add to Van Patten's analysis is that the majority of academic mobbings I have studied these past ten years have not arisen "from the right," that is, perpetrated by defenders of corporate interests, the kind of people who tend to be, in the United States, Republicans. In the majority of cases, the target has been a high-achieving truth-seeker whose research and teaching run counter to leftist orthodoxies about sex, race, sexual orientation, affirmative action, immigration, recovered memories, and so on. The leftist hijacking of academic purpose tends to be rooted these days in a strange, sanctimonious, cynical postmodernism. This mentality does not so much twist, constrain, and suppress truth in the manner of authoritarian churches and corporations, as deny the possibility of truth. All ideas are regarded equally, as somebody's self-serving ideology. No idea can be tolerated if it is contrary to the interests of some allegedly oppressed minority.

Not surprisingly, many recent mobbing targets have been heterosexual white males who are more committed to truth than to social justice. Richardson himself is an example, in so far as his ouster was effected by Toronto administrators on grounds that he offended some female students in an evening class. In *The Envy of Excellence, Workplace Mobbing in Academe,* and *Winning, Losing, Moving On,* at least a dozen cases are analyzed of professors whose crime was essentially offending a woman, a person of color, a homosexual, or a person with some kind of disability. Also in these books are cases of female proponents of politically incorrect ideas being run out of their jobs – sometimes with special venom on account of their being apparent traitors to the interests of their sex. In 2005, the president of Harvard, Lawrence Summers, almost lost his position when feminist scholars took offense from his honest, reasoned, empirically supported reflections on sex differences.

Many mobbing cases, I conclude, display the hijacking of the university not by dogmatic churches nor by corporate interests but by the faculty's own anti-ecclesiastical, anti-corporate, deconstructionist political movements. What we have in academe today, as many commentators have observed, is a culture war. Each side of this war finds it useful from time to time to identify a villain on the other side and humiliate that target utterly – oblivious that it is thereby enacting the age-old mobbing ritual. The perpetrators are sure they are acting honorably, upholding the highest ethical standards.

In institutions politicized by both right and left, academic administrators commonly find themselves caught in the middle, pressured by both sides. That was the case with Summers at Harvard. And like him, most administrators bend with the wind: if expression of honest views causes a job-threatening uproar, they retract and apologize for their honest views. More often, administrators do not voice honest views at all; they simply "go with the flow." In this respect, there was something refreshingly honest about the behavior of the St. Michael's administrators, also of Robert West, in the Richardson case: they believed in something, however narrow or vindictive, and acted accordingly. The Toronto administrators, by contrast, appeared mainly to be fulfilling role expectations: like a prosecutor handed a case and told to argue it by every trick in the book, on penalty of being passed over for promotion. The biggest single problem in today's universities, even worse than the culture war, may be the growth of a corps of professional career administrators who lack much feel for what truth-seeking means, care little about either side of the culture war, but are adept at what organizational theorists call "career-enhancing moves," whatever actions will safeguard their positions and help them climb up the ladder of administrative hierarchy.

That these are perilous times in universities for any scholar of independent mind goes without saying. Any such scholar, anyone who has what Dostoevsky called the illness of being an intellectual, a seeker of truth, risks threatening administrators, students, colleagues, or citizens outside the university, inciting them to gang up and get rid of the one they find threatening. Every mobbing case presents its own array of participants – maybe conservatives, maybe liberals, maybe truth-seekers convinced of different paradigms, or maybe just nasty careerists on all sides, jockeying for power. The task of the mobbing researcher is to sort out what is going on and why in each specific case, at the same time making clear that the university is diminished and unnecessary harm is done by any kind of ganging up. A culture that allows and encourages every professor and every student to inspect all relevant evidence for himself or herself, and then to express his or her own version of truth in a climate of reasoned, mutually respectful dialogue, serves the academic purpose best.

## Chapter Eight

# Canadian Gulag?
# Comparing the Elimination of
# Dissidents by Totalitarian Regimes
# and of Unwanted Professors by
# University Administrations

### Stan C. Weeber

The academic world is indebted to Kenneth Westhues for his book on administrative mobbing. The book calls the unfair firing of university professors by its proper name – administrative mobbing – and depicts the phenomenon realistically in its grotesque, animal savagery. Just as birds of a certain species will peck to death one of their own because it is smaller, deformed, or a different color, universities "kill" those of their own who differ in some way from an established norm. The norm involved may be general, even vague, yet it incites a diffuse kind of loyalty in the academic world. Among the more chilling insights in the book is that just about everyone in academe has been a party to the norm enforcement that Westhues calls mobbing.

Administrators play a direct role but faculty, staff and students, hearing rumors of an impending dismissal but doing nothing about it, contribute, by silence and inaction, to the norm's enforcement and to the mob action. This "ganging on" in the mobbing process has its animal counterpart: the man who has trespassed on the territory of Africanized bees may die from their attack, but no one sting definitively killed him. It was the collective effort, the combined effect of hundreds of stings. It is much the same with administrative mobbing.

The feelings of the University of Toronto community toward Professor Herbert Richardson are the kind found in a marriage gone bad, a partnership ruined, a covenant broken. Westhues describes the multiple social contexts from which the hostile feelings spring, being careful to draw out each source with detail, noting its unique features but also the complex way in which a particular context overlaps or interacts with others. The first context is that Richardson was a Protestant theologian and ordained Presbyterian minister teaching at a Catholic University. This contrariness in Richardson's situation appears at first to be the sole cause of the mob action awaiting him, and to set the stage for the sorts of abuse later inflicted on him. But Westhues carefully weaves in the cultural context of Richardson's hiring – the intellectual ferment of the 1960s, when free thought was valued and the oldest of traditions were opened for questioning and debate. The counterculture became the culture of the young, with its open-mindedness and rich public discourse. Universities struggled to keep up with their consumers. Richardson's hiring at Toronto fit the open, contrarian mood of the times, and the university was glad to have found such a bright young star.

The complexity of Richardson and of his situation became apparent soon enough. He offended the Aquarians with his first book, which was strangely conservative in orientation and opposed to the postmodern constructivism Richardson saw coming to theology. At the same time, he reveled in the more open ideological environment of the Vietnam era, with its free-wheeling thought and discourse, and he soon became an expert on sexual relations among students, a subject that would have been taboo years earlier. The new professor was brilliant, productive, controversial, inner-directed, and hard to figure out. He was both repelled by and attracted to the new world around him, yet he was bound by covenant to it. He was engaging: he made you think. According to Richardson, that is the whole point of teaching.

The contrarian nature of Richardson's teaching and research interests were most apparent and most carefully studied at a deeper philosophical level, the level to which administrators may delve as they try to invent ways to get rid of someone that they do not want, or may not want in the future. As Richardson's teachings and methods were running against Catholic doctrines early on, they were being quietly monitored by an unseen face deep within the Toronto bureaucracy. The unseen face whispers to another unseen face, then to another. Slowly, the headwaters of a mighty stream of opposition are formed. Richardson's embrace of new religions such as the Unification Church was especially offensive. Many considered Reverend Moon's new church a cult, its values at odds with mainstream society, even though its organization and practices did not fit the usual sociological definition of a cult. The professor viewed Moon's church as a healthy development, a counterweight to the secular trends he saw all around him. Nonetheless, Richardson's involvement with such a potentially "destructive" group was of great concern, and he was ostracized professionally within a fairly large network of colleagues and associates. Moreover, the new Edwin Mellen Press, Mellen University, and the University of Western Kansas that he proposed were increasingly perceived by the Toronto bureaucracy as off-beat, non-collegial, lacking in peer-review, "vanity" enterprises designed to line Richardson's pockets. It is worth pointing out that Richardson's innovations were essentially countercultural, products of an intellectually open era. They fit the time period in which they first began to germinate in Richardson's mind. Meanwhile, all the while, the professor's conservative detractors and enemies lurked in the shadows.

The hardest part of the book to get through is in Chapter 5, where the winds of cultural change move Toronto's theology program in a new and more conservative direction. Here we can see the beginning of the end of Dr. Richardson's fine career. At times, it is difficult to tell if the changes brought about in theology and religious studies were mostly local or wider and structural. It is difficult to ascertain whether these changes occurred because of Dr. Richardson's contrary style or in spite of it. I tend to think that the structural changes in St. Michael's College and the University of Toronto, plus the more conservative direction of the Roman Catholic Church, were the more important factors. In particular, I noticed that many of the conservative administrators who mobbed Richardson were newcomers to their roles, apparently anxious to make what they thought were worthwhile changes. Their ascendancy, their fervent seeking out of administrative roles, is not about money, as Westhues correctly notes, but about power – the power to frame problems, make decisions, and to have almost total control of a situation. This no doubt influenced the strong measures and the velocity of changes that occurred in the world of the mobbed professor. In any event, once the changes were in place (for whatever reason), they became the norm by which to judge Professor Richardson. The norm was general, diffuse. The peer pressure to conform to it was intense. So was the herd instinct of all watching the event, not wanting to be left out of the action. Dr. Richardson became officially a "deviant," a disvalued person, a spoiled identity, an expendable academic, who was forced out slowly at first and then more rapidly. The whisperers could now talk openly about getting rid of him, and they often did so.

The theme to be developed in this essay is yet another social context in which to understand Professor Richardson's experience. This context consists of the current systems of administrative rules in the university setting, their vagueness, and the arbitrary way in which they can be applied. This is a political context: it is about power and the ability to wield it. This exceedingly vague and arbitrary system of university rules and regulations has many parallels, I think, to the Soviet administrative law of the Lenin-Stalin era. In that period, those Russians who were intellectually opposed to the revolution were labeled as different, incapable of working within and for the Soviet system. They were counter-revolutionaries, "wreckers" of the Soviet program, or malingerers in it. They were "dangerous" people. To the revolutionary government that came to power in 1917, these people deserved death or severest imprisonment. Their fate was determined by extraordinarily vague law that was applied in the most arbitrary ways imaginable. Those not sent before firing squads were hauled off to gulags where the authorities worked on their attitudes. Here, the breaking of the spirit, the death of the soul, was the preferred outcome. The physical body lives on, and is able to expend its energies toward the numerous projects of Soviet construction. But when the soul dies, there is the total elimination of the prisoner *mentally*. Of course, there is no real "gulag" in Canada, no cold place comparable to Siberia where banished professors are sent. The academic gulag I will discuss is figurative, and I define it here as the whole process that professors undergo from the time they are initially identified in public as different or counter-revolutionary, through the post-separation phase. This gulag, though figurative, is real enough to those who experience it.

## Wrong Thinking under the Soviet Regime

The harsh treatment of political prisoners in the Soviet Union had its roots in the views of the master theoretician, Karl Marx. As most sociologists know, his social stratification system was basically a two-class system of proletariat and bourgeoisie. Yet a close examination of *Capital* (1936) and other works shows his belief that portions of the working class would become superfluous, a permanent "industrial reserve" sub-class that because of its circumstance in the process of capital accumulation, would sink into ever-deepening poverty, poor health, and general misery. Some proletarians might even plunge to the helpless debauchery of the pauper's world. At the very bottom, there was a kind of "untouchable" or "dangerous" class, consisting of criminals, vagabonds, drug-addicts, swindlers, beggars, pimps, brothel keepers, and other "lumpenproletarians" (Marx 1971a, 1971b). In *The Communist Manifesto* (1964), Marx describes this collection of misfits as a form of social scum that was, for the most part, unwilling and unable to contribute to a communistic society. If it played any role at all in the new revolutionary society, the lower stratum was to become a bribed tool of reactionary intrigue, impeding full implementation of the revolution.

Vladimir Lenin inherited the onerous task of implementing some of the ideas Marx wrote about. On the cusp of a successful revolution, Lenin suddenly realized that something would have to be done: a revolutionary society would have to emerge from the social structure left by the Tsarist regimes. Marx's work, already decades old, provided Lenin with little practical advice. Knowing very well that the state was not going to "wither away" as Marx had predicted, Lenin instead established a worker's state, based in part upon workers councils under the old regime (Lenin 1943). Furthermore, matters of law were going to be exceedingly complex in this new socialist society, and in the early days of the October Revolution it was clear that the new system of law and legal institutions would be a work in progress. The revolutionaries would make it up as they went along (Lenin 1975a).

Lenin shared Marx's wholly negative view of those unable or unwilling to contribute, and made it a point to expand the definition of the "dangerous classes" to include those individuals whose thought processes did not confine themselves to revolutionary socialism in the new Russia (Lenin 1975b). The intelligentsia, including professors, was particularly vulnerable. The bourgeoisie of the capitalist system was ending its rule as a class, but the ruling ideas of the bourgeoisie lived on in some intellectuals. These thoughts were difficult to extinguish. Lenin hated the intelligentsia in the most unqualified terms. Solzhenitsyn (1973, p. 328) recalled the letter that Gorky received from Lenin imploring him not to intercede in the trial of 28 intellectuals in the Tactical Center case. Commenting on the bulk of the Russian intelligentsia in the early 1920s, Lenin wrote: "In actual fact they are not (the nation's) brains, but shit ..." – worthy only of total elimination.

Correspondingly, early on in his new regime, Lenin simply voided the criminal code and began rounding up counter-revolutionaries, justifying this blanket action by the need to establish a stable and strict revolutionary order in the midst of civil war. Not long after that, and still during the civil war, he went after and arrested members of organized parties such as the Right Soviet Revolutionaries, the Mensheviks, the Anarchists, and the Popular Socialists, whose crime was nothing more than advocating and providing a source of counter-revolutionary ideas. They were guilty of nothing more than wrong thinking. This was followed by mass roundups of members of all parties other than the Bolshevik Party, and religious clerics as well, all guilty of wrong thinking.

As the revolutionary society settled in under Joseph Stalin's leadership, the regime got around to the task of authoring a new system of criminal law. Article 58 of the Russian Criminal Code of 1926 prohibited crimes against public order, organized gangsterism, and crimes against the state. Nowhere were any of those processed under this article considered political criminals. They were simply viewed as criminals. Many were guilty of wrong thinking, and this article of Russian law was applied to their behavior.

Section 1 of Article 58 is germane to our purpose here because it shows just how vague the law was and how arbitrarily it was applied. This section states that any action directed toward "the weakening of state power" was considered counter-revolutionary. This could include not only the overt organized activity of the Right Socialists or the Mensheviks who were considered "program wreckers," but also malingering, or failing to contribute to the revolutionary society. Broadly interpreted, this turned out to include such things as the refusal of a prisoner in camp to work when in a state of starvation and exhaustion. This was, incredibly enough, considered a "weakening of state power" that was punishable by execution. It is obvious that if this be "weakening" of the state, then almost any kind of behavior could be so labeled (Solzhenitsyn 1973, p. 61). Executions in fact took place for this reason during World War II. The goal was to completely break the prisoners' spirit or soul, so that they would never again even think of doing something against the rule. This use of terror for social control sent a chilling message to all who might misbehave in the future, inside or outside the labor camps.

Alexander Solzhenitsyn was convicted under Section 10 of Article 58. He was guilty of wrong thinking and the authorities hoped to identify a way to frame this as crime and also searched for a rule to apply to him. An artillery commander in East Prussia during World War II, he was bold enough to criticize Stalin in private correspondence with a friend, N.D. Utkevich. Stalin had been referred to in the letters with various pseudonyms, but the disguise was only thinly veiled. The regime understood that this was criticism of Stalin himself. This was unacceptable, especially coming from a military officer.

Solzhenitsyn, in his naiveté, thought it was not a crime to simply think bad thoughts about Stalin and his regime. His honest feeling was that Stalin had betrayed Leninism and was responsible for the defects in the first phase of the war, that he was a weak theoretician, and that his language was primitive. Admitting that he was both careless and reckless, he nonetheless put his thoughts down on paper. The letters were intercepted. His crime was wrong thinking but the actual charges were, under Article 58, anti-Soviet propagandizing and wishing to establish an anti-Soviet organization. Without even appearing before a three-man tribunal or "troika" of the NKGB (later,

KGB), Solzhenitsyn was sentenced to eight years of hard labor in a labor camp.

Section 10 read as follows: "Propaganda or agitation, containing an appeal for the overthrow, subverting, or weakening of the Soviet power ... and, equally, the dissemination or preparation or possession of literary materials of similar content." "Agitation containing an appeal" was enlarged to include a private letter. "Subverting and weakening the government" could include any idea which did not coincide with or rise to the level of intensity of the ideas expressed in the newspaper on any particular day. Anything that did not strengthen the regime must weaken it. Indeed, anything which does not completely fit in or coincides is subversive (Solzhenitsyn 1973, p. 66). Just about any thought, then, whether merely in the mind, spoken aloud, or written down on paper, was covered by Section 10 of the code.

Solzhenitsyn was convicted by a three person troika that he did not see or meet with. He signed his guilty verdict before Lt. Col. Kotov of the Special Police, and was sent off to jail. There he discovered that the screws are tightened on prisoners unwilling to cooperate with the regime. After refusing to teach mathematics as part of his sentence, he was transferred to the hard labor camps that became the raw experiential data for *One Day in the Life of Ivan Denisovitch* (1962), *The Gulag Archipelago* (1973), and other works.

The many years that Solzhenitsyn spent in the gulags render him well qualified to comment not only on the Russian prison experience but human life in general. The inmates that Solzhenitsyn said were at the "end of their tether," or "goners" as he called them, were made that way by their prison environment. By the time these individuals are completely "gone," they are showing signs of turning inward instead of outward, and isolating themselves rather than seeking help. One of Solzhenitsyn's first descriptions of such a person appears in *One Day in the Life of Ivan Denisovitch* (1962, p. 137). As supper was just about over at the end of the long cold day narrated by Ivan Denisovitch Shukhov, Shukhov notes that one inmate leaves the table and is replaced by another:

> Shukhov looked closely at the man. He held himself up
> straight – the other zeks sat all hunched up – and looked as
> if he's put something extra on the bench to sit on. There was
> nothing left to crop on his head: his hair had dropped out

long since ... His eyes didn't dart after everything going on in the mess hall. He kept them fixed in an unseeing gaze at some spot over Shukhov's head. His worn wooden spoon dipped rhythmically into the thin stew, but instead of lowering his head to the bowl like everybody else, he raised the spoon high to his lips. He'd lost all his teeth and chewed his bread with iron gums. All life had drained out of his face but it had been left ... hard and dark like carved stone. And by his hands, big and cracked and blackened, you could see that he's had little opportunity of doing soft jobs.

Notice the man's vacant look, the self-absorption, and the presentation of self that exudes with all the affect of one whose spiritual being and personality were totally destroyed by the prison system. Physically and mentally exhausted, such people survive for each moment and live in it. Solzhenitsyn in later works would portray the goners in the daily life of the work-group as being the butt of many jokes and a minor irritant to all in the camp, including fellow workers and the work foremen. The goners are weak, always looking for a break, and absorbed in their own miserable condition. For example, in *The Love-Girl and the Innocent* (1969), the goners' plight provides a morbid but comic levity that contrasts with the book's more serious themes.

Solzhenitsyn was sentenced to eight years of hard labor, the purpose of which was to destroy his very soul. The Soviets wanted to evict from his being any thoughts of doing anything even remotely "wrong" or criminal again, including the crime of wrong thinking. If his soul breaks, he would join the ranks of the goners who have lost their will to live. To the Russian officials, to be "gone," actually, was the desired condition of the prisoner. Even after being spiritually broken in this way, the Russians wanted to save the physical body for whatever construction work could be squeezed out of it. From Solzhenitsyn's works one learns that most goners could and did work in Soviet construction projects.

About a month after completing eight years of prison labor, Solzhenitsyn received an administrative order granting him a sentence "in perpetuity," or without limit. He was sent to a camp in southern Kazakhstan to begin serving the sentence. This was not a special measure directed at Solzhenitsyn but a very common procedure at the time (Kodjak 1978).

### The Law in Today's University

Readers may be skeptical, even incredulous, of any likening of today's university to the Soviet regime under Lenin and Stalin. After all, university rules appear to have the trappings of Western law, including an "adversarial" proceeding and due process. I would be skeptical myself, had I not read Westhues's account of administrative mobbing and seen the animal savagery unleashed in the mob actions against professors. It is the similarities, not the differences, between the two systems that to me are most striking. In both Solzhenitsyn's case in Russia and Richardson's case at the University of Toronto, the procedure was the same: find something objectionable about the person, redefine it as crime or deviancy, and then apply any rules that may exist to justify getting rid of the person under scrutiny.

University rules guiding the evaluation and disciplining of professors have developed in a kind of administrative hinterland between criminal and civil law. In this respect, academia is truly its own little world. The criminal law is applied to those special situations where the professor's conduct violates the law, as when he kidnaps a student, forges his credentials, or embezzles research funds. In situations lacking criminal intent, civil law may apply to cases where a professor along with the university is being sued for civil damages, often in a class action.

The rules governing internal evaluation of the professor, however, exist in a kind of gray area suspended between criminal and civil law, and when disputes arise about the professor's conduct, action is often delegated by university administrations to a tribunal of some kind, an academic troika. These tribunals, as administrative systems, are by nature fickle and arbitrary, designed by imperfect human beings with little public oversight. Proof beyond reasonable doubt is not required, just the weighing of probabilities. Charges need not be specific. Rules of evidence are not strict. Most of the professors sitting in judgment have no formal credentials in law, and procedures are informal, haphazard and free of the presumption of innocence. However, on most campuses it is the only internal system available for judging an accused professor. An individual school's evaluative rules may follow the general guidelines suggested by the American Association of University Professors, (or its Canadian counterpart, Canadian

Association of University Teachers) but often with a local twist. These local twists reflect the personalities and imperfections of the administrators in charge at any given time at any given school. That was the case at the University of Toronto, where departments followed a series of professorial evaluation rules set up by a former administrator named John Crispo.

In Westhues's presentation of the "Crispo Rules" at Toronto, there were four categories for evaluating faculty: (1) academic output; (2) teaching ability; (3) administrative committee work, and (4) everything else. The first three are the recommended AAUP/CAUT categories and are pretty much standard at all universities, even the lower ranked "teaching" institutions. In most departments at most schools there are at least a few objective standards concerning what is or is not satisfactory performance in the three areas, though in the final analysis, this is left to the discretion and judgment of the department head. In the absence of reasonably objective criteria, the head has much discretion, and may be as logical or as whimsical as he wants. Moreover, these standards may vary widely depending upon the reputation of the school, its primary mission (teaching versus research), and its strategic plan at any point in time. At the end of the day, the head has enormous power to apply whatever system he or she would like to determine satisfactory performance. This power is all the greater if the head enjoys the confidence of the Dean and the Dean's superiors, and is customarily backed by them.

The fourth category may be spelled out in some detail at Toronto, but it is largely unspecified elsewhere. At most institutions, the "everything else" means in practice that when approaching tenure, it is best to keep one's name out of the papers and not to stir up a lot of controversy. It may also mean hiding a personal peccadillo or weakness from public view, at least until tenure is earned. As formally written at Toronto, however, it covers the academic remainder of the professor's life and his or her personal life and business affairs inside and outside of the university, anything that may affect the professor's day-to-day life at the school. Basically it is expected that whatever happens in this sphere will not detract from or hurt in any way the professor's job duties or his interactions with students, faculty and administrators. Professors in good standing are often given a wide berth with respect to this rule, provided that they

are satisfactory performers on the other three criteria and get along
well with the head and other administrators.

### Richardson in the Gulag

The administrative process against Richardson is really over
before it begins. By the time he receives the letter from Rev. Michael
Fahey dated January 7, 1987, Richardson has already been deemed
expendable. The letter pronounces both judgment and sentence. It is
the combined opinion of an unseen troika, or more, within the
bureaucracies of St. Michael's College and/or the larger university.
Fahey is the messenger, just as Lt. Col. Kotov was for Alexander
Solzhenitsyn. In a letter that is amazingly frank as academic letters
go, Fahey is telling Richardson to leave. Richardson's request for
leave has been denied. That reality, in the eyes of the administrators,
should give the professor a strong enough hint that it is time for him
to quit the university.

What crime is Richardson guilty of? He is guilty of counter-
revolutionary wrong thinking, the entertaining and imparting of
prohibited ideas. His thoughts run against the norms of his college.
The administrators now wonder if he will go quietly or not. That is
probably what Kotov thought upon sentencing Solzhenitsyn: would
he accept his sentence quietly, or create problems?

The cumulative whispering and murmuring campaign against
Richardson must have been going on for a long time for the matter to
come to such an abrupt head with the Fahey letter. With this letter, the
covenant is broken. As a wrong-thinker, Richardson's views on
matters of all kinds related to theology no longer fit with the more
conservative norms put in place. Richardson's wrong-headedness was
confirmed by his refusal to sign the collegium's new by-laws
pertaining to theology. With this refusal to sign, Richardson showed
no indication of bowing out gracefully. He looks instead to be digging
in.

The failure to sign the Catholic "loyalty oath" also ushers in a new
stage in the evolving conflict with the administration. Now, he is
essentially refusing to go along with the new program. Now he's no
longer a nuisance or someone who is inconveniently in the way. He is
now officially a program "wrecker" or "impeder" by virtue of his
intransigence. He is not only someone who does not fit, he has

become *dangerous*. At this point in Solzhenitsyn's career, he was transferred to the hard labor camps.

For Richardson the "loyalty oath" was the kind of document that he must reject on the basis of his conscience. A cooler head, or a less conscientious one, may have signed the document and then made changes in his approach and attitude. To Richardson, this was a frontal attack upon his entire academic life, and after his long service to the university, he felt that he had the right to be left alone. How different things were from the days of his initial appointment, when both Richardson and the administration rejoiced in the new covenant being formed! Now as then, he was passionate about his work, and he felt bound by higher principles to refuse to sign the document. The administration felt otherwise. The screws were being tightened upon Professor Richardson.

When the professor would not go quietly, the administration felt that there was no choice but to define his deviancy in a public way that was a violation of university rules. Thus the hunt was on for the proper "article" or section of the university rules to apply to his case.

Once labeled a deviant by the letter of January, 1987, which undoubtedly worked its way through the rumor mill at Toronto, the formal charges against the professor were nothing more than a ganging up or piling on to make sure that at least something worked, or something "stuck" to defile Richardson publicly and identify him as unfit to continue at Toronto. (For the Soviets persecuting Solzhenitsyn, this process is easy in that the many vaguely stated laws under the Criminal Code of 1926 are given the widest possible interpretation). It is here that Richardson's behind-the-scene enemies, the whisperers, become bolder, press onward with their charges, and speak openly. It is a basal, primitive kind of herd instinct as well as a bold strategy to make sure that Richardson will be gone, forever. It is a pitiful attempt at the trappings of a "Western" proceeding, where charges must be clearly stated. Unfair as this figurative gang violence may be, it is not without precedent. Thomas Szasz (1988) wrote of a similar procedure in cases where a defendant is suspected of being mentally ill. The district attorney could commission several psychiatrists to independently interview the defendant, hoping that more than one would declare the defendant incompetent to stand trial. By doing so, at least one charge would "stick," and the D.A. could recommend incarceration in a mental facility as an alternative to a jury trial.

Toronto did not use psychiatry against Richardson, but judging from the charges drawn against him, they threw in all but the kitchen sink in their effort to sink the errant professor. Unfortunately for Dr. Richardson, there was enough evidence, just barely enough, to substantiate one of the charges against him: the charge of not doing enough administrative work at the university. This was formally a violation of part 3 of the Crispo rules. It is true that he did very little administrative committee work in his last years at the school. But as any faculty member knows, this is as much the fault of the department head and the administrators at the university as it is Richardson's. If the university does not make committee assignments available to the professor, it is very difficult for that person to "hustle" one's way onto one or more committees. After all, the committee work is considered a "plum" by some faculty and as job security by others. Professors are not usually willing to "share" this work with others, despite its drudgery. Nor do many opportunities spring up for professors to "volunteer" for such work independent of being assigned to it by their superiors. If administrators want to "freeze" someone out of the department by not giving them committee assignments, they can do so within the rules. If that in fact happens, what is the targeted professor to do? He is given no administrative tasks and then fired for doing no administrative work.

In my experience, the embattled professor in this circumstance will retreat to the familiar fold of what may be scores of loyal colleagues, friends, and former students now teaching at other schools. This is a lot more comfortable for most professors, and far easier, than the unpleasant task of trying to curry favor on their home campuses. The professor may well be, like Richardson, immensely popular with this remote group, even while despised at home. However, for the administrator who is freezing out the professor, this is exactly the desired response. By turning inward toward his own set of professional friends, the mobbed professor further isolates himself from his departmental colleagues and triggers what could be one of many negative experiences that culminate in an inclement state of the mobbed professor's mental and physical health.

The charge that Richardson misused his medical leave, officially subsumed under Part 4 of the Crispo rules, is incredibly weak by just about any standard imaginable. The school charged him with fraudulently taking medical leave at a time when he was not sick. A private investigator discovered that Richardson had traveled a good deal at a time when he was supposedly too ill to teach. In retrospect, the whole episode appears to be a misunderstanding. Such a misunderstanding between the university and a professor in its good graces is usually shrugged off or blamed on department staff. Clerical workers are the most likely to be blamed, and fired. I suppose it is true that Richardson did not communicate effectively with staff and higher-ups. But consider the context of this episode: this is a man marginalized and beaten down by the stress of his scholarly workload and the efforts needed to fend off the charges against him. By not communicating effectively, Richardson had done something wrong, but in no way is this reasonable justification for firing the man. Dr. Richardson was beaten down, exhausted, preoccupied with self, and most likely incapable of communicating effectively. He may well have been viewed as a hapless and pathetic "goner" by the administration, and we can only wonder what behind-the-scenes levity his case may have provided for the administrators.

When I read Westhues' account of how Richardson had been beaten down physically and mentally by the charges against him, I immediately thought of the "goners" in Solzhenitsyn's books. The cumulative effect of the charges against Richardson put him at the end of his tether; this was the reason that he needed a medical leave in the first place. The administration treated him horribly for being ill, citing the "abuse" of his medical leave as a reason to get rid of him. He is worn down to a nub by the Toronto bureaucracy and then penalized for being tired and not communicating properly. How much different is that than the Soviets calling an exhausted person who cannot work one who "weakens the state?" The Soviets showed no mercy on the goners. Toronto showed no mercy on Richardson.

Although Richardson's experience parallels Solzhenitsyn's in many ways, the comparison must not be overdrawn. Richardson had at least the trappings of Western law, or the gentlemanly academic approximation of them. Four charges were put on paper by the administration. Solzhenitsyn, by contrast, had no lawyer, could not get a copy of the criminal code he was charged with violating, nor a copy of the criminal procedure that he was operating under.

Richardson had legal representation, and he was able to present evidence in his behalf in order to rebut the charges.

Yet – and Richardson seems to have understood this very well – the charges against him were part of an administrative law system that functioned mostly upon the whim of those running it. It was essentially the tool of the administration. It is here that further comparisons with Solzhenitsyn are in order.

I think Professor Richardson, on the inside at least, knew the futility of what he was doing at his tribunal – as Solzhenitsyn knew upon meeting Kotov. He knew that he was receiving the short end of justice. He would concur with Westhues that the tribunal was a wallaby court, a smaller version of the kangaroo court where justice is a sham and it is produced in a quick way that is not necessarily just. In reality, the judgment and the sentence had already been rendered in the initial letter. The "court proceeding" was simply a show trial: not only for an administration eager to send waves of *angst* over faculty who might contemplate being as wrong-headed as Richardson, but also for Richardson himself, who had the forethought to know that history is long and that someday his cause might be vindicated. Richardson, unlike Russia's most famous prisoner, got a real troika that he could see; but in circumstances that paralleled Solzhenitsyn, it was the "unseen" troika that unseated him. He was already gone at his own hearing, figuratively dead and laboring under the stresses that prompted his medical leave.

The university had no prison, no building project that Richardson could work on, as the Soviets had for Solzhenitsyn, so when his academic days were over, he would have to leave. Importantly, they had nothing else for him to do of any academic or administrative significance, and offered him no opportunity at all to stay on at Toronto in any capacity. And the actions taken by the university after he left the school indicated a further desire not only to keep Richardson at arm's length from Toronto but to prevent him from ever teaching again or belonging to a scholarly community, at Toronto or anywhere else. A kind of total destruction of the target, an exercise of absolute power over him, appeared to be the order of the day. The university aimed for his sentence to be "in perpetuity" – among the most frightening of the Soviet sentences. This is the angry bees swarming, the gang circling with weapons in the air. This is the breaking of a professor's scholarly soul, so that he might never to do anything scholarly again. It is also a message to any of his colleagues who might dare to think wrong thoughts. As a social scientist, I see this as the academic version of a standard ploy of totalitarian regimes, the use of terror as a form of social control. It worked for the Russians and it works in academe today.

What happened after Richardson left his school and after Solzhenitsyn left the gulags adds an important further chapter to the story. Solzhenitsyn continued to be pursued by the Soviet regime. His writing and publishing in the West was questioned and he was harassed to the point of leaving the Soviet Union for the United States, where he would settle down and continue his writing career (Solzhenitsyn 1980). Richardson, after being dismissed from Toronto, was harassed further by the university, which denied a lump sum payment of his pension. Even after his career at Toronto was over, he still had to fend off the swarming Canadian mob. At least they did not succeed in destroying his publishing house, headquartered across the border in the United States. Like Solzhenitsyn, Richardson continues to write and work today.

## Conclusion

We cannot conclude from this essay that the system of academic rules and regulations concerning professorial conduct in Canada and other Western countries is as vague and arbitrary as were the systems of Soviet law under Lenin and Stalin. On its best days, regularly and predictably, the system of administrative rules is overseen by reasonable, honorable individuals who act reasonably and honorably toward others. Yet a review of Professor Richardson's case raises serious concerns. We would like to think that what he endured was a deviant or unusual, perhaps a case of one lone university administration that was out of control. According to Westhues, this is not true. There are literally hundreds of cases like Richardson's that surface each year and maybe many more that are privately processed that we do not know of. The "worst days" of the academic administrative systems may be becoming more numerous. It may no longer be a case of a few rotten apples in the barrel, but of progressive "rottening" of the whole barrel (see Westhues 1998).

What's needed now is a book that compares the academic survival strategies of people like Richardson and Westhues. At first glance, I suspect Westhues sought more outside help and went more on the offensive through public relations. Richardson may have been too far gone to attend to himself adequately. He was too exhausted and inner-directed, mired too deeply in his busy scholarly and professional life, whereas Westhues was more detached and able to shake loose from that life, at least long enough to put up a defense and rally others on his behalf. If that turns out to be a winning formula when several cases of "winning" are accumulated and studied, then that is a formula that needs to be communicated to professors everywhere as a matter of professional survival.

The real tragedy of cases like Richardson's is what happens to mobbed individuals after the elimination process is complete. It is important to follow up to see what becomes of them. I do not have any idea what the endgame of this process really is. Many are already in ill health physically, mentally, intellectually and spiritually. My suspicion is that their health spirals downward from the total weight of the abuse put upon them. They have been removed from everything they have worked for their entire lives; I assume that they die sooner than expected, either from the combined effects of stress or from acting out suicidal ideation. This renders them "goners" in the total sense that the university would like to see. How distant is the day when a surviving spouse or child of a mobbed professor sues the school for wrongful death? Even if many do not reach this "final" stage, how many lives spiral downward into severe depression, psychosis, or the abuse of alcohol and drugs?

Alexander Solzhenitsyn had many long and difficult days and nights in which to ponder the real purpose behind the brutal and arbitrary Soviet system of justice. In one of his Russian-language books, he stated that the purpose of it all was the total absolute control and the crushing of the personalities of opposers, the terrifying of potential opposers, and the enslavement of the entire population. In a state that could do as it pleased, no one was safe (Carter 1977). I am confident that at the universities where mobbing takes place, administrators seek a similar kind of state-like total control, where professors are scared to death and each one feels unsafe, personally vulnerable to a mob that could await them in any given semester. The ultimate expression of this control is the Soviet sentence of "in perpetuity," handed to Solzhenitsyn in real life and fictionally to the character Oleg Kostoglotov in *The Cancer Ward*

(1968). The ugly, bitter pursuit of Richardson's soul after his Toronto career ended is as ugly as the campaign against Solzhenitsyn. Richardson's sentence, like Solzhenitsyn's, was "in perpetuity."

Solzhenitsyn was once asked how the people of the former Soviet Union could have consented to the reign of terror that reached its full fruition under Joseph Stalin. Solzhenitsyn attributed the rise of tyranny to the herd instinct, the fear of remaining alone, outside the community, which leads to the voluntary acceptance of other people's errors (Carter 1977). Is this not the same instinct that Westhues is writing about? If Solzhenitsyn is right, then the herd instinct must be a part of human nature that both allows mobbing and fuels it. The academic world, for its part, tolerates considerable diversity and individuality, but it does not deal well with loneliness or the experience of being a loner. When someone shows the tendency toward academic loneliness, it's like an identifying mark is placed upon the head: a bulls-eye. Set against these processes deeply rooted in the human condition, how can we possibly hope to halt the tide of academic mobbings?

Perhaps more disgusting than sad is how the administrators involved in Richardson's mobbing received promotions. A message is sent that eliminating an ill-fitting colleague is acceptable. What happened in this case was an abomination. Richardson was attacked with animal savagery by the officials of an administrative law system that, at its worse, rivals Soviet law. As a tribute to Professor Richardson's scholarly career at Toronto, we should continue to learn all we can about the phenomenon of workplace mobbing in academe – especially how to proactively avoid it – and share what we learn via the Edwin Mellen Press to all those vulnerable to being mobbed. As Westhues suggests, that is just about every single one of us.

# References

Carter, Stephen, 1977. *The Politics of Solzhenitsyn*. New York: Holmes and Meier Publications, Inc.

Kodjak, Andrej, 1978. *Alexander Solzhenitsyn*. Boston: Twayne Publishers.

Lenin, Vladimir I., 1975a. "All Out for the Fight Against Denikin!" Pp. 184-199 in Vol. 3 of *Selected Works*. Moscow: Progress Publishers.

_____, 1975b. "Letter to the Workers and Peasants Apropos of the Victory over Kolchak." Pp. 216-222 in Vol. 3 of *Selected Works*. Moscow: Progress Publishers.

_____, 1943. *The State and Revolution*. New York: International Publishers.

Marx, Karl, 1971a. "The Class Struggles in France, 1848-1850." Pp. 154-242 in S. Padover (Ed.), *Karl Marx on Revolution*. New York: McGraw-Hill.

_____, 1971b. "The Eighteenth Brumaire of Louis Napoleon." Pp. 243-328 in S. Padover (Ed.), *Karl Marx on Revolution*. New York: McGraw-Hill.

_____, 1964. *The Communist Manifesto*. New York: Monthly Review Press.

_____, 1936. *Capital: A Critique of Political Economy*. New York: The Modern Library.

Solzhenitsyn, Alexander, 1996. *Invisible Allies*. Washington, D.C.: Counterpoint Press.

_____. 1980. *The Oak and the Calf*. New York: Harper and Row.

_____, 1973. *The Gulag Archipelago*. New York: Harper and Row.

_____, 1969. *The Love-Girl and the Innocent*. New York: Bantam Books.

_____, 1968. *The Cancer Ward*. New York: Dial Press.

_____, 1962. *One Day in the Life of Ivan Denisovitch*. New York: Penguin Books.

Szasz, Thomas, 1988. *Psychiatric Justice*. Syracuse: Syracuse University Press.

Westhues, Kenneth, 1998. *Eliminating Professors: A Guide to the Dismissal Process*. Lewiston: Edwin Mellen Press.

# Response

Weeber's essay calls to mind a classic quotation from Everett C.
Hughes, a Chicago-School sociologist who helped establish the
discipline in Canada in the mid-twentieth century. For a graduate
seminar I used to teach in comparative sociology, I customarily put
Hughes's words at the top of the course syllabus:

> Some of the students of man's doings should be creatures
> ready to invade the territory of others, both figuratively and
> literally, and to compare anything with anything else
> without shock or apology. It is a friction-generating and
> improper pursuit. Any social situation is in some measure
> dear to those in it. To compare it with others is to seem to
> dull the poignancy of the wrongs of the underdogs, and to
> detract from the merits of those who have the better place in
> it. (L. White, ed., *Frontiers of Knowledge in the Study of
> Man*, Harper & Row, 1956, p. 92)

Weeber is exactly the kind of researcher Hughes had in mind. He
sets the administrative procedures at the University of Toronto by
which Richardson was dismissed (as described in my book) alongside
the administrative procedures in the Soviet Union by which dissidents
were convicted of and punished for thought crimes (as described in
Alexander Solzhenitsyn's books), and then identifies similarities
between the two. Weeber's comparison will generate friction with
readers who think it belittles the wrong done to the Soviet dissidents
and unfairly demeans the Toronto administrators.

I can think of only one comparison more offensive than Weeber's:
a likening of workplace mobbing to what was done to Jews in Nazi
Germany. Leymann made the latter comparison, entitling a book
chapter on the last stage of the mobbing process, the target's
elimination, *"Die Endlösung,"* the word the Nazis used for their
intended final solution to the existence of Jews. Other mobbing
researchers, me included, have made comparisons along the same
lines – to some readers' horror. Is not the suffering of the millions of
Holocaust victims diminished when the mere dismissal of professors
is said to be in some ways similar? And is it not slanderous and low to
paint university deans and presidents acting in good faith with the
same brush as Nazi war criminals?

We humans crave enemies, utterly alien others, as symbols and archetypes of evil against which to juxtapose the virtue we claim for ourselves. In today's mainstream Western culture, Nazi Germany and Stalinist Russia have been elevated to this alien status and imagined to embody pure evil, thus to be altogether unlike our own society. Pointing out similarities between these archetypes and societies more recently defined as our enemies – Milosevic's Yugoslavia, Saddam's Iraq, or the Taliban's Afghanistan – is legitimate, indeed comforting. On the other hand, any similarities suggested between these archetypes and our own society are seen as specious, spurious, indeed preposterous, because they undermine our own sense of superiority.

The comparative researcher's rebuttal, the response of the seeker after truth, comes down to, "If the shoe fits...." If evidence supports identification of similarities, then they must be admitted – as well as balanced by whatever differences the evidence supports. The comparative researcher's attitude thus tends to suppress the human craving for enemies, maybe even to sublimate demonizing impulses into compassion and an ethic of live and let live. In research on mobbing, this attitude leads to the repeated demonstration of the empirical falsity of dividing humanity into sheep and goats, good (or evil) perpetrators and evil (or good) targets.

Weeber acknowledges the differences between the Canadian academic and the Soviet Russian systems of administrative law. He admits that the academic gulag to which Richardson was condemned is figurative. No incarceration or physical privation was involved in this case (though the target was indeed jailed in other Canadian and American cases I have studied of mobbing in academe). The gulag Weeber refers to is the process an academic undergoes from the point of first public identification as a wrong-thinker to the post-elimination phase. Weeber is right: to the target of this process, the gulag is real.

Having but limited acquaintance with Solzhenitsyn's work or Soviet history, I was surprised and fascinated by the parallels Weeber describes between the Soviet system of thought control and the procedures Richardson and other academic mobbing targets have been put through. The parallels are chilling enough to recommend critical study of the very field of administrative law. John Evans, the tribunal chair for Richardson's dismissal hearing, is among Canada's foremost experts in the area, co-author of a standard text. After studying his report on the Richardson case, I am left wondering if perhaps the field itself is but an instrument for enforcing managerial authority. It must assume at the start that the person on trial, the one faced with possible punishment and humiliation, is not the free citizen of criminal jurisprudence but a citizen whose rights are already reduced and circumscribed by employment in a corporate entity. It is plausible to me that domestic or house tribunals within these corporate entities, operating on principles of administrative law, might often resemble the troikas of totalitarian states. In Canada at least, the master-servant relation still underpins much of labor law.

In its decision on the Richardson case, the Evans tribunal applied the legal term *fiduciary* to him – and by implication, to any professor in his or her relation to the university employer. If this view were upheld, the professor would owe to the university the same duties of loyalty and care that a parent owes to a child or one partner of a business to the other partners: an obligation to place the university's interests ahead of his or her personal interests, indeed to the exclusion of any contrary interest, including, presumably, an interest in seeking truth. The professor would also have little right to privacy, being required to disclose to the administration any activity or involvement that might conceivably impinge on what the administration defines as the university's interests. If professors were fiduciaries of the university, their right to conduct independent research and freely publish the results would take second place to their duty to serve the university's institutional priorities.

It is to Richardson's credit that when he appealed the Evans decision to the Ontario Court of Justice, he directed his lawyers to challenge the identification of professors as fiduciaries of their home universities. It is to the credit of that court, moreover, that it accepted this complaint against the Evans decision, and ruled that professors are *not* correctly described as fiduciaries. The public court thus rolled back the extension of a university administration's authority over professors that the Evans tribunal had sought to impose. This correction of the Evans decision did not, however, prevent the Ontario Court from upholding Evans's overall conclusion, that Richardson should be dismissed.

In 1994 and again in 1996, I myself faced troikas constituted under the ethics policy of my home university. One was chaired by a lawyer on the Waterloo faculty, the other by a PhD-holding former dean. On each occasion, the proceedings were so untruthful, fanatic and punitive, so biased in favor of administrative preferences and so prejudicial to me, that I was embarrassed to witness their occurrence on our campus. To call them kangaroo courts would be generous. On the second occasion, having taken a lesson from the first, I felt obliged to walk out, leaving the troika chair fuming over his lack of subpoena power and recommending that I be severely punished. I shudder to think what that troika would have done to me if it had had the power its counterparts had in Soviet Russia. In the wake of publicity about my second case, publicity that reflected poorly on the university, Waterloo's board of governors abolished our ethics tribunal in 1998. It was a major blow to savagery on our campus.

Most of the mobbing targets I have studied, including Richardson at Toronto and Warden and Watson at Medaille College, faced tribunal proceedings just as unfair as the ones I went through. Only a few of the resultant decisions (like mine or those at Medaille) were subsequently overturned. A common theme, as Weeber points out, is elasticity of the charges. Words like *abuse, harassment, hate speech, interference, uncollegiality,* and *intimidation* can be stretched to apply to almost anything if the felt need to punish a target is strong enough.

Everett C. Hughes, the sociologist I quoted at the start of this response, was a man of slight stature, soft speech, and brilliant mind. One of his students at McGill, a scholar who went on to similar prominence, was Hubert Guindon, a big, burly man with a booming voice. At a testimonial dinner for Hughes, Guindon boomed out his warm recollection of being the guest of honor's student: "I was scared of you." Should Hughes have been faulted for frightening a student, as Richardson was faulted at Toronto? Offenses vaguely defined, aribtrarily enforced, and relating more to the defendant's intentions than to actual deeds, are the hallmark of tribunal proceedings that do much harm, in universities as in totalitarian states.

Efforts to reform inadequate administrative structures run in two directions, different though not necessarily opposed. One is to insist on similar procedural safeguards as in criminal courts: mainly the rules of natural justice (like the right of the accused to be present, to be informed of the charges, to adduce evidence, to face and question the accuser and other witnesses, and to be represented by legal counsel) but also training for tribunal members and insulation of them from organizational authority. The other direction is toward abolition of tribunals altogether, letting disputes and conflicts be resolved by line administrators in the routine course of their jobs rather than by quasi-judicial procedures, with any appeals being handled by authorities altogether outside the university (public courts or professional arbitrators).

Both these directions of reform deserve support, but especially the latter. If there is evidence that a professor has breached the criminal code, the police should be informed. If charges follow, the professor will have the benefit at trial of the procedural safeguards of criminal law. These are no guarantees against wrongful conviction in the courts, but the odds of it are lower than in domestic tribunals. If the matter falls short of criminality, it is best handled by the chair, dean, or vice-president, as has been the case for alleged ethical violations at the University of Waterloo since 1998. For all of human history, grass-roots discussion, debate, and dialogue have been the usual means of resolving most disputes. These means deserve far more trust than they get in today's colleges and universities.

Finally, the word *goner* that Weeber draws from Solzhenitsyn hits home with me, as I reflect on the cases of mobbed professors I have studied. Not Richardson, Warden or Watson. None of these was defeated so completely as to merit the label of *goner*. The same cannot be said of many other targets of academic mobbing. The saddest part of my research has been to witness once vigorous, robust professors weeping uncontrollably, hallucinating, hypervigilant to the point of clinical paranoia, rendered zombie-like by alcohol or drugs, hospitalized for depression or stress-related physical disease, or driven to suicide. How much humiliation can be endured before something gives varies from one person to the next, and people also vary in what gives first. To structure our universities so as to prevent professors from becoming "goners" is a worthy goal.

# Chapter Nine

# A Good Reason for Mobbing

## Jo A. Baldwin

Power from on high was the element missing in Rev. Herbert Richardson's life when he experienced the ordeal described in Westhues's book. On the basis of information provided there, I believe the attack on Rev. Richardson was induced by the Holy Ghost to position him to see salvation in a different light from Calvin's theology. Rev. Richardson was not "saved" from the mobbing and for good reason.

Westhues defines, explains, and elaborates on the phenomenon of mobbing using Rev. Richardson as his main subject. From Westhues I gleaned that mobbing is a spiritual act, taking into consideration the spiritual forces of good and evil within people. A passage in the Bible speaks of Jesus telling his disciples – James and John – that they do not know what manner of spirit they are of, referring to good and evil. They were in Samaria determined to go to Jerusalem and the Samaritans would not receive them. So James and John tried to get permission from Jesus to call down fire from heaven to destroy the Samaritans. It is here that Jesus tells them they do not know what spirit is operating in them at the time, both good and evil being present (see Luke 9:51-56).

Previously a candidate for ordination of the Word and Sacrament in the Presbyterian Church U.S.A., I am now an elected and ordained Itinerant Elder in the African Methodist Episcopal Church, and I can see how Rev. Richardson's Calvinist theology factored into some of his behavior described in Westhues's book. I also want to warn readers that most of my comments on what happened to Rev. Richardson are based on Scripture.

Westhues's direct and to-the-point writing style connected with me as well as his analytical judgments. He says,

> The reality brought to bear on this professor was thus not just loss of position but a full year of public shaming. ... No professor in Canadian history has been so publicly humiliated. ... [And] the intertwining of Richardson's life with the lives of decent people was frazzled, frayed and undone. He was transformed into the sort of person with whom upstanding citizens would not identify, and whose suffering they would not share. (p. 17)

This says to me that what was designed to harm Rev. Richardson God meant for good. There is a story in the Bible about Jacob's son Joseph whose brothers plotted to kill him. They threw him in a pit to die but then reconsidered and, instead, sold him into slavery in Egypt. As it turned out, Joseph was made second only to Pharaoh and ended up saving people from starvation during a seven year famine. Included in the people he fed were his father and brothers (see Genesis 37:2-50:20). What appears to have happened to Rev. Richardson is that Jesus made him privy to his mind and emotions during his passion when he was falsely accused, spat upon, beaten, stripped, and hanged on the cross, and for good reason.

Westhues analogizes Rev. Richardson's ordeal to the process of elimination, "encompassing both *defecation* and *urination* ... the expulsion from the body of noxious waste: matter which, if retained, would cause disease and death. ... The identity placed upon the target is of a foul, filthy, polluted person, good for nothing and deserving to be separated utterly and completely from the social organism" (p. 19). Jesus, too, was eliminated from society and literally for three days. Rev. Richardson was figuratively eliminated but was still made privy to Jesus's mind and emotions, which is no small privilege with Rev. Richardson's being a man of the cloth. "Many are called but few are chosen" (Matthew 22:14) for such an intimate understanding of Jesus.

All are saved who believe in Jesus but few are made privy to his mind and emotions.

Westhues talks about *swarming,* saying it describes

> a collective attack by a gang of teenagers to rob a targeted individual of money, jacket, hat, or other status symbol, but basically of dignity and self-respect. The apparent goal is to trumpet the power of the group by humiliating someone who has, intentionally or not, challenged it. ... Swarming illustrates social elimination more directly when the group turns against one of its own.... (p. 20)

Westhues says, "the essence of swarming is exclusion and humiliation – whether violent or not" (p. 22). Again, Rev. Richardson was made privy to Jesus's mind and emotions. Both were swarmed. Judas, one of Jesus's twelve disciples, betrayed him. All the disciples ran away when he was captured in the Garden of Gethsemane, and Peter denied him three times during his trial. Rev. Richardson too was humiliated. But the interesting point here is that Jesus did not save Rev. Richardson from the shame of the exclusion he experienced and for good reason.

Westhues talks about how people feel a sense of triumph and satisfaction when participating in destroying someone's life (p. 23). I am reminded of the jeering crowd at the foot of the cross, who railed at Jesus saying, "If you are the Son of God, come down from the cross" (Matthew 27:40b). The chief priests, scribes, and elders were included in the bunch. Westhues says that elimination "requires detection of a spirit, force, or current" (p. 24) that moves toward premature death from a broken heart. Jesus wept for the City of Jerusalem before he was crucified saying that they killed the prophets and stoned people he sent to them and that he longed to gather them as a hen gathers her brood under her wings but they would not let him (see Matthew 23:37). In this case the tables were turned. Jesus was speaking figuratively. Rev. Richardson's physical heart trouble was literal.

I gleaned from Westhues that mobbing is akin to sexual arousal and orgasm. He mentions the American South and the lynching of Black people (p. 39). I am a Black woman, educated, and see lynchings as sexual acts. I was told by older Black people who had firsthand knowledge of the practice that men would take their wives and children to see the event and the women would dress up like they were going out on a date or to church. The spectacle was like foreplay for the adults that planted perverted seeds of future glee in the children. I said after completing Westhues's book that I would write about humiliation and say that it is the foundation of evil and that if Satan were to be relegated to human status, then the sexual side of Satan is satisfied through humiliation, but I changed my mind. Then I started to say that humiliation is Satan's ultimate source of sexual release and that if Satan is sexually active with a hearty appetite, it follows that humiliation would be exercised frequently and with enthusiasm and vigor, but I changed my mind again. It is enough to see how humiliation negatively affected Rev. Richardson and God himself.

Humiliation is an abomination to God. From my studies of the Bible I see that Jesus went out of his way to keep people from being humiliated. The first miracle he performed was at a wedding in Cana of Galilee. He turned water into wine when the wine ran out at the reception to keep the bridegroom from being humiliated before his guests (see John 2:1-11). In Jerusalem a woman was brought to him who had been caught in the act of adultery and Jesus bent down and wrote on the ground before her and her accusers. He did not want the woman to feel even more shame by looking her in the face and he did not even want to see the guilt on the men's faces that were accusing her, allowing them, instead, to walk away one by one (see John 8:2-11). It is as though God says, "If anyone intentionally goes about humiliating someone, 'let him be Anathema Maranatha'" (1 Corinthians 16:22b). Yet it is a human pastime.

Bullying and the desire to control are prominent in the elimination process. "Research amply shows, moreover, that the effects of being bullied are all but identical to the effects of being mobbed: powerlessness, rage, self-doubt, listlessness, and the physical and psychological forms of stress-induced illness" (p. 45). Here the analogy of Jesus and Rev. Richardson ends and turns. Jesus came into the world to die for the remission of sins. He chose the cross as his means of execution, having been able to escape his captors in the first place not to mention being able to call down a legion of angels to rescue him from the tree once he was nailed up there (see Matthew 26:53). But Rev. Richardson did not choose any of what happened to him and could not stop the elimination process once it started. The success of the mobbing indicates that Rev. Richardson did not have much power. He certainly did not have power from on high like Jesus did.

"Rational thought should guide action" (p. 64) and that is true. But more than rational thought is expected from people of the cloth. Westhues quotes Rev. Richardson as saying, "The deepest insight from theology, I believe, is that men are created for communion with God and the universality of being" (pp. 96-97). But more than that, people are created for receiving from God good gifts, the greatest of which is satisfying peace through Jesus Christ, which is the gift of his Holy Ghost. For us – people of the cloth – the Holy Ghost or Holy Spirit guides our thoughts and actions. The Third Person of the Godhead is supposed to influence our behavior. He is present to protect us from others and even from ourselves. But it is obvious Rev. Richardson was outside the arc of safety when he was mobbed and in some of what he did before the mobbing that gave his enemies ammunition.

"Politics, Richardson summarized, is 'a practical enterprise devoted to creating a contingent and ever-changing order by compromising and balancing diverse and competing interests against one another'" (p. 100). There is, of course, politics in the Church. However, compromise has no place in the worship of the resurrected Jesus of Matthew 28:18.

Richardson pointed out that … Christianity rejects not only the claim that the king is God, but also the claim that God is like a king: "Christianity affirms that what is higher than all earthly kings is not some heavenly king, but the suffering crucified Christ." … The thrust of Richardson's critique was to insist on religion's autonomy *vis-à-vis* the political and economic order. The bond he would defend was not that of allegiance to a state, nor even that of membership in a nation, but that of surrender to a transcendent God. Only such surrender, such faith, can keep human power in check (p. 102).

But all that is contingent upon having a working knowledge of who Jesus Christ really is, knowledge that Rev. Richardson did not have at the time of his mobbing and still may not have. "The suffering crucified Christ" was limited by choice in his incarnated state but after the resurrection went back to being king of heaven and earth with all power (see Matthew 28:18), irrespective of the human faith needed to "keep human power in check." So what happened to Rev. Richardson was for good reason.

A case in point that shows Rev. Richardson did not have power from on high when he was mobbed is his involvement with the Unification Church. Westhues says that Rev. Richardson

> came to count it his professional duty, as a Christian, Calvinist theologian, to secure legitimacy for the Unification Church in the United States and Canada, and to protect this and the other new religions from persecution by the forces of secularism. (p. 113)

That he wanted to defend the Unification Church's right to exist is understandable, but what threw up a red flag for me was his wanting to protect "other new religions from persecution." My reason for being taken aback with that is Christian ministers who know who Jesus is and have a personal relationship with him are about conversions and wanting people to be Christians, not supporting other religions that oppose Jesus and compete with Christianity for converts. According to Westhues Rev. Richardson never joined the Unification Church. But Westhues says that Rev. Richardson asked Rev. Sun-Myung "Moon if he was the messiah" (p. 117) and that really disturbed me. Rev. Richardson supposedly appreciated "Unification's commitment to missions, 'not just converting people to Jesus Christ but also building a unified world.' [And], the Unification movement's priority on personal transformation and efforts toward individual self-perfection: 'Part of the way that better people are formed is through the work of Jesus Christ in the soul, the task of the church [being] to bring this to pass'" (p. 117). Rev. Richardson said "that he did not see the Unification Church as a new religion, but rather as a renewal movement within the church" (p. 118). Still, associating Rev. Moon with the Second Coming of Christ was implied in his question. It appears to me that neither minister knew Jesus at the time and who he is. Hence the main reason for my writing this essay: to say that Jesus wants Rev. Richardson to know him and be born again.

As a member of the African Methodist Episcopal Church, I believe it is possible for a person to intellectualize him or herself right out of the kingdom. Rev. Richardson is an ordained minister of the Word and Sacrament in the Presbyterian Church (U.S.A.) and could very well be a victim of the Church's doctrine of the elect and its vigorous Trinitarian emphasis. What "saved" me from watering down Jesus was divine intervention. The Holy Ghost pulled my coattail.

Rev. Richardson intellectualized himself right out of a tenured faculty position, but I believe divine intervention dominated his situation and that what happened to him was for good reason.

Newspaper writer Warren St. John wrote in a 1993 article in *Lingua Franca* "that Richardson 'had sacrificed his own reputation and the reputation of his publishing company by preaching tolerance towards the Unification Church'" (qtd. on p. 125). Tolerance in Rev. Richardson's case became a weapon used for self-inflicted wounds. He should have known better than to ask Rev. Moon if he were the Messiah. Ignorance of who Jesus is evidently prompted the question, which is why he was not "saved" from the mobbing ordeal for good reason.

"The structure of [Richardson's] book says a lot about Richardson's Calvinist theology, in particular his commitment to politics as he defined it: pluralism, diversity, tolerance of dissent, free debate" (p. 179). However, much of that is in name only. Calvinism protects its Zion. Proof of that is in the hoops a person has to jump through to get ordained in the Presbyterian Church (U.S.A.). And, much of Calvin's theology is not based on Scripture, which is problematic for me. But, that is another story and another paper.

I do agree with Calvinism, however, when it comes to the sovereignty of God, particularly in Rev. Richardson's case. For example, Calvin says that everything is God's will, even evil because being sovereign God can make good out of evil. "Calvin, like Augustine, contended that some things happen according to God's will which are at the same time against his will" (Leith, p. 89). God is sometimes made a victim of His own sovereignty. By Calvinism, that is, but not in this case. What happened to Rev. Richardson was for good reason, that is, to enlighten him that Jesus is not just the Savior but the Eternal God.

Rev. Richardson was accused of bad teaching – among other things – to serve as fuel for the mobbing, "the objective of every elimination process [being] not just to correct or punish misdeeds but to unmask a fundamentally flawed human being" (p. 211). God made Rev. Richardson privy to his mind and emotions not because misery loves company but to initiate a personal relationship that Trinitarian emphasis hinders. What I mean by that will be explained at the end of this essay.

"Richardson's this-worldly asceticism and his embrace of private enterprise to serve godly ends are consistent with his American Calvinist theology" (p. 241), but the Presbyterian Church (U.S.A.) is losing members every year by the thousands mainly, I believe, because of the Church's Trinitarian emphasis. By that I mean, the Godhead's titles are used in sermons and Sunday School classes rather than calling his name. This practice precludes their lifting up the name Jesus and receiving the power from on high he promises for calling on his name.

The remainder of Westhues's book elaborates on the goals of mobbing and the elimination process then suggests ways to remedy the problem.

> The point at which an accused person's life shifts from normal to a state of crisis comes well before the verdict of a tribunal or court. The shift comes when the charge is laid, that is, when the indictment is served. From that point on, the person's identity is under siege. In the moment of indictment, the accused ceases to be a "regular Joe," a person within the normal range of relation, whose pluses and minuses are incorporated into the routine of life. The accused becomes a questionable character. His or her moral worth becomes an official subject of debate.
>
> Conviction matters, of course. It is the answer to the questions raised. Yet even after an acquittal, the questions do not go away. "He was charged, you know, but they couldn't prove anything and he got off scot-free." Who wants to be the one about whom this is said? (p. 229)

Jesus's trial before Annas, Caiaphas, and Pontius Pilate (see John 18:12-40) show the accusers' predetermination to condemn Jesus to death by crucifixion (see John 19:1-42). It was predetermined by the powers that be at St. Michael's College, University of Toronto, that Rev. Richardson be ousted. Lies were told on Jesus even after he rose from the dead thousands of years ago and are still being told. Rev. Richardson is still being talked about disparagingly in spite of his academic and financial success. A marred reputation is a permanent residual of successful mobbing.

> As Muse explains, Foxe regards the degradation ceremony as the primary locus in which a person's faith is tested, a locus more critical even than the scaffold or the stake. The

target or perpetrator is properly obliged to *stand*, often in a literal sense but more importantly in the sense of Luther's famous phrase, "Here I stand, I can do no other." (p. 259)

But a person can stand more securely with power from on high.

Regarding his publishing house, Rev. Richardson wrote the following and he is to be commended for it:

My friends tell me that I need to pretend the decisions [about manuscript selections for publication] are more anguished and complicated – and mystified. I'm supposed to consult "readers" and have "reports" and "committee meetings." In this way, everything gets shrouded in "mystery" and that mystery is what gives authority to the process of acceptance and publishing. It just occurred to me that I'm a Calvinist-Puritan. That is, I don't like mystifying liturgy. I just like plainspeak – and for books to speak for themselves, evidencing their own worth. (qtd. on p. 282)

That part of Calvinism is admirable: speaking plainly and clearly. However, Scripture contains mysteries that it takes the Holy Ghost to demystify. For example, the Apostle Paul speaks in code in his epistle to the Romans, and it takes power from on high to decipher the code. A person can think he knows something but be wrong and stand just the same. Also, speaking plainly in error is just as bad as speaking a lie. What I am trying to say is this. A lot of what happened to Rev. Richardson was the result of what he did not know about Jesus. But "man's extremity is God's opportunity" (see Job 35:15-16).

Westhues elaborates further on Rev. Richardson's situation saying "there is much intellectual satisfaction in unraveling the process by which a Protestant theologian's refusal to sign Catholic bylaws led to a threat of dismissal for abusing students, then two years later, actual dismissal for spending too much time publishing books and for taking a stress leave on doctors' orders" (p. 291). He further says, "the only bad guy is the status quo, which oppresses everyone. Liberation lies in transforming the status quo" (p. 292). I agree. Status quo Christianity should be transformed by way of preaching the "New Millennial Covenant," the title I coined for my ministry based on knowledge I received from the Holy Ghost through divine revelation. My sermon on which the "New Millennial Covenant" is based is at the end of this essay for Rev. Richardson's sake.

Westhues study was done for the purpose of "human betterment."
He says more is expected "from social research than intellectually
interesting reflections on how things are ... [but] guidance toward
how things might become. ... The purpose of social research is first
of all to understand, and on this basis to construct, to build, to
somehow enable action that will leave all concerned and the earth
itself, better off" (p. 292). Power from on high is what makes the
difference.

Westhues goes on to say, "taking away one person's dignity does
not serve the dignity of anybody else. Nor is there anything especially
creative about cutting one person off from others. That is a well-
beaten path. True creativity means finding ways to build prospective
scapegoats in. This is not always possible, in workplaces or society at
large. The common good sometimes requires exclusion. It never
requires celebrating it, or doing it without a compelling reason – and
sorrow" (p. 295). "For workplace mobbing, as for any affliction, the
preferred solution is not recovery or remedy but prevention" (p. 303).

> Supporters evince a utopian outlook, confidence that
> through rational planning and social engineering, we
> humans can put in place a decent society, one that does not
> humiliate people but instead satisfies our highest aspirations
> for social justice. Opponents display a skeptical, anti-
> utopian mentality, mindfulness of human sinfulness and the
> limits of reason, therefore suspicion of planning and higher
> priority on pluralism and freedom. The difference can be
> traced back to two fifth-century theologians: the more
> idealistic Pelagius, who thought people are naturally
> innocent and good, and the more realistic Augustine, who
> believed in original sin and doubted that any City of Man
> could match the City of God. (p. 306)

I agree with Augustine. Human beings are born in sin. Human beings
need a Savior. Human beings need to know who the Savior is. Human
beings need to know the Savior's name. And, my personal belief is
that human beings need to call on the Savior's name and often.

Westhues says he wrote his research findings to encourage people
"to reflect on this material freely and critically, in light of their own
experience, to discuss and debate it, and to draw whatever
conclusions fit the context of their lives" (p. 308). That is what I did
and that is why I am including in this paper a sermon I wrote to

explain to Rev. Richardson what was missing in his life at the time of his ordeal and his just barely surviving it.

"Upon the foundation of factual knowledge, the subversion of mobbing and social elimination can be achieved" (p. 309). I disagree. Only power from on high can defeat sin.

Westhues writes about "Reciprocity in Workplace Relations" saying, "workmates take turns talking and listening, respond to one another in a spirit of mutual challenge, and surrender to a common extrinsic goal beyond what can be specified beforehand, trusting that the pursuit of it will produce a mutually satisfying surprise" (p. 310). That is just another way of practicing The Golden Rule (see Matthew 7:12). Connecting "with one another in constructive human ways" (p. 310) is Christ-like behavior also.

Westhues summarizes mobbing saying that it

signals a near-total breakdown of reciprocal relations in a workplace, especially a university. All the power is massed on the mobbers' side and drained completely from the target's side. The latter is not listened to, unless with groans of contempt. The object is to deprive the target of any say in what goes on, to turn the target into such an untouchable that even chatting with him or her in the corridor pollutes respectable colleagues. If reciprocity is a dance wherein people move their bodies with and against one another, bringing one another fully to life, mobbing is a free-for-all in which ten or twenty people sit on top of and crush one colleague by their collective weight. (p. 311)

This analogizes Jesus's trial and crucifixion as well.

"Mobbing destroys reciprocity in relations not only between mobbers and target, but also *among* the mobbers. They are not allowed to speak and act freely either" (p. 311). Such was the case with Nicodemus – a master of Israel who came to Jesus by night – with his colleagues in the Sanhedrin (see John 3:1-21).

"The first chapter of [Westhues's] book began by noting the widespread and well-founded doubt in our time about the judgments of public courts. Even with all the procedural safeguards of criminal law, and even with judges specially trained to be unbiased and fair, courts make mistakes. They sometimes nail the wrong person for an offense or unnecessarily cut the defendant off from respectable company" (p. 313). But, more to the point, it is shown in Jesus's trial and condemnation that courts can be intentionally perverted.

I agree with Westhues when he says that he endorses education as a preventive measure for mobbing (p. 314), which is why I am including my sermon in this essay. Educating preachers, pastors, evangelists, teachers, and other ministers to the nature of God and God's identity will do much to help believers receive power from on high. Of course, the Holy Ghost makes the final decision as to who receives the power. But, our minds and spirits are quickened to determine "who has ears to hear" (Luke 8:8) and who will be obedient.

"On the whole, giving others the same right one claims for oneself to think, speak, act, and live with the consequences, brings out the best in everyone and results in a more decent society. Humanity's biggest mistakes have come from trying to force everybody into the mold of some overarching system of thought. Betterment is not too much to hope for. Perfection is" (p. 314). Of course, people need to be aware that the devil is a liar and the father of lies (see John 8:44). All too often humans have bought the lie that freedom is the goal of life. Even Christianity teaches the freedom to live forever. But freedom has its downside. When elected officials feel free to rob people of dignity and human rights through slavery and slave-wages and to exterminate races of people through genocide and war, freedom becomes an enemy. When corporate and political leaders feel free to steal people's pensions and retirement funds and remove employment opportunities, freedom becomes a tool for thieves. And, when greed provides the means for people to self-destruct with drugs and alcohol, then freedom gags people to death.

It takes power to fight a powerful enemy. It takes power from on high to fight evil period. Therefore, the good reason for Rev. Richardson's mobbing is that it set the stage for Kenneth Westhues's book and for me to review it and for him to read a sermon I wrote. The Holy Ghost gave me this Word for Rev. Richardson: "I have loved you with an everlasting love. Therefore, in loving kindness have I drawn you. Again, I will build you" (Jeremiah 31:3-4a).

As a minister of the "New Millennial Covenant" that was given to me through divine revelation, I celebrate the initiative Jesus takes in bringing people to himself out of his great love (Revelation 3:7-13).

## Power From On High

Christian ministers need power. More to the point, Christian ministers need power from on high. So I shall do three things in this sermon. One, I shall tell you the source of the power, two, what the power is, and three, how to get power from on high.

First of all, we have to deal with Jesus. We've been taught certain things about Jesus like he was called the Son of God and the Son of Man. He had a mother named Mary and sisters and brothers. Two of his brothers were named James and Jude.

The Scripture tells us that Jesus walked the earth and "went about doing good" (Acts 10:38). He healed the sick, fed the hungry, cast out demons and walked on water. He even raised the dead. He wept and he prayed, calling God "Father" (see Matthew 6:9). But some things about Jesus are hard to understand like when he says in John 10:30, "The Father and I are one." What did Jesus mean by that, and how can that be?

So I will tell you a story now about the Trinity. You know what I mean: God the Father, God the Son, and God the Holy Ghost, Holy Ghost and Holy Spirit being interchangeable. The story was given to me through divine revelation and it explains how God is three in one. And it explains how Jesus could say what he did in John 10:30.

Once upon a time God was in heaven and God allowed chaos to rule the world. There was no order. Everything was helter-skelter and all over the place. Well, when chaos ruled the world, God was thinking. God thought for thousands – if not millions – of years. But one day God made a decision. The decision God made was to do something. God would speak and turn chaos into an orderly universe. The universe would consist of everything that exists, including people.

God decided to make the world by speaking the world into existence. Now thoughts are words, so Jesus, the Word, was before the foundation of the world. But when God uttered sound – the "Big Bang," if you will – that's when Jesus was begotten. What I mean is Jesus is the voice of God (see Ps. 29) and the words God spoke. To put it another way, Jesus is the articulation of divine thought. Now stay with me. God's thoughts are wisdom, understanding, counsel, might and knowledge (Is. 11:2), among other things I am incapable of comprehending.

As soon as God opened God's mouth and spoke, what God said happened; for example, when God said, "Let there be light" or "light be" – as my husband who is a Hebrew scholar told me – there it was. When God said, "Let there be land" or "land be," there it was. As soon as God said it, it happened. So, when God spoke and things happened, that was the work of the Holy Spirit.

All this occurred at the same time. That is, all three things happened at once. God thought, God spoke, and every time God said something, it happened. That's how God is three in one. I was given the phrase thought, word, and deed – a familiar phrase – to help me remember.

God the Father is the original thought, supported in Isaiah 14:24, God the Son is the articulated Word later made flesh in John 1:1, 2, 3, and 14, and God the Holy Spirit is deed, the activity or movement of God in Genesis 1:1-2. It is through the Holy Spirit that God called those things which be not as though they were in Romans 4:17. And, it is the Holy Spirit that "sounds" the Word. So the Triune God – meaning Father, Son, and Holy Ghost or Spirit – is thought, Word, and deed.

Stay with me now. Thousands of years after the world was created, God made another decision and that was to come down from heaven and walk the earth. That's called the Incarnation, God in the flesh. So God as thought who decided to speak became a man, born of a woman, which means the Word was made flesh.

Jesus grew up and learned the carpentry trade from his stepfather Joseph. He lived 33 ½ years. His ministry lasted about 3 ½ years before he was killed. He was crucified, died and was buried. However, it is after he rose from the dead that we learn of another divine decision.

Jesus says in Matthew 28:18, "All power is given to me in heaven and in earth." He means all power everywhere. This indicates that God as thought deferred to his spoken word after the resurrection. Or to put it another way, defer means to yield. God respectfully yielded his thoughts to what he said after he rose from the dead.

Stay with me now. Referring to the Holy Ghost Jesus says in John 15:26, "When the Comforter comes, whom I will send to you from the Father, even the Spirit of truth who proceeds from the Father, He will testify of me" (emphasis mine). So after yielding to the Word, meaning Jesus, the Holy Ghost confirms the Word as the foundation of God. Do you see what I'm saying? God is sovereign. God defines God's Self. God does what God wants to do.

Colossians 2:9 says that Jesus is "all the fullness of the Godhead bodily," and Matthew 28:18 says that Jesus rose from the dead with all power. So we learn from Scripture God's divine plan established before the creation of the world.

Now you've probably noticed that I'm still on my first point: the source of power from on high. And, I'm not done yet. But don't worry. The other two points can be covered in just a few sentences.

My explanation of the Trinity – which is thought, Word, and deed – gives rise to the question, "How is God addressed?" especially when praying, which gives me the opportunity to share yet another revelation. You need to know that most of my God-thought and God-talk comes from Scripture and divine revelation. It goes like this.

The enemy – meaning the devil, also known as Satan – can be called "god" because Yahweh – God in Hebrew – said, "Thou shalt have no other gods before me" (Ex. 20:3). The enemy can be called "father" because Jesus called the devil the father of lies (see Jn. 8:44). The enemy can be called "lord" because Jesus used the term generically. He made reference to the lord of the vineyard (Mk. 12:9), the lord of the virgins (Mt. 25:11), the lord and his servants (Mt. 25:19).

The enemy can be called "master." Jesus talked about the master of a house (Mk. 13:35) and said, "No [one] can serve two masters" (Mt. 6:24). He even referred to Nicodemus as "a master of Israel" (Jn. 3:10). But the enemy has never been and can never be called Jesus Christ. Therefore, the Holy Ghost told me to say when I pray, "Dear Lord Jesus Christ."

The reason for that is words like Father, Lord, God, Master, and Christ are titles like Mr., Mrs. and Dr.; they are not names. The name of God is Jesus and in the world to come his name will change from Jesus to The Word of God (Rev. 9:13). And know this. Christ is not Jesus's last name. Like I said, Christ is a title meaning the Messiah, or anointed one.

Well, preacher woman, you ask. What about the prayer Jesus taught his disciples where he says "Our Father?" My answer is, during the Incarnation, again meaning when God walked the earth in the flesh, God's thoughts stayed where they were – in heaven, because the thoughts of God are more than the flesh can contain or comprehend.

God says in Isaiah 55:8-9, "My thoughts are not your thoughts, neither are my ways your ways. As high as the heavens are from the earth so are my ways higher than your ways and my thoughts than your thoughts." However, God's *spoken* word became flesh in the person of Jesus born of the Virgin Mary.

After his death and resurrection Jesus went back to the Father, meaning divine thought. To make it plain, Jesus went back to himself. Or, Jesus went back to his mind, his original thoughts. He sits at the right hand of the Father but that is root power, not a location. I repeat. Sitting at the right hand of the Father is not a geographical location. Revelation 7:17 says Jesus is in the midst of the throne, and there is only one throne. Hear me now. The Word is the foundation of God. And understand this. The Incarnation caused a separation that the resurrection reunited. But that's another sermon.

I just want you to know that when you do say, Father or Lord or Master or Christ, Jesus is the God you're referring to. Jesus is the One true God. He came down from heaven, walked the earth, went back to heaven and sent his Holy Spirit back down here to live in us.

So to summarize point one, the source of power from on high is the resurrected Jesus with all power. Jesus is God, the Word made flesh, the articulation of divine thought; the power of God, the wisdom of God. When Jesus walked the earth a distinction was made in the Godhead but after the resurrection that distinction no longer applies, because Jesus was raised with all power in heaven and on earth. So hear me well. The Holy Ghost told me to tell you that he is the Eternal God and that his name is Jesus, and he is the source of power from on high.

That being said, my second point explains what power from on high is. It is the supernatural manifestation of the Holy Ghost. Power from on high enables a person to move in the gifts of the Spirit for greater service to humanity. This Holy Ghost power is what makes you able to prophesy and work miracles.

You can heal the sick, speak in tongues, teach, preach, and comfort. This power gives you the ability to hear the still small voice of Jesus, and obey him. But most of all, power from on high is having the love of Jesus in your heart and the *shekinah* glory on your face.

"So preacher woman," you say, "get to your third point. How does one get this power from on high?" Well, our text gives us the answer. Revelation 3:8b says, "I know that you have but little power, and yet you have kept my word and have not denied my name." Jesus is talking about obedience and knowing him personally.

We receive power from on high when we obey the Word and lift up the name Jesus because we know who he is. Jesus is the Eternal God. When we believe on his name and preach his Word, he gives us his Holy Ghost, which is power from on high. What we ministers should do is have a personal relationship with Jesus and every time we preach say his name and not just use his title.

In every sermon we preach we should say Jesus and say it often, because there's power in the name. Jesus says in John 12:32, "If I be lifted up from the earth I'll draw all people unto me." You lift him up by calling on his name. Now using titles sometimes is unavoidable. I mean, we have to say God, Lord, and Father sometimes to preach the Bible. But if you want your church to grow, lift up the name Jesus in your sermons. If you want Holy Ghost power in your worship services where people are healed and delivered, lift up the name Jesus in your sermons. If you want to pray for the sick and they get well and rebuke the devil and make him flee and speak in tongues to receive divine revelations, call on the name Jesus when you preach and pray, for Jesus tells us repeatedly, "Do not deny my name."

Now I would be remiss if I didn't make this point. The church is political and we ministers suffer. There is jealousy, resentment, and persecution on every side and sometimes rejection. But Jesus promises to make us stand if we do not deny his name. We ministers have to confront evil. The devil walks about like a roaring lion seeking whom he may devour. Ole Slewfoot stays on our case. But Jesus promises to shield and protect us if we do not deny his name.

We ministers need power from on high so we have to be obedient to receive it. When Jesus says, "Do not deny my name," he means it.

Jesus says, "Whosoever shall be ashamed of me in this adulterous and sinful generation, of them shall I be ashamed when I come in my glory with the holy angels." (Mk. 8:38)
Do not deny my name.

Jesus says, "You did not choose Me, but I chose you and appointed you that you should go and bear fruit, and that your fruit should remain." (Jn. 15:16)
Do not deny my name.

The Word says, "My kindness shall not depart from you, neither shall the covenant of my peace be removed, for I will have mercy on you." (Is. 54:10)
Do not deny my name.

Jesus says, "I give you authority to tread on serpents and scorpions, and over all the power of the enemy: and nothing shall by any means hurt you." (Lk. 10:19.
Do not deny my name.

Jesus says, "These signs shall follow them that believe; In my name shall they cast out devils; they shall speak in new tongues; ... they shall lay hands on the sick, and they shall recover." (Mk. 16:17-18)
Do not deny my name.

The Word says, "Remember not the former things neither consider the things of old. Behold I will do a new thing." (Is. 43:18-19a)
Do not deny my name.

Jesus says, "Go into all the world and preach the gospel to every creature." (Mk. 16:15)
And, do not deny my name.

There is power in the name Jesus.

It is power that lifts up our cast down heads.
Power that straightens up our bent down bodies.
Power that heals our feeble flesh.
Power that soothes our troubled minds.

It is power that delivers us from evil.
Power that saves our sin sick souls.
Power that removes the sting of death.
Power that grabs us up from the grave.

It is power that will one day chain down Satan in the pits of hell.

It is power that raises us up from the dead.

It is power that gives us eternal life.

Who is this power?
His name is Jesus!
What is this power?
It's his Holy Ghost, Holy Ghost, Holy Ghost, Holy Ghost!

It is power that makes the wind and the rain.
Power that makes the lightning flash and the sea billows roll.
Power that calms the raging storms.
Power that heals our weary land.

Who is this power?
His name is Jesus!
What is this power?
It's his Holy Ghost, Holy Ghost, Holy Ghost, Holy Ghost!

## Work Cited

Leith, John H., 1993. *Basic Christian Doctrine*. Louisville, KY: Westminster/John Knox.

# Response

A number of readers have said my books on mobbing have made them uncomfortable by awakening memories of their own past involvements in eliminating unwanted colleagues. Baldwin's essay is likely to make even more readers uncomfortable, on account of its explicit foundation of Christian Scripture and undisguised standpoint of faith in Jesus Christ. That is one reason I was pleased that Mellen accepted this essay for publication. If the study of academic mobbing is to progress, we students of the subject need to grapple with a wide variety of approaches, perhaps especially those that leave us squirming a little in our academic chairs.

Like the overwhelming majority of professors in the public universities of Europe and North America, I teach and write within a world-view that has been purged of specific religious commitments. I intend that my work should be based on reason and evidence, that it should be no more or less intelligible to a Protestant reader than to a Catholic or Jewish or Hindu or Muslim or atheist reader. I hold to the Enlightenment ideal of science as a path to truth – the hard vocation that Max Weber said leads also to disenchantment of the world. Richardson has called me an "astringent sociologist." I would wish to have stood with Galileo in the seventeenth century, and with Darwin in the nineteenth. I was glad for the chance, on a visit to Paris, to pay respect in the Panthèon at the tombs of Voltaire and Rousseau.

How should secular scholars like me react to Baldwin's essay? With disdain or contempt? Hardly. Instead with the same kind of respectful, critical thinking apparent in her reaction to my work. Science is a high value, but dialogue is higher.

Across the street from the Panthèon in Paris is the church of St.-Etienne-du-Mont, the shrine to Ste.-Genevieve, and therein the tomb of Blaise Pascal, the mathematician who claimed that "the heart has reasons that reason does not know." I have paid respect at his tomb, too. Not that I have ever had a conversion experience like Pascal's. I have not craved one either. Maybe, like Weber, I am not religiously musical enough. Mundane experience and study led me to the view even in my youth that commitment to science need not and should not be to the exclusion of religious faith. Who would want to spend a lifetime in one of the actual historical outcomes of human efforts to reshape society solely on the basis of reason, with a ban on the cult of what lies beyond reason? Does the terror of revolutionary France seem like fun, or the concentration camps of the Third Reich, or deportation to Siberia in Stalin's Russia? In my view, any social theory that pretends to be all-encompassing, a blueprint for some city on a hill, whether that theory is supposedly scientific or supposedly inspired by God, should be promptly scorned before a movement forms to set it in place.

The tough, practical question is how to mix reasoned analyses with a deep bow of surrender to the larger mystery that remains. Some professors combine meticulously secular scholarship with membership in a church, synagogue, temple or mosque. Others cultivate diverse private spiritualities. In my own case, I admit and feel no shame that my scholarship is tinged with the Catholicism of my upbringing. Until graduate school, most of my teachers were monks, nuns, or priests, and I am grateful to them. Every reasoned scholar's work is tinged with something beyond reason. I draw the motto for my gardening from St. Bernard of Clairveaux: "You will find something more in woods than in books. Trees and stones will teach you what you can never learn from teachers."

More threatening than churchgoers, nature mystics, and spiritual seekers are scholars like Baldwin in whose work faith and reason, Sacred Scripture and secular knowledge, are explicitly intermixed. This is the mix that defines their work as theology. Richardson is another example, though the mix in his case involves a lighter sprinkling of faith and a heavier dose of reason. That may be why Baldwin faults Richardson. She says he "intellectualized himself right out of a tenured faculty position." She finds him too Calvinist and Trinitarian, insufficiently simple in his faith, not ready enough to invoke the name of Jesus and to receive in return power from on high. In her view, God let Richardson be mobbed to give him "working knowledge" of who Jesus Christ really is, to make Richardson privy to Jesus's own mind and emotions when he was crucified. Baldwin's "good reason for mobbing" is from a supernatural viewpoint.

Being a sociologist rather than a theologian, I cannot agree or disagree with Baldwin on this score. By my reading of Richardson's scholarship, he is indeed a worldly, world-affirming theologian. This fact helps explain why most of his work has been intelligible to me, a more secular scholar. It may also be, however, that the sociological analysis of Richardson in my book understates the faith dimension of his scholarly life. I expect that would be his view. On every day of his dismissal hearing, he placed on the table in front of him a holy card of Joan of Arc, to whose mind and emotions at the time of her trial Richardson felt himself more privy than he ever expected to be. Years earlier, in 1990, when faced with the college's demand that he sign the new Catholic theology bylaws, Richardson begged President Alway in a letter "to let this cup pass from me."

What impresses me most about Baldwin's essay is how Christian faith has enabled her to grasp thoroughly what mobbing is about. Secular respondents to my work have sometimes struck me as so out of touch with people's emotions, so oblivious of the deep interiority of human life, that they cannot quite wrap their minds around the go-for-broke seriousness of workplace mobbing, its unleashing of elemental impulses. Baldwin, by contrast, has read my account of Richardson's dismissal against a background of meditation on the stories of how Joseph's brothers ganged up on him and of how Jesus's enemies and even his friends coalesced in the collective aggression that led to his torture and death. As a Christian, Baldwin is not surprised that humans sometimes form themselves into mobs. Like Augustine, she is keenly aware of human sinfulness.

I do not believe Baldwin is correct when she says she "gleaned" from my book that mobbing is akin to sexual arousal. That is her own insight, but I believe there is truth in it – at least in so far as mobbing awakens blind passion that finds orgasmic satisfaction in the absolute conquest of the target. Baldwin's description of lynchings as sexual acts is not unlike Orlando Patterson's analysis of lynchings as human sacrifice (in his *Rituals of Blood*, Civitas/Counterpoint, 1998). What happens when humans join themselves into a crowd for the humiliation of the designated prey is not casual, not routine, not like a typical convocation for conferral of degrees. It is something people get "swept up in" just as much as when they are "swept off their feet" in romantic love. True revulsion for another evokes feelings just as deep as erotic attraction does. In *Eliminating Professors* (1998), my first book on academic mobbing, I said it was like the bullfight or the hunt, no playful romp. In their different ways, Baldwin and Patterson make essentially the same point.

Baldwin's further point, rooted even more directly in her Christian faith, is that humiliation, which she describes as "the foundation of evil," is an abomination to God. To illustrate this all-important contention, Baldwin recounts the story of Jesus's rescue of the woman caught in adultery. Here, then, is a Christian theologian asserting in religious language, and from a standpoint of faith, the same hallmark of Judaeo-Christianity that René Girard has discerned in his more disinterested study of myths (reported in my second paper on Medaille College, Chapter Three herein). Christianity, at its very core, stands for the wrongness of collective humiliation. In story after story of this faith tradition, its "good news," lies the moral that in the long run, the mob or crowd does not win. Joseph, as Baldwin points out, ends up in the second highest position of Egyptian rule. Jesus rises from the dead.

It is not only people of virtue, according to the Christian Scriptures, who should not be ganged up on, but also people who have misbehaved. In the story about the first stone, the woman whom Jesus rescues is not falsely accused of adultery. This is not a case of wrongful conviction. No, the woman was caught in the act and therefore deserved to be put to death, according to law. But Jesus said no. Girard claims he can find few other myths of that era so opposed to the dominance of the collective over the individual. Do not judge, Jesus preached, lest you also be judged. As a Christian believer in our own day, Baldwin precisely illustrates Girard's point.

This brings me to a final reason for not dismissing Baldwin's essay, despite its having been written from the explicitly Christian viewpoint that is generally sneered at in the secular academic culture of our time. It is an empirical fact that Christianity spawned and nourished what came to be called Western Civilization, what we today take for granted as our own way of life, with its unparalleled safeguards of individual liberty and human rights. To be sure, Western civilization includes monstrous violations of the Christian proscription of humiliation, many of them sponsored by Christian churches: Torquemada and the Spanish Inquisition, massacres of Protestants by Catholics, of Catholics by Protestants, and of witches, Jews, and infidels by both Catholics and Protestants. Still, the Christian message endured for almost two millennia as the religious bedrock of the West. Never was its central place in public culture challenged so widely and fundamentally as it came to be in the late twentieth century. Does this mean that Western civilization has risen to a threshhold even higher than the Christian ethic for condemning collective humiliation of targeted individuals? Or does it mean that these recent generations and our own are loosening the fetters on mobbing tendencies that the Christian ethic formerly, with many exceptions, kept in place?

In *Nineteen Eighty-Four,* Orwell claimed that beside modern forms of group tyranny over individuals, the tyranny of medieval Christendom pales. Studying mobbing episodes in today's formally rational, secular, bureaucratized universities, I have often suspected Orwell is right. If he is, an essay like Baldwin's deserves a place of honor on the plural landscape of contemporary academic thought.

## Chapter Ten

# When the Bastards Grind You Under: Conflict Theory versus Social Exchange Theory

### Anson Shupe

Kenneth Westhues's two companion volumes (1998, 2003) on workplace mobbing and faculty elimination, in particular his account of the pillorying of well-known theologian/author/publisher Herbert Richardson by two Canadian academic administrations, have been disturbing to me, a tenured full professor in sociology, for two reasons.

First, over the years (earlier in my career more than later) I have admittedly been part of the feeding frenzy sometimes occurring in tenure and promotion committees when like-minded senior colleagues have passed judgement on marginal and ill-liked faculty members. In a few cases we did not even wait for the ultimate tenure decision to rub the person out of the institution's memory.

Second, thanks in part to Westhues's analysis, I can in hindsight see some of my own conflicts with my administration as due to their attempts to lower my profile in committee service and start a rumor mill down the line of administrators, redefining my personal idiosyncrasies, research interests, or resistance to certain administrative initiatives as somehow a personality problem on my part. In addition, I have seen other colleagues demonized more or less as if the administrators and eliminators were acting in an ideologically pure atmosphere while those who objected to the former's groupthink were simply obstreperous by nature ("He's a congenital malcontent") or consumed by attributed personal problems spilling over into their professional roles ("She's going through a divorce" or "he drinks too much" or "she's going through a mid-life crisis").

During the past three decades a good deal has been published on the political economy and professional behavior of actors in higher education: as fictional satire (Hynes 1997; Waugh 1967), humorous critical (Mitchell 1981), and serious critical (Roche 1994; Sommer 1995; Mandell 1977; Postman and Weingartner 1969). Professor Westhues in his two volumes has done an admirable review of the additional considerable research literature on both administrative and faculty reactance to the elimination process, even if many of the narratives read like hospice career overviews.

Before I offer my perspective on the issue of universities sacking or driving out senior faculty members, I want to make one preliminary observation. My original understanding as a young assistant professor, both at Alfred University (in New York state) and the University of Texas at Arlington, was that tenure was a traditional device used to provide productive faculty with job security and insulate those pursuing cutting-edge, even controversial research from political and social forces outside the university that might object to the findings. Years later I now see a more important internal function: to protect faculty from administrators, particularly when the latter do not share the same discipline, paradigmatic models, politics, or – as in the Richardson case at a parochial college – religious denomination. Tenure is not always an effective defense. The public, including alumni, may temporarily criticize or call for the head of a professor but those winds subside; administrators, on the other hand, are well-placed to carry on grudges and resentments that may take years to operationalize into faculty dismissal.

## The Interplay of Two Sociological Models in Academic Eliminations

I will settle for Westhues's characterization of administrators' attempts to expunge faculty member from their institutions as "mobbing," but I want to point out that the elimination is not technically "mob" behavior. It is too rational and deliberate. It is not spontaneous. Elimination is more like a social movement or systematic campaign: it possesses identifiable leaders, agenda, organization, and goals. But to the extent that members of a mob cannot clearly reflect on their intentions and are oblivious to how disinterested persons would regard their passions, then Westhues's use of the term "mobbing behavior" in academia is useful. I would term it "ganging-up-on" behavior, but the phenomenon is the same. There is something here akin to a lust, or drive, for purification of faculty by administrators that takes on a sanctimonious nature: we need to purge within our own ranks, we can purge our own, we will purge our own. It becomes a show of chest-pounding efficacy at the expense of the targets (and as a latent function, it brings more solidarity within the ranks of administrators since they, too, have likely been under counterattack from the targets in the purging process).

There were two models at various times framing the understanding of the administrative campaign to eliminate Herbert Richardson from both the University of Toronto and its "satellite" affiliate, Saint Michael's College. These were the conflict theory approach and the social exchange approach.

## Conflict Theory

There are three points with which any conflict theorist would agree:

- all social order and appearance of harmony in society and any organization of any size ultimately rests on force and coercion.
- conflict, because of limited resources available, and competition are inevitable and normal.
- elites who benefit from whatever system of inequality is in place try to mask or rationalize the conflict or stigmatize it when it breaks out.

Not to attempt to put too fine a point on parallels between the Marxist theory of class conflict and administrative/faculty relations in the academy, the comparison is apt even so. In Marx's terms, the administrators of a college or university are the bourgeoisie (some, by *double entendre*, are remarkably petty bourgeois). They ultimately control the resources (course offerings, salaries, raises, bonuses, grants, sabbatical leaves, and so forth) or the means of production. The faculty, on the other hand, are the proletariat. Alongside janitors and secretaries, faculty members are where the rubber meets the highway. Moreover, they are the intermediaries who largely provide the institution with whatever reputation it has through their research and who regularly teach and advise tuition-paying students. The latter, in turn, along with the credit hours they generate, are the units of production. But in the grand scheme of things administrators have the upper-class status in the relations of production.

If this comparison seems somewhat of a stretch, consider the funding formulae for many public universities as well as the typical distribution of raise monies (wealth) between faculty (of whatever rank) and administrators (of whatever level). Many upper-level administrators, like CEOs, even have "golden parachutes" prepared as they approach retirement.

*Social Exchange Theory*

A tenet of the social exchange model is that persons generally pursue rewards (or profits), eschew costs, and remain in what they perceive as equitable or future equitable exchanges in personal and professional relationships. There are in virtually every culture *norms of distributive justice* that define what equity means. The important point in cases such as Richardson's is that one can see in hindsight that the demise of his institutional role was planned without his knowledge, yet he apparently perceived a distributive justice still at work until late in the game. This prolonged the elimination process, such as engagements in considering early retirement by both sides. Conflict involves victory or surrender, not compromise or finding common ground.

The Richardson case presents what seemingly started out as a dialogue where clarification of positions and negotiation of how to interpret his behavior left open the possibility of a non-dismissal resolution, at least from Richardson's viewpoint. This explains the frequent exchange of superficially cordial memoranda between him and various administrators expressing hints of considering contrition and further exploration of concerns, usually ending in "Best Wishes" and similar memo exits. Thus there appeared to be for some time an exchange of information and the possibility of salvaging Richardson's appointment in Toronto.

The fact is that two years after his dismissal, Richardson sued (unsuccessfully) a second-tier journal, *Lingua Franca*, for libel in negatively and erroneously describing his previous professional activities, and university administrators fed at least in part off the previous media coverage during their mobbing of Richardson. Thus a conflict model may make a better fit with many elements of Richardson's experiences, such as the administration's otherwise curious withholding of student criticisms of his classroom demeanor for over a year and Kafkaesque refusals to divulge the names or numbers of them. In an honest exchange, such information is ethically imperative in order to provide a colleague facts when his or her livelihood is at stake. But his dismissal was not really at stake; it was already a *fait accompli*. A cynic might conclude that the various administrators allowed Richardson to believe there was hope to find a resolution short of dismissal, at least lending the color of due process to a mobbing. Let me say it more strongly. The correspondence of the early 1990s in which Richardson was required "to explain himself," i.e., with students in his classes and his relationships to The Edwin Mellen Press, Mellen University, and the Unification Church, seems in retrospect a pretext to dodge the impression of mobbing

## Lessons

Before giving some conclusions, allow me briefly to describe an incomplete late 1990s attempt by administrators at my institution to mob several senior faculty members. I'll set the stage with a single case.

The Chancellor of our campus, it was learned first-hand by the President of the Faculty Senate, kept files in Nixonesque fashion on selected faculty members. He had a particular file on Professor X, the contents of which claimed that the professor was so emotionally unstable that his wife had left him and his grown daughter had moved out of the house. The claims had a spin-doctored truth to them: the wife *was* spending weekdays taking classes toward a ministerial degree at a southern Indiana seminary in another city, returning home on weekends, and the daughter *had* moved into a dormitory in West Lafayette, Indiana, but to start her freshman year at Purdue.

The real issue was revealed. Professor X had a tenured appointment in the Philosophy Department and had developed an interest in sports ethics, eventually becoming our institution's liaison with the National Collegiate Athletic Association. In that capacity he had discovered recruiting violations by the men's basketball coach (soon gone), but before they were sent on to the NCAA, his office was burglarized by persons unknown and the critical documents removed. (Professor X retired soon after.)

The Vice-Chancellor for Academic Affairs, meanwhile was himself something of a mobbing expert, having literally co-authored a book on how to do it successfully (many times more cynical than Professor Westhues's volumes) and how to manipulate the media in the process. When his wife assumed the Deanship of the School of Education, claiming to have been tenured at a southern university, a suspicious assistant professor contacted that university and discovered that the wife had in fact been denied tenure. After her investigation became known, the junior faculty member was mobbed but finally won a lawsuit against the university. There is an important point in not just recognizing mobbing but understanding the social psychology of a number of mobbers: they will play hardball until the end, then moments before the lawyers enter the courtroom they will agree to a settlement. I have seen that scenario played out over and over in just sixteen years at just one university.

A string of such incidents about the same time (even the same year) prompted something unprecedented in my academic experience. According to our faculty handbook, a circulated petition to the faculty receiving two-thirds of their signatures would initiate a pair of campus-wide convocations in which *any* faculty-staff member could step up to a microphone and speak his or her mind. Administrators could attend but were not allowed to speak.

The auditorium was standing room-only. The local television and print media were there, and while the speakers were not always of the same mind, the administrators had more critics than defenders. (In private a number of junior faculty had urged senior faculty, presumably insulated by tenure, to speak out "because we don't dare.")

In the administrators' minds, I imagine, this was a case of reverse mobbing by faculty. But, true to the conflict model, they had their petty revenge in the ways Westhues (1998) has described. Suddenly some senior faculty were no longer invited to lunch with the Chancellor and Vice-Chancellor, the former's racketball partners were no longer called for matches, and rumors began being passed down the line to Deans about other faculty members' instabilities. Inquiries were made about who showed up for class precisely on the second, and who was using university travel funds to go where. It appears that one initial sign of mobbing is a sudden micromanagement by top administrators, when management of faculty affairs by, say, department chairs is the norm.

So it goes.

The polite language used in memos, many of the sort exchanged between Richardson and administrators as thoroughly documented by Westhues, has a collegial tone but is often a subterfuge. An astute faculty member being mobbed has to read between the lines. He or she also has to assume a certain paranoia in interpreting even casual comments by fellows and in responding to administrators' requests to "drop by." One even watches what one says in the main office in front of the secretary.

Administrators sometimes also may count on spinning natural reactance or even defensiveness by a marked faculty member into a self-fulfilling prophecy: see, we told you so, there *is* evidence that Professor W is unstable, holds hatred for the institution, and generally demonstrates a non-cooperative attitude. One professor at a former university where I taught ended up mobbed and did not receive promotion/tenure when I did. Exasperated, he sent copies of his curriculum vitae to a host of nationally prominent sociologists soliciting their evaluation of his record. Of course, most had never heard of him (or perhaps even of the institution) but nevertheless as a courtesy sent back pleasant-to-positive letters praising his progress. This professor then, probably out of institutional spite, taped them (over three dozen) to his office door and the walls on either side from floor to ceiling. It only confirmed to mobbers and the larger faculty that he was ego-damaged and slightly bizarre. Quipped one professorial mobber, "Anyone with such glowing endorsements should have no problem finding another job." By then the exasperated professor was further contributing to his ostracization and justifying the mobbing. Thus, once targeted, marked, or labeled, administrators *and* fellow faculty retrospectively and ongoingly impose on the faculty member what deviance theorists term a "master status" that overrides all his or her otherwise good qualities and even reinterprets otherwise good achievements as inferior.

Finally there is a nasty possibility that I can testify to anecdotally but could be tested more generally by an aggressive doctoral student studying professors' and administrators' resumes: many professors might squeak by in the tenure process with minimal accomplishments and later move into middle-management administration because their new status gives them an excuse not to engage in the arduous work of researching/publishing/teaching/grading/advising, and additionally because administration often pays better. I suspect some become invidious of their faculty fellows who *do* excel in their endeavors and therefore become zealous in questioning the latters' accomplishments. This might possibly underlie Harvard-educated Herbert Richardson's case, a man who started a thriving academic publishing house, created an unique university, and had an impressive publication record in theology and social issues. But that is only an hypothesis.

## References

Hynes, James, 1997. *Publish or Perish*. New York: Picador USA.

Mandell, Richard D., 1977. *The Professor Game*. Garden City, NY: Doubleday.

Postman, Neil and Charles Weingartner, 1969. *Teaching as a Subversive Activity*. New York: Dell.

Roche, George, 1994. *The Fall of the Ivory Tower: Government Funding, Corruption, and the Bankruptcy of American Higher Education*. Washington, DC: Regnery.

Sommer, John W., ed., 1995. *The Academy in Crisis*. New Brunswick, NJ: Transaction.

Waugh, Evelyn, 1967. *Decline and Fall*. New York: Dell.

Westhues, Kenneth, 1998. *Eliminating Professors: A Guide to the Dismissal Process.* Lewiston, New York: The Edwin Mellen Press.

Westhues, Kenneth, 2003. *The Trial, Degradation, and Dismissal of a Professor: AdministrativeMobbing in Academe*. Lewiston, NY: The Edwin Mellen Press.

# Response

Shupe's short essay is long on insight, displaying keen appreciation of what academic mobbing involves. Not surprisingly, since he and I are both sociologists, we seem to be on the same wave-length in the effort to make sense of campus politics. I want to respond to three of his insights that seem to me especially perceptive and constructive: the difference between conflict and exchange perspectives, the divide between administration and professoriate, and finally the word *mobbing* itself, how it is defined and understood.

A basic component of the sociology curriculum, usually conveyed in required courses in sociological theory but often also in introductory and other courses, is a review of competing perspectives on what life in human societies is basically about. Conflict theory and social exchange theory are ordinarily two of the perspectives reviewed. In the first of these, life is seen as a clash between people with more power and those with less, and specific events are analyzed in terms of how the more powerful try to cling to advantage and ward off challenges by the less powerful. In the exchange perspective, by contrast, life is seen as a process of ongoing trade-offs between groups and individuals, as each one gives and takes according to its own purposes. Each of these perspectives is spelled out in an array of concepts and hypotheses, but they boil down to the basic question of whether life is a fight, a contest to win and make an opponent lose, or a parley, a negotiation for working out terms of living and letting live.

Obviously, real life includes both conflict and exchange. Which perspective is more useful for sociological explanation depends on which scene of human interaction one is studying. If the subject matter is everyday life in most marriages, exchange theory yields many useful insights. If the subject matter is divorce court, conflict theory probably gives a more adequate account of what is happening.

Shupe is correct in preferring conflict theory for present purposes, and his saying so enlarges our understanding of workplace mobbing. This pathology can be understood as the breakdown of the normal process of social exchange. In any workplace, academic or not, negotiation and trade are the everyday routine. Issues arise. You win some, lose some. Workers balance each other, trading on each other's strengths. A worker's stock fluctuates over time, higher then lower, depending on ever-changing priorities. Things seem to "work out" –

not perfectly, but more or less. In sharp contrast, on the rare occasion when some worker is mobbed, there is a squaring off. Perpetrators line up on one side as a strong, united force. Their object is to defeat the target, who faces them alone or with a scatter of defenders. The principles of conflict theory come into play.

Shupe sees relevance for conflict theory even apart from mobbing episodes. In Marxist language, he casts administrators as bourgeoisie, professors as proletariat. I would add two points. First is that such bifurcation in university politics has increased over the past half century as institutions have grown larger and more bureaucratized, as the gap has widened between administrators' and professors' salaries, as the goal of credentialing students and making them marketable has displaced the goal of educating them, and as administration has come to be viewed as a career of its own rather than as interruption of a career in teaching and research.

The second point I would add is that most mobbings are accurately seen as ways of enlarging administrators' power over faculty. This is obvious, of course, in a case like Richardson's or those at Medaille College. But even when the attack on a professor arises initially from students, colleagues, alumni, or an outside interest group, an administration strengthens its position over faculty by taking charge and putting the target in a pillory. Anne Llewellyn Barstow (in *Witchcraze*, HarperCollins, 1994) has argued that medieval witch hunts, even when arising from the masses, served the interests of the emergent state authorities, as the latter stepped in to hold a trial, convict the witch and kill or punish her, thereby "solving" what was popularly regarded as a problem. Barstow's point applies equally to a university administration that responds aggressively to clamor by others over what some professor has said or done.

Now finally to Shupe's reservations about my use of the word *mobbing* to describe incursions on a professor's job and reputation of the kind observed in the Richardson case and similar ones. Shupe argues that such administrative elimination of professors is too rational and deliberate to qualify exactly as mob behavior. He would sooner call it a social movement or a kind of "ganging up."

No label is perfect. A rose is a rose. In the late nineteenth century, the British philosopher Ferdinand Schiller proposed to William James that the kind of philosophy the two of them, along with John Dewey, C. S. Pierce, Henri Bergson, and others, were doing should be called *humanism* rather than *pragmatism*. James agreed, but it was too late. The latter name had already caught on. These philosophers have been called *pragmatists* ever since.

I have no objection to applying the term *ganging up* to the cases of social elimination analyzed in this and my other books. I use the phrase myself. The term *social movement* also fits. But Shupe is correct: the main label I have used in my research is *workplace mobbing*. One reason is that this term has already caught on in Europe, as a result of Heinz Leymann's and others' research. The substantive reason is that the word *mobbing*, as used long before Leymann's application of it to events in the workplace, encompasses four key attributes of what I have seen on a micro-level in the cases I have studied:

1. *Mobbing implies surrender of individuality to the collective*. In the formation of a mob (*crowd* is a synonym), the plurality of voices, each expressing an opinion a little different from the rest, this normal state of human affairs, gives way to a single voice. The mob is all for one and one for all, whether the archetype be the Boston Tea Party of 1773, the storming of the Bastille in 1789, the lynchings once common in the US South, or the roving masses of youth that sometimes form after British soccer games or other sports events. Mobs strike terror because they signal the loss of the usual roominess of life. People no longer go their separate ways, one doing this, another that. They have set aside differences and are locked in tight embrace. This is also the key defining attribute of mobs in nature. Ethologists call it mobbing when ten crows quit their respective activities and congregate in a single screaming chorus for harassment of an owl. When dogs form a pack, they forget the differences that normally keep them scattered, variously occupied, and fighting with one another, and give themselves over to a common cause.

2. *Mobbing is situation-specific, an unusual event*. We do not apply the word *mob* to the commonality, the absence of individuality apparent in peasant communities, totalitarian states, or total institutions like armies and monasteries. In nature, an everyday anthill or flock of sheep is not called a mob. The latter term is reserved for exceptional occasions when individuals normally separate and diverse dissolve enthusiastically, as if mesmerized, into a single pulsating mass.

3.  *A mob is about eliminating a person or thing; it aims to destroy.*
    The Boston Tea Party was held to waste tea. The Parisians who
    stormed the Bastille aimed to tear down the monarchy (in the
    shorter term, they beheaded the Bastille's governor and paraded
    his head on a spike). The focus of a lynch mob is on torturing to
    death the person being lynched. Mobbing among birds is for the
    purpose of killing or driving away the targeted bird. In almost all
    uses of the term, mobbing has a destructive purpose. An
    exception is when fans are said to mob a rock star or sports hero;
    even in this usage, mobbing is not understood as an altogether
    friendly act, since it involves objectifying the hero, rushing and
    possibly harming him or her.
4.  *Mobbing involves passion.* It is not something you do just for
    pay. Participants have their hearts in it. They are sure of
    themselves. There is fury, loud or silent, in a mob.

These four defining attributes justify Leymann's, my, and others'
extension and application of the term to that pathological process in
workplaces whereby, in a specific circumstance, normal diversity of
thought and action gives way to an impassioned, single-minded,
collective push to humiliate and eliminate a targeted worker.

The concept of *workplace mobbing* also differs, of course, from
*mobbing* in its older, classic sense. Here are five differences:

1.  The classic mob has hundreds of participants, a workplace mob
    only a handful, or rarely (as in Richardson's case) some dozens.
2.  Classic mobbings involve literal bloodlust and violence, while
    workplace mobbing is usually bloodless and polite.
3.  Classic mobbings last a day, a few days or weeks, but workplace
    mobs often act slowly, over months or years.
4.  Lawlessness is undisguised in a classic mobbing, while mobbing
    in workplaces brims with pretense, subterfuge, and sophistry.
5.  As Shupe points out, the classic mob is usually less planful, less
    step-by-step in its thinking, than is a workplace mob.

It is also worth noting that the word *mobbing*, like *lynching*,
*swarming*, and *bullying*, but unlike *collective behavior* or *social
movement*, has an edge, a pejorative connotation, a suggestion of
something wrong. That is fine with me, as a pragmatist sociologist. A
lynching is not just collective behavior; it is a very rotten kind of it.
And workplace mobbing is not just a social movement.

## Chapter Eleven

# A Review of Literature on Tenure

# and Dismissal of Professors

**Barry W. Birnbaum**

In 1994, Professor Herbert Richardson was released from his tenured position at St. Michael's College, University of Toronto. Professor Richardson held an enviable reputation during his years at the institution. He was a highly esteemed scholar who held international status. He produced scholarly materials, published, and met all the requirements one would need to seek, be granted, and hold tenure. His dismissal, however, raises questions about the process of tenure and its future within the academic community.

In many situations, the process of being awarded tenure is lengthy and somewhat difficult. Different institutions establish different requirements. However, the award of tenure is supposed to be given for a lifetime and implies a certain sense of job security that one takes for granted. In the case of Dr. Richardson, he was denied due process and the rights granted with this award.

Chait (2002) defines tenure as a "permanent" or "continuous" contract for employment that is normally granted until the person resigns or retires and that only "just" cause can be used for dismissal. Tenure is definitively linked to academic freedom as well as economic security that makes the "profession attractive" to potential faculty members. In some instances, tenure is extended to mean a guarantee of salary and a promise of no demotion in rank. At Asbury College (as cited in Chait), tenure is a "voice in the formulation of the academic policies" of the institution. It is important to note that tenure provides a wide array of rights and privileges once it has been granted and that, in most cases, these rights are inalienable.

Wilke (1979) states that professors are ranked according to a pre-determined system. This system includes academic rank and tenure status. Wilke further states that tenure is a "procedural right" that gives an individual some type of standing within the academic institution as well as within the courts and while tenure does not provide an "absolute job guarantee", it protects the professor from capricious dismissal. While Wilke states that tenure does not give any specific guarantees, it does provide some power that can be used by its holders.

In most instances, tenure is granted to professors who meet certain criteria such as length of service, quality of student evaluations, holding of terminal degrees, recommendations by colleagues already on tenure, and approval by the administration of the institution (Wilke, 1979). In the case of Professor Richardson, he had met these requirements when he was granted tenure and therefore, should be entitled to all the rights, including those related to academic freedom. There was no indication at the time tenure was granted that Dr. Richardson had not fully met the criteria.

As mentioned earlier, many institutions implement new policies as to how an individual earns tenure and promotion. These new policies apply only to those individuals being employed at the time of their implementation. This would not impact Dr. Richardson because he had met the requirements for tenure years before. He demonstrated skills in publishing, teaching, and service to the university and cannot be judged by a different set of criteria. While some of these new standards are implemented in order to avoid granting tenure to professors, it is not practical or moral to change the criteria after the fact and expect someone who was already granted tenure to meet these revised requirements.

As universities have grown, so has their need for a centralized administration (Wilke, 1979). This system removes any meaningful contact between the faculty member and the administration and makes it more difficult for the institution to monitor the behavior of faculty members. This is usually left to the college or the department. There is no indication that Dr. Richardson had done anything that would have caused his dismissal. In most cases, individuals are dismissed because of institutional financial hardship that requires the termination of a program, or serious malfeasance at the professional level. These reasons for dismissal did not apply in this case.

What inevitably happens is that institutions that indiscriminately dismiss professors who are on tenure gain a reputation that keeps potential candidates from applying for work. The institution loses trust and respect within the community and it becomes more difficult for the university to find individuals who are willing to work for it. The same holds true for colleges that are censured by the American Association for University Professors (AAUP).

With a limited number of applicants for each position, universities need to be concerned about how they are perceived by potential candidates and those that have a reputation of denying tenure or terminating tenured faculty will have a more difficult time hiring and retaining qualified individuals. This operates as a disadvantage to those seeking positions (Wilke, 1979), and also does not bode well for the university. Since tenure is a goal and an award given for hard work in academic circles, those institutions that have a history of not granting tenure or revoking it will be less likely to hire highly qualified candidates.

Academic positions are one of a kind because of tenure, the product of teaching and research, and the quality of employment (Trower as cited in Chait, 2002). Kuh (1998) found that most institutions should be careful in their awards of tenure because of research issues. In some instances, tenure is used to take the place of higher salaries that individuals could earn outside of academe (Bowen and Schuster, 1986).

Finkin (1996) found that threats to academic freedom and lack of job security are two areas that concern potential hires. Universities that are known for violating academic freedom and that do not provide some sense of job security are less likely to hire competent people. Institutions of higher education must be responsive to their environment and that younger people are becoming concerned about working or staying at an institution that does not grant tenure. Many of these individuals see tenure as the only viable option to ensure that their career will not be interrupted (Baldwin and Chronister, 2001).

Academic freedom is an important aspect of tenure and one that was denied to Herbert Richardson. Chait (2002) states that academic freedom entitles teachers to "full freedom in research and publications" that are compared to "adequate performance of other academic duties." Chait adds that any limitations due to religious aspects of the institution should be given in writing before an individual begins working. Richardson was employed in a program of religious studies, but he was not provided anything in writing that described any limitations to academic freedom before he was hired.

Byrne (1997) states that academic freedom must be protected by having policies and rules in place. While private institutions may not provide the rights to academic freedom as regularly as public ones, the Supreme Court has consistently upheld that the First Amendment to the US Constitution protects academic freedom. Sometimes, the courts misjudge academic freedom and its intention. If the individual has been provided and promised this right, the pursuit of it must be handled in the courts when the need arises (Byrne). Additionally, the institution is expected to provide a fair internal-appeal mechanism when dismissal is based upon violations of academic freedom. The right to file a grievance should be awarded to each faculty member who feels his or her right to academic freedom has been violated.

Byrne (1997) states that the majority of individuals who serve on grievance committees should be professors so that the rights appertaining to academic freedom are not compromised. Professors should be judged by their peers and they should be expected to demonstrate that their rights or entitlement to academic freedom have not been violated. At this point, the burden of proof should move from the professor to the institution. Byrne further states that all members of the university community have a very strong concern in defending their rights to academic freedom.

De George (1997) defines academic freedom as freedom of research, freedom of teaching and freedom to engage in governance. De George defines freedom of research as the right of the faculty to pursue research for the purpose of disseminating it to peers. De George also states that research must be allowed to occur as long as the individual conducting it is knowledgeable and competent in the field of study. This area should be broad and no individual should be held to a "restricted specialization." New discoveries are made because scholars go beyond their narrow field of study and pursue new avenues. Richardson's research was extensive and he pursued other arenas, as well. Additionally, he created a publishing company that has been unfairly criticized and he established a university that was named after the publishing company.

De George (1997) states that research is a form of teaching but that more restraints are placed against faculty members in the area of teaching. De George also mentions that the freedom to teach includes "the freedom to learn" and that faculty accountability is more at stake here than in any other area. The quality of teaching is evaluated prior to the award of tenure and is normally judged by student evaluations. The accountability as to the quality of teaching is between the faculty member and the student. Richardson's dismissal had little to do with this important area and was not an issue during his tenured years at St. Michael's.

Faculty members must have a voice in all matters pertaining to the university (De George, 1997). This voice is a crucial part of any decision made by the institution and, as mentioned earlier, is important in the hiring, awarding of tenure, and termination of employment of professors within a particular academic institution. De George states that there are only minimal areas where faculty should not have a say and decisions that shape departments should be left to the faculty. Even in matters of financial exigency, faculty should have a say as to how the university or college will be restructured so that as many jobs as possible can be saved.

De George (1997) addresses several ethical issues related to academic freedom. Universities that have as their main goal the "advancement of knowledge" are most likely to have a broad definition of academic freedom. While this may be less true in private or religious institutions, it is still a widely accepted belief. The protection of civil rights of the individuals should be tantamount to anything else, however, in some cases; it receives less attention than should be required. Most of the threat, according to De George, to academic freedom comes from legislation, board of directors, and the public. Historically, witch hunts have taken place solely for the purpose of denying academic freedom to professors. De George directly mentions the McCarthy era as being one of the worst times for academics to express themselves. In the case of Richardson, a witch hunt scenario seemed to be the custom.

In many instances, power plays an important role in the denial of academic freedom (De George, 1997). It is a search for truth that allows differing opinions to prevail. When power gets in the way, however, the search for truth becomes very limited in scope. Some say this is nothing more than a ruse played out in the wide array of fields found within the university community. In some instances, the attacks from outside the university can be as brutal as those that come from within.

Today, political correctness is used to silence those with divergent opinions or thoughts. Doing so is an infringement of academic freedom and a violation of individual rights. In today's world, as in the Richardson case, many of these rights and freedoms are becoming confused and muddled. Academic freedom does apply to speaking about religion and practicing whatever beliefs one wants. The freedom of religion is sometimes determined in the courts and can also relate to issues of political correctness that violate the freedom of expression (De George, 1997).

The Richardson case was based upon issues surrounding religion. Professor Richardson was employed as a teacher in religious studies, however, he was asked to teach in an area that was not his expertise. His basic freedoms of speech and religion were brought to the forefront of the case and were violated outright. His dismissal was predicated upon charges that were in no way related to any cause that would warrant termination of tenured employment.

De George (1997) states that nontenured faculty are more at risk of losing academic freedom because they must please the administration and faculty who will vote upon granting them tenure at some later date. If tenured faculty become concerned about the amount of academic freedom they may have, then the issue is whether or not this freedom is truly even necessary. Once academic freedom is challenged, the status of the institution is exaggerated in a negative way.

Chait (2002) states that college and university professors are "members of a learned profession" and "officers of an educational institution." When these individuals exercise their rights to speak or write their freedom from censorship or discipline should be protected. This was not the case in Professor Richardson's dilemma while employed at St. Michael's College, University of Toronto. While outsiders may judge an institution by what its professors say, it sometimes becomes necessary to temper comments that are more appropriate for dissemination to the general population (Chait). Dr. Richardson in no way did anything that compromised the reputation of the institution where he was employed nor did he do anything that would be considered out of bounds in the arena of academic freedom. The AAUP (as cited in Chait) further states that academic freedom reaches beyond tenured faculty and should be granted to those hired on a probationary basis.

Chait (2002) found that 200 institutions from the Faculty Appointment Policy Archive (FAPA) had statements that related to academic freedom. Thirty-seven percent of these institutions set exceptional teaching as the most important aspect of gaining tenure while 3% placed research above teaching. Four percent require that teaching and one other category (research or service) be outstanding while 6% allow the individual departments to determine the criteria for granting tenure. Based upon these facts, Dr. Richardson had consistently demonstrated high marks in the area of teaching, research, and service and had not violated any policies that would have resulted in his dismissal.

Access to students is an important factor for determining whether or not a professor has achieved objective qualities (Tierney and Bensimon, 1996). The expectation is that professors will drop everything in order to meet with students. This usually shows in the teaching evaluations completed by the students at the end of the term. Those individuals who have a closed-door policy usually will have it noted in these course evaluations and will have to make significant changes in order to be eligible for continued employment. Much weight and emphasis is placed upon student evaluations at teaching institutions and these scores are used regularly to qualify for tenure and promotion. Nothing appeared to have changed from the time Dr. Richardson was granted tenure and the time he was dismissed. He met the stated criteria to earn the award of tenure as it relates to teaching and continued to receive positive comments from his students. Therefore, he did not exhibit any dereliction in this regard to his performance.

In the area of research, Professor Richardson exemplified what a tenured professor should. He published, established his own publishing company, and was well-respected by his colleagues. Tierney and Bensimon (1996) state that research should serve the profession in a professional manner and that is what Dr. Richardson did. He published in areas that were relevant to his field. He appeared to enjoy his research and accumulated sufficient writings in books as well as publications.

While service is the least important activity in many institutions (Tierney and Bensimon, 1996), it is still usually a requirement for tenure. The expectation is that individuals will serve on different committees at various levels, including department, college, and university. Larger research universities normally require less service than do larger ones.

The expectation is that faculty work hard in one or all of the areas required for tenure and the assumption is that the faculty member will continue to do so after the fact. Herbert Richardson demonstrated a high level of commitment in his field in all areas after he received tenure and it appears he continued to do so at the time of his dismissal. Therefore, it seems as though his dismissal was inappropriate and morally wrong.

In many institutions, junior faculty find themselves working "all the time" (Tierney and Bensimon, 1996). Large amounts of time are spent developing lesson plans, writing grant proposals, conducting research, or writing up results of studies for potential publication. In some instances, teaching becomes less important to research, but the expectation is that one will accomplish the goals set forth in order to earn tenure. The hope is that all the work an individual accomplishes will lead to tenure and promotion. Some senior faculty may not be as energized as their junior counterparts to work toward excellence; however, this was not the case with Dr. Richardson. It appears that he kept a strong teaching and research agenda during his years at his university. There doesn't appear to be any reason to doubt otherwise.

There are other ethical questions that need to be raised concerning the granting of tenure and the termination of tenured faculty (De George, 1997). The strength of the department is important when determining the status of its faculty. Each department must hire the most competent people and try to keep them. Weak departments consist of faculty members who are also weak. Departments are responsible for sharing with new faculty members their obligations and duties. The lack of collegiality within departments can cause problems at a higher level. This lack can harm the institution.

In the case of Professor Richardson, the higher levels of the administration seemed to dismiss his relationship as invaluable with his colleagues and his students. What was considered best for the university was not necessarily best for the department or the college. It can be argued that Richardson's performance was not measured fairly across a multitude of domains and that the decisions that were made were done so in order to please the higher levels of administration. This becomes an ethical dilemma that places a burden upon the institution to prove its motives were truly in its best interests.

Dismissal and due process are synonymous terms (Finkin, 1996). In one case cited by Finkin, extensive tracking of a professor's performance was recorded and due process, including a hearing before the faculty senate was conducted. The committee was composed of faculty who met to hear complaints under the tenure code of the university. The professor was allowed substantial documentary discovery and a pre-hearing conference was held. Although the committee did recommend termination, the university board provided the faculty member with a one-year extension of a probationary year. This was done to ensure that due process was provided, thereby avoiding a retracted legal battle.

Finkin (1996) states that due process must be provided, especially when something as serious as dismissal is being considered. Adequate notice of the charges must be provided as must the opportunity for the accused to meet with his or her complainants. Additionally, the professor who has been accused of malfeasance must be given the chance to present evidence, cross-examine witnesses, and have the right to a fair and impartial hearing. Finkin finds that these processes are intended to protect individual freedoms. This protection extends beyond just the university but also affects the larger community. It is important for the entire community that due process be provided so that citizens feel their freedoms have not been threatened.

The chair of the department must be involved in this process since any dismissal will impact the entire branch. Faculties are expected to participate in matters that affect the unit and the chair is responsible for seeing that this is accomplished. Richardson did work closely with his division and didn't become derelict in his responsibilities. If problems are not resolved at the department level, then the next step is to involve the program dean (Finkin, 1996).

In its report on faculty tenure, the Commission on Academic Tenure in Higher Education (1973) finds that tenure guarantees a faculty member the right to hold an academic appointment until the age of retirement as long as competence has been established. Only in cases of extreme malfeasance where due process has been provided can an individual be dismissed from a position. It becomes a point of interest as to whether Herbert Richardson's accusers read the report and understood its content. It appears that they did not.

The politics of tenure certainly were apparent in the Richardson case. Tenured faculty, according to Williams (1999), are expected to be allowed to be uninhibited in assessing theories, "widely held beliefs", as well as criticizing the administration at which he or she is employed. The university is supposed to be a safe place that is usually exempt from everyday constraints (Haskell, 1996).

Williams (1999) further states that tenure describes academics as professionals who contribute to one's field. There is no doubt that Richardson had done this not occasionally, but rather consistently. The level of contribution to one's field is a prime determiner of whether or not someone receives and is able to hold tenure until retirement. The charges against Professor Richardson did not indicate that he did otherwise.

Tenure reviews are often used as mechanisms to dismiss faculty. Misconduct accusations are usually the most common way that this occurs (Euben, 2003). Post-tenure review is full of false accusations about the performance of individuals and is used widely by universities to develop just cause for dismissal. Many of these charges begin as rumors rather than fact and are allowed to spread like wildfire without any intervention. There is no question that these rumors are created for the sole purpose of trying to get a tenured faculty member to resign or be brought up on charges of dismissal.

Appropriate assessment during misconduct charges, as in the granting of tenure, must be provided to each faculty member as well as written documentation of the charges (Euben, 2003). In the event the charges cannot be proven, the individual is entitled to face these charges in a documented form. Euben states that an appropriate "careful assessment" must be given so that the individual has time to read and respond to charges against him or her. It is also essential, according to Euben, that the individual who is charged be given any and all opportunities to be represented before any committees that will hold hearings concerning the allegations.

Any post-tenure review should be formative and summative (Licata & Morreale, 1997). The summative component should include accurate and detailed information about performance that can be used to make decisions concerning personnel. The summative review should reflect strengths and weaknesses of the individual and should be used as a tool for improving performance. How accurate any post-tenure review of Professor Richardson was remains in question.

The formative component should be developmental and, where needed, should include a professional development plan (Licata & Morreale, 1997). This phase should emphasize plans for the future while providing support to the faculty member. It is unclear as to whether Richardson received this type of plan or if any "concerns" were readily addressed.

Not only should post-tenure review be evaluative, it should also be driven by policy (Licata & Morreale, 1997). The policy should include nine principles as listed by Licata & Morreale. These areas are (a) academic freedom, (b) academic tradition, (c) articulation of purpose and consequences, (d) accurate, defensible, and useful information, (e) decentralized control, (f) peer review, (g) feedback, (h) flexibility and (i) institutional support. While peer committees are usually responsible for post-tenure review, the manner in which this is conducted varies widely. A committee looks at both the formative and summative aspects of performance and provides feedback for the faculty member. The committee is made up of a divergent constituency from the university that represents its different facets. In other instances, the department chair solely makes decisions about post-tenure performance issues.

Licata and Morreale (1997) state that the most important part of the post-tenure review practice is outcome-based. These outcomes are "expected and unanticipated." The purpose of these reviews, once again, is to continually improve performance while enhancing career growth. If a faculty member's performance is less than acceptable, most times a practical remediation plan is developed. All these reviews should be based upon realistic objectives and outcomes and specific remedial techniques should be included. This normally starts either with the review committee or the department chair. Others can, as needed, engage in creative thinking that helps the individual remediate any weaknesses or deficiencies.

The action that is taken if the individual does not improve performance is a question that has been debated for years. In most cases, the institution will not seek dismissal because of the cost involved, both in terms of finances, and its reputation within the academic community. Sometimes, buy-outs or early retirement are options given to the individual (Licata & Morreale, 1997). With the current trend toward accountability, many more universities are looking at the dismissal route; however, few feel they have enough substantive data to warrant such an approach.

In many cases, the post-tenure review is part of the negotiated settlement between the university and several faculty organizations (Licata & Morreale, 1997). The dean and chair normally evaluate the overall input of the faculty member while evaluating research and scholarly activity. In most cases, the faculty member is evaluated on departmental criteria and is judged on long-range plans that contribute to both the university and the unit. In most instances, the faculty member retains the right of appeal should she or he disagree with the post tenure evaluation. Usually, the purpose of the review is either formative or summative, but it tends to be the former.

The AAUP maintains a censure list of universities they claim mistreat or deny tenure to faculty members (Knight, 2003). In some instances, institutions remain on this list for years and some administrators claim that being on this list doesn't bother them. This has been a practice that has gone on since the 1930s and began as a "nonrecommended list" that followed an extensive evaluation of the facts. In many cases, the issues related to academic freedom and tenure.

Tenure is a usually misunderstood concept that usually falls prey to individual interpretations (Olswang, 2003). While some administrators consider tenure to be an obstacle to some level of flexibility, the only other profession that awards tenure is within the court system. Tenure does not allow faculty to become offensive to others and does provide certain rights and limitations. The AAUP assures that all individuals are given their due process rights before placing a university on their censure list. This remains the one mechanism that professional organizations have to enforce the rights of individuals who may have been denied academic freedom, lost their jobs while on tenure, and have been persecuted for their beliefs.

This review of the literature intends to provide the reader with an overview of how tenure and academic freedom are perceived. Comparing these findings to the case of Professor Herbert Richardson indicate he was not provided full due process in his dismissal from the College of St. Michael's at the University of Toronto. The dismissal was a ruse in order to deny a scholar the right to continue teaching that was based upon erroneous information.

The reader is left to conclude what he or she may, however this particular case is worthy of further investigation. A man's reputation and livelihood were compromised in order to establish a power play between the faculty member and an institution. The reputation of the university should be negatively impacted and tarnished based upon what it did to a proven and reputable scholar.

## References

Baldwin, R.G. & Chronister, J.L., 2001. *Teaching without Tenure*. Baltimore, MD: The Johns Hopkins University Press.

Bowen, H.R. & Schuster, J.H., 1986. *American Professors: a National Resource Imperiled*. New York: Oxford University Press.

Breneman, D.W., 1997. *Alternatives to Tenure for the Next Generation of Academics*. New Pathways Working Paper Series, Inquiry no. 14, Washington, D.C.: American Association for Higher Education.

Byrne, J.P., 1997. *Academic Freedom without Tenure*. (American Association for Higher Education Inquiry # 5). Washington, D.C.: American Association for Higher Education.

Chait, R.P., 2002. *The Questions of Tenure*. Cambridge, MA: Harvard University Press.

Commission on Academic Tenure in Higher Education, 1973. *Faculty Tenure*. A Report and Recommendations by the Commission on Academic Tenure in Higher Education, San Francisco, CA: Jossey-Bass.

De George, R.T., 1997. *Academic Freedom and Tenure: Ethical Issues*. New York: Rowman & Littlefield Publishers, Inc.

Euben, D.R., 2003. "Misconduct accusations in tenure reviews," *Academe* 89 (1), p. 78.

Finkin, M.W. (Ed.)., 1996. *The Case for Tenure*. Ithaca, NY: Cornell University Press.

Haskell, T.L., 1996. "Justifying the rights of academic freedom in the era of power/knowledge," in *The future of Academic Freedom*. Chicago, IL: Chicago University Press.

Knight, J., 2003. "The AAUP's censure list," *Academe,* 89 (1), pp. 44-59.

Kuh, C., 1998. Off-tenure track employment and the labor market. Paper presented to the Workshop on Higher Education, National Bureau of Economic Research, National Research Council.

Licata, C.M. & Morreale, J.C., 1997. *Post-tenure Review: Policies, Practices, Precautions*. (American Association for Higher Education Inquiry # 12). Washington, D.C.: American Association for Higher Education.

Olswang, S., 2003. *The Future of Tenure*. Change. 35(3). 36-38.

Tierney, W.G., & Bensimon, E.M., 1996. *Promotion and Tenure: Community and Socialization in Academe*. New York: State University of New York Press.

Whicker, M.L., Kronefeld, J.J., & Strickland, R.A., 1993. *Getting Tenure*. Newbury Park: Sage Publications.

Wilke, A.S., 1979. *The Hidden Professoriate: Credentialism, Professionalism, and the Tenure Crisis*. Westport, CT: Greenwood Press.

Williams, J., 1999. "The other politics of tenure," *College Literature,* 26 (3), pp. 1-12.

# Response

My response to Birnbaum's methodical application of basic principles of academic governance to the Toronto mobbing case is brief, lest I repeat points made in Chapters One (my overview of the Medaille Project) and Three (the second paper on the Medaille conflict) about academic freedom and AAUP's emphasis on it. Birnbaum's essay reads much as a report by AAUP (or its Canadian counterpart, CAUT) would probably have read, if one of these organizations had intervened in the Richardson case. Birnbaum's understanding of academic freedom, its relation to tenure and the basic purposes of a university, is consistent with AAUP's 1940 "Statement of Principles on Academic Freedom and Tenure," and later revisions thereof.

Point by point, Birnbaum applies this dominant thinking to the Toronto case. He says Richardson's dismissal "was predicated upon charges that were in no way related to any cause that would warrant termination of tenured employment," that Richardson "did not exhibit any dereliction" in his devotion to students, that he "accumulated sufficient writings in books as well as publications," that "he kept a strong teaching and research agenda," and finally, that the "dismissal was a ruse in order to deny a scholar the right to continue teaching that was based upon erroneous information." I essentially agree with these points, also with Birnbaum's emphasis on due process and appellate rights in any post-tenure review or dismissal proceeding.

Having spent untold hours of my life in meetings of tenure and promotion committees, I can vouch that a good part of the time, decision-making in such committees proceeds by the principles Birnbaum reviews. The presiding administrator, other professors, and sometimes a student or two, review evidence about the candidate's research, publications, teaching performance, and committee service, voice reasoned judgments about whether the evidence puts the candidate above or below expectations, and then vote.

Such decision-making processes are rarely free of irrational elements. Committee members sometimes show prejudice for or against candidates of a particular sex, sexual orientation, race, age, ethnicity, political slant or theoretical orientation, to the neglect of personal achievements and abilities. Still more often, unreason of a ritualistic kind creeps in. Is an average score of 2.4 on the course evaluation instrument high enough, or should 2.5 be the minimum?

How can this candidate be promoted with seven articles in refereed journals and one monograph, when last year a candidate was turned down who had eight journal articles and one co-authored textbook? Are three letters from external referees enough? Nonetheless, there is usually a lot of rationality in academic personnel decisions, and appellate committees often catch and overturn wrong decisions.

In an academic mobbing, however, a coterie of administrators and/or colleagues feels such antipathy for the targeted professor as to preclude normal decision-making. Established procedures may be jettisoned altogether in favor of *ad hoc* action – secret meetings and urgent petitions for the target's immediate humiliation. More often, established procedures are followed but in twisted, topsy-turvy ways. Words acquire new meanings (like *turpitude* in the Medaille cases). Inevitable ambiguities in policy manuals and collective agreements are seized upon to demonstrate how some action or inaction by the target warrants severe sanction, even dismissal. Committees meet, tribunals hold hearings, witnesses testify, evidence comes under scrutiny, and decisions are handed down. It may seem routine at first glance, but it is not. Collective hostility toward the target has turned standard, reasonable procedures into a burlesque, due process into a charade. The hypocrisy by itself can drive a person mad.

The mobbing research adds to our understanding of life in universities and other workplaces by suggesting *why* and *how*, in certain cases under identifiable conditions, normal decision-making breaks down. This research goes beyond pointing out violations of academic freedom, robberies of tenure, and distortions of due process; it *explains* these aberrations.

In his famous novel, Chinua Achebe drew classic lines from the Irish poet, W. B. Yeats, to capture the turning upside down of Ibo society by European colonizers. Those same lines from Yeats, penned in 1920 in the wake of the Great War, capture how workplace mobbing turns normal decision-making upside down, even while authorities assure all concerned that everything is on the up and up:

> Things fall apart; the centre cannot hold;
> Mere anarchy is loosed upon the world,
> The blood-dimmed tide is loosed, and everywhere
> The ceremony of innocence is drowned;
> The best lack all conviction, while the worst
> Are full of passionate intensity.

## Chapter Twelve

# Dreams and Reflections

# on a Sad Chapter

# in Canadian Academic History

## James Gollnick

When I received an invitation to write commentary on Ken Westhues's study of Professor Herbert W. Richardson's dismissal from St. Michael's College at the University of Toronto, I had mixed feelings. On the one hand, I felt that I had nothing to add to Westhues's detailed analysis of the historical, cultural and political aspects of this most celebrated academic dismissal case in Canadian history. After all, I have never researched such cases, and I was no longer teaching at the University of Toronto when this case came to trial. I remember reading some newspaper accounts of the trial, but I really had no knowledge of what was going on behind the scenes of what from all accounts seemed to be an extraordinarily painful process.

On the other hand, reading Westhues's book precipitated a flood of memories and dream images of my time at the University of Toronto, where I studied and worked for almost a quarter of a century before moving on to the University of Waterloo, where I am a professor in the Department of Religious Studies. As I read

Westhues's chapters on the biographical and cultural context of the case, I realized how much Professor Richardson's history was part of my own. Reading these chapters stirred vivid memories of the excitement and high expectations that accompanied Richardson's arrival at St. Michael's College in the Fall of 1968. The striking contrast between this promising beginning and the sad conclusion, his dismissal in 1994, was startling, and made me want to piece together in my own mind what brought about this dramatic turn of fortune. It occurred to me that the one thing I might be able to contribute is my personal impression of certain aspects of this unhappy story. I want to share my vantage point because such memories and impressions may help to keep in mind the personal story behind the public proceedings.

### Dream Images: Flashback to 1968

As a dream analyst and psychotherapist, I spend a lot of time reviewing and examining the past. Dreams constantly bring up images of the recent and distant past to reveal how we feel at a deep level about what is going on in our lives. Dreams help to monitor our emotional life and often provide a sense of where things are going. The memories stirred by reading Westhues's book invaded my dreams. The images that came to me in the night took me back to an exciting but tumultuous period in my life. Some of these dream images recalled the circumstances of my coming to the University of Toronto and the major events of that time — images of angry protest, a disastrous war, and the promise of a more humane society in Canada. In late August of 1968, I packed my bags in Wisconsin and headed north for St. Michael's College at the University of Toronto, where I had received a four-year scholarship for graduate studies. In the United States, the Vietnam war was tearing the country apart, but in Canada hope was on the rise as Pierre Trudeau cast his spell and generated enthusiasm and optimism almost everywhere he went.

Other dream images took me back to my first years in Toronto. St. Michael's College at that time was one of the most fertile locations in North America for studying religious thought. J. Edgar Bruns, a meticulous scholar and able administrator, was the Director of the Institute of Christian Thought, a graduate division of St. Michael's College. Gregory Baum had been teaching there since 1959 and was already famous for his insightful writings on the Second Vatican

Council and the ecumenical movement it inspired. Leslie Dewart stirred international controversy with his daring *Future of Belief*. Arthur Gibson was exploring the faith of atheists and scientists, and Walter Principe, attached to both St. Michael's College and the Pontifical Institute of Medieval Studies, was well known as a scholar of medieval Christian thought. These were just some of the bright intellectual lights of St. Michael's College at that time. John Kelly, longtime president of St. Michael's College, fully supported and defended the avant-garde group of thinkers who were assembled there.

In 1968, Herbert Richardson joined the faculty of St. Michael's College. He arrived with outstanding credentials from Harvard University, a man who at the age of thirty-seven was already considered a leading thinker among the next generation of Protestant theologians. As a student just starting graduate studies, I was almost overwhelmed with the academic riches available at St. Michael's College and the University of Toronto. In my first two years of graduate study I took as many courses as possible from the outstanding array of creative thinkers there — all of the people mentioned above, as well as Marshall McLuhan and Northrop Frye. I also took Richardson's graduate seminar on Christology, a very traditional subject which he taught in a lively and thought-provoking manner.

I was amazed at Richardson's command of history, his ability to see connections between diverse thinkers from widely different periods of Western civilization, and his capacity to analyze the inner coherence of various systems of thought. I quickly learned that he was an expert, but no narrow specialist. His reading and understanding ranged over many disciplines, including history, philosophy, theology, psychology, sociology, and anthropology. Word of this remarkable intellect and teacher spread quickly and soon his seminars and undergraduate courses were filled to overflowing. Hundreds of students packed Carr Hall at St. Michael's College to hear his analysis of both historical and contemporary problems. He developed a reputation as an exciting thinker and a spell-binding teacher. It seemed the sky was the limit for Richardson at St. Michael's College and the University of Toronto.

## Storm Clouds Gather

But even in this auspicious beginning the seeds of later discontent can be found. For one thing, Richardson was more interested in raising questions and discerning patterns of thought than he was in giving traditional answers, even though he was well-versed in the great thinkers of Western civilization. His attitude seemed to be consonant with the spirit of the late 1960s, with its search for new paths and its critique of established ways of thinking. His approach to theoretical and practical issues made some faculty members and students uneasy. Although he won the University of Toronto distinguished teaching award, some people were put off with his style and sense of humor. What was exciting and creative for some, was threatening and offensive for others.

Among some faculty members, there seemed to be a growing resentment as large numbers of students were drawn to his undergraduate classes. Some of the less popular teachers seemed to feel that he must be a popularizer rather than a serious scholar because he appealed to so many students. At the graduate level too, a disproportionate number of students wanted Richardson to direct their thesis projects because of his growing reputation as a scholar, writer and editor. Over the years, he directed more than sixty theses, and most of these have been published. That is an astonishing record, but a record that irritated some who felt they were being overlooked in the wake of Richardson's charisma. But even with the resentment and antagonism increasingly expressed toward Richardson as a result of these circumstances in the 1970s, there was no way to anticipate how acrimonious and vengeful attitudes were to become by the late 1980s.

## Fast Forward

By the mid 1970s I had completed my M.A. and Ph.D. In order to develop further my understanding of clinical approaches in the psychology of religion I began the training program for therapists at the Gestalt Institute of Toronto, which I completed some years later. In the following decade I entered the training program for Jungian analysts in Zurich and continued that process in the form of a three-year analysis with Fraser Boa, Canada's first Jungian analyst. During that time I lost touch with the politics surrounding St. Michael's

College. By the 1980s the atmosphere at St. Michael's College seemed to have changed considerably from the exciting and open ecumenical spirit of the 1960s that inspired my early dreams.

J. Edgar Bruns and John Kelly, who had been broad-minded and strong leaders at St. Michael's College in the late 1960s and early 1970s, were now gone. Both had greatly appreciated Richardson's unique contribution to St. Michael's College and defended his creative Protestant perspective. But the times were changing. Defenders and admirers of Richardson had moved on or died. As Westhues put it, Richardson "no longer fit the college's definition of its purpose" (p. 86). This statement perhaps reaches to the heart of the change that reshaped St. Michael's College and Richardson's relation to it. Westhues has described these changes in great detail and there is very little I can add to his thorough account.

Westhues also recounts the charges brought against Richardson regarding student complaints and questions about his involvement with the Edwin Mellen Press. These are complicated matters that I do not claim to fully understand. I know that Richardson was not always very careful or diplomatic in dealing with students and that he did at times offend some of them. On the other hand, I am aware of how many young North American scholars he helped to get started through his personal generosity, astute editorial advice, and publishing know-how. I know that Richardson would not back down from a fight for principles he believed in. His unbending attitude may have precluded a happier and less public resolution of the impasse with St. Michael's College and the University of Toronto. I may be wrong about this, but I suspect it was ultimately the changing circumstances at the college, combined with a number of personal animosities, that provided the incredible energy, motivation, and expense to carry through this lengthy and unfortunate dismissal process. It is to Westhues's credit that his illuminating analysis of this case allows the moving story of a brilliant but embattled scholar to emerge from behind the cold proceedings of the public record. It is that personal story of a remarkable man in difficult times that remains alive in my dreams.

# Response

Mobbing is universal in the sense that it happens in all societies in all historical periods. One could not cite a single year in American or Canadian academic history in which some professors were not ganged up on and run out of their jobs.

Yet the incidence of mobbing is clearly greater in some places and times than others. Witch trials, *autos da fé*, and lynchings have all occurred more often in certain settings and eras than in others. Certain social conditions seem to unleash human instincts to form a pack and find some prey to humiliate and destroy.

Gollnick's reflections, at once factual and personal, on how things changed at St. Michael's from the late sixties, when he was among Richardson's admirers there in an exciting, avant-garde intellectual climate, to the mid-nineties, when Richardson was brought down, raise the question of whether conditions in universities over the past half century have become more conducive to mobbing and related craziness. Gollnick's is not the only essay in this volume to raise such a question. Van Patten lamented the disappearance of what he called the "boundless joy" of collegiality. One doubts that Weeber would have characterized universities so harshly in the 1970s as he does today. Is academic life generally on a downhill slide, away from a lively, constructive, collaborative search for truth, toward destructive, internecine conflicts?

Any answer to so broad a question is necessarily tentative. It bears mention that Richardson himself, in his writings and teachings in the 1960s, detected a demonic tendency in the intellectual trends being spawned at that time, trends that have strengthened ever since. The rise of metacritical, relativistic scholarship, he argued, the assessment of ideas in relation to power instead of by some independent, external yardstick, would result in steadily more intense and irreconcilable ideological conflict. The antidote Richardson proposed was ardent, mature Christian faith, the kind he sketched in his own theology. I devoted Chapter Five of *Administrative Mobbing* to this cultural context of Richardson's careeer. Here it is enough to note his own gloomy prognosis, forty years before his dismissal: that the rise of relativism and the demise of religion would put people more and more at each other's throats.

Another commentator on my *Administrative Mobbing* book, the Japanese-Canadian sociologist Mitsuru Shimpo, has offered a similarly gloomy prognosis, but from a different angle. Shimpo has spent decades studying aboriginal cultures in Canada and Australia, fairly isolated peoples functioning close to a subsistence level. In them he has found a degree of decency, tolerance, mutual respect, and reciprocity that is rare in the advanced industrial mainstream. Shimpo therefore finds my proposal of reciprocity as the remedy for mobbing in our own society unrealistic. Let me quote with thanks his own words:

> I found Westhues's conclusion very interesting – namely, that the development of reciprocal relations will be the solution for mobbing. In this regard, I have two questions. (1) How can one develop reciprocal relations in a workplace with problems? (2) Are "reciprocal relations" as universal as "mobbings" are?
>
> In my opinion, the second point needs further theoretical refinement. Richardson's dismissal took place in North American society, which has abundant social and economic resources. Westhues pointed out that this quarrel consumed almost half a million dollars. What would have happened in a less affluent society?
>
> One of my areas of study has been Japanese society. Japan is now considered to be a rich country, but when modernization began in 1868, it was estimated that Japan was as poor as Burma. In Japanese peasant society, there were approximately ten sets of social relations which required cooperation among community members: initiations, weddings, funerals, births, construction of a house, travelling, fire-fighting, flood conditions, and disease. When a community member was branded as a social deviant, eight sets of social relations were discontinued against both the individual and the family to which he belonged. The exceptions were funerals and fire-fighting. Funerals represented a loss to the labor force in the community and fires could destroy the whole community. In other words, social sanctions were not applied to the limit.
>
> How about a society with only a minimal amount of resources for survival? Take the case of Australian

Aborigines whom I studied during my sabbatical year. In their society, there are no equivalent words for "thank you." Words are not considered sufficient to repay for what you have received. You must repay your social and economic obligations with your own deeds and material things. This is an extreme case of "reciprocal relations."

From the above, I would say the amount of resources in a given society will affect the degree of reciprocity. If resources are minimal, then reciprocal relations are full. If the resources are abundant, then reciprocal relations are hard to realize. Many cases will be at some point on the continuum. Richardson's case is certainly at one extreme.

If I understand Shimpo's hypothesis correctly, it means that affluence, conditions of material abundance, may unleash eliminative impulses and remove checks on the destruction of designated enemies more than do conditions of material scarcity. Poor societies place high value on cooperation because all available hands are needed – not just for fighting fires but for producing food, caring for children, and doing all the other things necessary for the society to endure. Hence norms arise that, so far as possible, build people in. A rich society, by contrast, can afford to eliminate some members from time to time, even totally, because they can easily be done without. Social extermination thus becomes more common.

To confirm my understanding of Shimpo's scary point, I sent him the preceding paragraph for his comments. He responded by citing a film he had just seen, Ingmar Bergman's "Saraband," which depicts relations between an educated and wealthy retired music professor, the successful lawyer who is his former wife, and his son from a previous marriage, also a retired professor. The harshness of the professors toward each other and toward life itself sends shivers down the spine. There is scant milk of human kindness in these men. The father's living ex-wife, powerfully portrayed by Liv Ullmann, the son's deceased wife, and the son's still-innocent teenaged daughter, are the foil against which the pathetic self-absorption of the two twisted old professors leaps out in horror. Shimpo comments:

> My wife and I agreed that the film is Bergman's warning to the Swedes that unless they cultivate a cooperative spirit, their future will be one of cold, icy human relations.

Each professor lives alone in his own house. The social

welfare programs in Sweden are so well developed that an individual can survive without help and cooperation from others. If an individual can survive without others' help, he tends to be independent, a loner, rejecting interference from outside. As a result, whichever way he turns, he faces only hostile, uncooperative people.

In a subsistent economy, no individual can survive without belonging to a group: a family, some kind of cooperative community. In such a society, human relations almost have to be warm and reciprocal.

Shimpo's broad hypothesis gains plausibility from applying it on a smaller scale. I have observed in my research that professors are less likely to be mobbed in fields where there is a seller's market. "We need this guy's expertise," administrators and colleagues seem to say, "and we are not likely to be able to replace him; therefore we have to put up with him." In those sectors of the academic labor market where there is a buyer's market, by contrast, the reasoning is opposite: "Scholars with his expertise are a dime a dozen, so let's dump him and find somebody easier for us to get along with." Richardson's situation at St. Michael's was thus doubly inauspicious: not only were Protestant theologians in oversupply, but the Catholic college did not value their expertise.

I followed a mobbing case in a Canadian city some years ago, wherein a firestorm of moral outrage arose against a well-known physician whom police caught trying to procure the services of a prostitute. He was humiliated in the media, and there were demands for his ouster from the medical profession. Then the news came out that he was one of the city's few specialists in cardiac surgery, and that if he were decertified, many heart patients would be deprived of needed operations. Almost as quickly as it had flared, the uproar died down. The doctor's sin was glossed over, apparently forgiven. So far as I know, his work in the operating room continues as before.

The broader reference of Shimpo's hypothesis is troubling: that the farther above subsistence needs our society rises, the more dispensable people become – and the more vulnerable to being "taken out" by angry crowds. Our universities may be on the leading edge of the trend, at least in the humanities and social sciences. For here is a whole organization secure in its basic subsistence needs and radically removed from mundane concerns like the production of food, clothes, and shelter. What purpose it serves for the larger society, however, has become steadily more doubtful and ambiguous, the old canons of literature, philosophy, theology and history having broken down. Academics on the arts side of campus may be like the generously endowed "boatload of knowledge" Robert Owen steered down the Ohio River in 1826, hoping this assemblage of high-minded utopians would create a perfect society in New Harmony, Indiana, on the American frontier. The experiment lasted scarcely two years before crumbling under the weight of internal strife.

Shimpo and I are regularly exposed to the incredible abundance of our society, and the worry about what it will lead to, through our involvement in the Working Centre, a community organization in Kitchener, Ontario, aimed at building community especially among poor and marginalized citizens, and providing them along the way with access to food, clothing, shelter, and the tools by which to regain control of their lives. The centre reminds me again and again that very many people in our rich society feel utterly alone, unneeded, unwanted, dispensable, worthless. These people do not lack intelligence, talent, skills, or heartfelt desire to contribute to Canada in a positive way. They respond eagerly to programs at the centre that allow them to develop and exercise their skills cooperatively for the common good. Mainly, what they lack is a credential and specialized skill that would enable them to occupy some niche of employment in our complex economy.

Something else strikes me even more at the Working Centre, and at the soup kitchen and used-goods store it operates: that poor and marginalized people no longer depend on the actual charity of others to keep body and soul together. Only a fraction of the food served in the soup kitchen and of the second-hand clothing and furniture made available at low cost is donated by people who "miss" what they have given away. In the main, the donors have not sacrificed anything in order to provide marginalized people with the necessities of life. These necessities are no longer scarce. On the contrary, the bulk of the food, clothes, and furniture the Working Centre provides to poor people is *waste*: groceries, for instance, that are slightly past their best-before dates and would be trucked to the landfill if not distributed for free, clothes that would be bundled and sold for almost nothing to rag merchants if they were not recycled onto poor people's backs, and functional household appliances that have been replaced by newer models in affluent homes and that would be hauled away in garbage trucks if they were not stocked in the Working Centre's store called "Worth a Second Look."

Others learn in different ways what the Working Centre teaches Shimpo and me: that the extent of material abundance in today's Western World, our emancipation from the need to cooperate day by day and face to face in the production of necessities of life, is without precedent in history. That this heady condition might result in a gradual weakening of norms of reciprocity and the ethic of live and let live is a scary prospect, maybe also a likely one.

I share the pessimistic outlook suggested in different ways by Richardson and Shimpo, and in still other terms by Martin Buber, Pitirim Sorokin, Werner Stark, Christopher Lasch, and other theorists. Yet like them, I do not let my mind dwell on gloom too much. The important distinction (Lasch spells it out nicely in *The True and Only Heaven*, Norton, 1991) is between optimism and hope. The former is just a forecast. The latter is a deep-seated trust in life, the kind Gollnick, Richardson, Shimpo, and many more express in Christian faith. One can be pessimistic, obliged by evidence to predict nastier forms of social relation in the future, but still hopeful that by determined, joyful, reasoned, cooperative effort, we can reduce the incidence of mobbing and other kinds of harm for future generations. The concluding chapter of this book is founded on such hope.

# Conclusion:

# The Waterloo Strategy for

# Prevention of Mobbing in

# Universities[1]

In this final chapter, my aim is not to summarize the earlier ones or my own and others' previous work, nor to document the pathology further, but to draw lessons from the Medaille and Mellen Projects, and the other cases of academic mobbing I have studied. The lessons offered here are not so much for personal defense. Suggestions of this kind are found mainly in other volumes of this series, especially Part Six of *Workplace Mobbing in Academe* (2004) and the chapter by Ross A. Klein in *Winning, Losing, Moving On* (2005). The focus here, by contrast, is on practical implications mainly at the organizational level: ten specific administrative measures for prevention of this bizarre social process, and beyond that, for making academic workplaces more truthful, productive, and decent.

---

[1] This chapter is a slightly revised and adapted version of a paper I presented in the session on "Institutional Power and Equity (or Fairness): Taming Academic Imperialism," sponsored jointly by the Canadian Societies for the Study of Education, Higher Education, and Educational Administration, at the Congress of the Canadian Federation of Humanities and Social Sciences, University of Western Ontario, London, 2005. Thanks to Nancy Fenton (Brock), Joan Friedenberg (Southern Illinois), and Jan Gregersen (Akershus), for their comments on the earlier paper.

I assume here that the preceding chapters have conveyed, from varied points of view and through diverse examples, an understanding of what workplace mobbing is and how it happens. Readers still in doubt or seeking further evidence can consult the other books in this series and the wider research literature. References given at the end of the introductory chapter are useful starting points.

I assume here also, and trust readers will agree, that workplace mobbing is not inevitable, that its occurrence can be reduced through reasoned human intervention. Lynchings, duels, and blood feuds were at one time counted regrettable but common and ineradicable realities of life, part of human nature. By now in North America, they rarely happen. Yet mobbing is today widely accepted as part of normal academic politics, as if nothing can be done about it except try to escape being targeted oneself. This concluding chapter, even more than the preceding ones, is founded on a rejection of this view, a confidence that by reasoned study of workplace mobbing, we can devise ways of lowering its incidence, as was earlier achieved for certain other kinds of harm.

Yet a third assumption bears mention: that the way to prevent mobbing is to change the structure of the workplace, the conduct of governance and administration. This is not to deny the importance of good will and good faith; it is to steer attention away from motives and mental states to actual practice. The proposals made here are pragmatic in William James's sense: focussed on behavioural, organizational measures that promise to achieve the desired outcome even when people's motives are mixed and their intentions are not altogether pure. This paper is not a call to repent of wickedness, but a plan for holding in check the wickedness that lurks in all of us.

To anyone willing to grant these three assumptions – that mobbing in universities is a real pathology, that it is not inevitable, and that identifiable administrative techniques can make it less prevalent – the concluding important question is, "Which techniques?"

## The Waterloo Strategy vs. the Criminalization Strategy

The ten interrelated techniques proposed below constitute what I call the Waterloo Strategy for prevention of mobbing. I do not mean to suggest that my home university is a paragon of virtue or has formally adopted this strategy. The two basic measures on the list, to which most of the others are corollary, have been officially adopted by Waterloo's administration. Mainly, I have packaged these ten measures as the Waterloo Strategy in grateful recognition of the university that has hosted and supported my research over the past dozen years – rarely with enthusiasm, but faithfully even so.

Calling this package the Waterloo Strategy is also a shorthand way of contrasting it to a different preventive strategy that is widely proposed, what might be called the Criminalization Strategy. The latter rests on the same three assumptions (those listed above) as the former, but its defining tactic for preventing mobbing is to formally proscribe it in an anti-mobbing policy, an anti-mobbing clause of a collective agreement, or an anti-mobbing law at the state, provincial, or national level – in much the same way as sexual harassment has been criminalized in many jurisdictions. Psychologists Gary and Ruth Namie are leading proponents of the Criminalization Strategy in the United States, and law professor David Yamada has drafted a model statute against what he calls "status-blind harassment." The idea is to define mobbing empirically and then outlaw it. The anti-mobbing policy, clause, or law typically provides for the adjudication of alleged violations by a quasi-judicial tribunal, arbitrator, or court, and mandates penalties up to and including dismissal for participation in mobbing activities.

The Criminalization Strategy has been adopted by numerous corporations in Europe, notably Volkswagen A G, and at the state level by France and Italy. In 2004, Quebec became the first North American jurisdiction to pass anti-mobbing legislation, which has been introduced in the legislatures also of Ontario and several American states. Policies against mobbing and bullying have also been established in some branches of the public service.

While respecting the good intentions that lay behind the Criminalization Strategy and while granting its value for raising awareness of the problem, I doubt that it works: that is, reduces the incidence of mobbing or raises levels of decency and productivity on the job. Clogged courts, wasted resources, subtler mobbing techniques, distrust and hard feelings are more likely consequences, as have been observed in France since enactment of anti-mobbing legislation.

The concluding chapter of my book, *The Envy of Excellence* (2005), spelled out my reservations about the Criminalization

Strategy. Here, in a more positive vein, I suggest some elements of a different approach, the Waterloo Strategy, which emphasizes practice more than policy, politics more than law, and administrative as opposed to judicial or quasi-judicial procedures.

## Ten Administrative Measures

*1.     "Focus on the **situation, issue,** or **behaviour,** not the person."*

This first measure is in quotation marks because this is how it is succinctly phrased on the webpage of Waterloo's human resources department and in posters displayed across campus, which identify it as the first principle for the UW workplace. By definition, only a person can be mobbed. A situation can be remedied, an issue sorted out, a behaviour corrected, and a problem solved, but none of these can be mobbed. That is why these matters should occupy our minds rather than the personalities of our co-workers. Workplace mobbing represents a collective turning inward, a shift of energy and attention away from situations and issues, away from extrinsic organizational objectives, toward going after the SOB down the corridor. At the most basic level, prevention of mobbing requires us academics to keep our minds, day after grueling day, on getting the work of teaching and research done, rather than on separating bad guys from good guys.

Professors X and Y are at loggerheads, disagreeing sharply about something or other. X goes to the dean. Here are three responses by which the dean can set the stage for a mobbing: (a) "Y is a woman of impeccable integrity; I cannot believe she is acting in anything but good faith"; (b) "Y is a perpetual malcontent and there is no way to please her"; or even (c) "I'm not sure what to do, because I like you, but I like Y, too." Instead of inept responses like these, which focus on Y's personal character and lay groundwork for mobbing either her or her opponent, a dean mindful of the first anti-mobbing measure hones in on the specific issue that X and Y at this moment are fighting over, brings evidence and reason to bear on it, seeks out and weighs conflicting viewpoints, looks for common ground, searches for whatever solution will best serve the university's purposes. X, Y, and the dean all live to fight another day, and no witch gets burned.

2. *Replace quasi-judicial campus tribunals with administrative decision-making.*

An adversarial, court-like proceeding wherein an accused person is indicted, tried, and judged, is the single best example of what sociologist Harold Garfinkel called, in his classic article (*American Journal of Sociology*, 1956), a "degradation ceremony." It is a sweetly effective tool for transporting a disliked colleague into disrepute. Removing such proceedings from university governance structures therefore deprives prospective mobbers of one of their most effective tools, and lowers the odds that any professor will be mobbed. This anti-mobbing measure is generically similar to gun control as a means of reducing the murder rate or nuclear disarmament for lowering the risk of total war. By making the tool for doing harm less available, less harm is done.

So enamoured of courts has our society become that this proposal to do without courts on campus may seem utopian. Our actual experience at Waterloo therefore deserves emphasis: that in 1998, the Board of Governors of the University of Waterloo *abolished* our campus tribunal, the UW ethics committee, that had for sixteen years been adjudicating complaints of sexual harassment, racial discrimination, and similar ethical violations (my detailed documentary history of the tribunal is published on the web; google my name and "ethics committee"). In the eight years that have passed (at this writing) since 1998, such complaints have been handled by chairs, deans, and other administrators in the routine course of their jobs. The sky has not fallen. Professors and students have not run ethically amok. We now lack, moreover, an intoxicating organizational instrument by which to run collectively amok in mobbing a colleague.

Court procedures for deciding disputes are usefully compared to surgical procedures for healing diseases. The former, like the latter, are sometimes the best alternative in the circumstance at hand. All agree, however, that no surgical procedure should even be attempted unless stringent specific conditions are all met: careful diagnosis and pre-operative preparation of the patient, an absolutely sterile and well-fitted operating room, a surgeon, anesthetist, and nurses who are highly skilled, rested and focussed, freedom from interruption, careful observance of tried and true techniques, all the necessary tools and equipment, a recovery room, and after-care. We insist on these conditions because for all its possible benefits, surgery is risky and dangerous, and can easily do more harm than good. The patient may die. This same logic should be applied to any court or court-like procedure wherein a professor's name and position are at stake. Adjudication will likely do more harm than good unless all the requisite conditions are met: careful diagnosis that this procedure is appropriate for this case, careful preparation by both sides, an absolutely unbiased setting, judges who are impartial, learned, wise, rested and focussed, freedom from interruption, meticulous observance of due process, all the necessary documentation, a functioning tape recorder, time for recovery, and so on.

That these stringent conditions are often unmet in public courts is demonstrated by the frequency of wrongful convictions and of decisions overturned by appellate courts. But in campus tribunals, these conditions are virtually never met, despite the best of intentions on everybody's part. They were certainly not met in the cases of Therese Warden and Uhuru Watson at Medaille College, nor in the case of Herbert Richardson at the University of Toronto. It is easy to find professors willing to sit in judgment of their colleagues, especially when importuned to do so by university authorities – a circumstance that by itself undermines impartiality. It is almost impossible to satisfy the conditions that would raise campus tribunals above the level of kangaroo courts. That is why quasi-judicial procedures should have no place within a university.

Currently at Waterloo, disputes that are not resolved through normal administrative decision-making (negotiation, mediation, horse-trading, cajoling, compromise) may be taken to external arbitration – or in the case of criminal conduct, to public courts. This system is not perfect, but it affords at least some distance from campus politics, it is usually public, and rules of evidence and due process are generally observed. Empirically, it has proven more successful than our earlier system of internal ethics and grievance tribunals. I played a significant part in this procedural overhaul, and I am proud to have done so. Any would-be defender of campus tribunals should walk in the shoes of Warden and Watson at Medaille, or of Richardson at Toronto, or in my own shoes as I was going through the three tribunal proceedings at Waterloo years ago. The experience was akin to undergoing a major surgical procedure in a toolshed at the hands of a drunken dropout from medical school who is not wearing scrubs and has not washed his hands in a week.

Administrators' decisions are more likely to be wise, of course, when they are subject to the countervailing power of senate, board, media, faculty association, and the varied committees through which faculty and students share in university governance. When reasoned, dialogic, nonforensic mechanisms of dispute resolution are in place, the need for court procedures is greatly reduced – just as healthy lifestyles and appropriate medications greatly reduce the need for expensive, invasive, life-threatening surgical procedures. Tribunals and courts should always be a last resort for resolving administrative issues in a university, always external to its own hierarchy of authority, and never even contemplated unless the full list of stringent specific conditions has been met.

3. *Unless evidence compels them, avoid forensic words like allegations and charges.*

This third technique for preventing mobbing follows closely on the first two. The use in academic discourse of language drawn from courts of law distracts from solving problems and threatens people personally. It is a step toward squaring off for a fight.

Professors disagree a lot. They take offense and get angry. In the realm of ideas, disputes can be fierce. In such a context, skilled administrators refrain from gratuitously imposing forensic language on diffuse statements of concern, as in, "Even if not explicitly, Professor X, you have made allegations of serious misconduct against Professor Y, and I am therefore obliged to commence an investigation of these charges according to university policy." Far better to solve the problem, to sort out and resolve Professor X's concerns. In universities (unlike in courts), disputes need not be win-lose. Rarely is there need to pronounce anyone guilty of anything. Even the threat of such pronouncement casts a pall on the lively, free-wheeling inquiry, discourse and debate by which academics (on good days) reach new thresholds of truth.

I count myself lucky to have been able to observe closely for many years an exceedingly effective principal of a successful private school. How did he manage so well? By ignoring many of the squabbles parents and teachers got into, by resolving some squabbles creatively, by recoiling from forensic language – meanwhile focussing fanatically with consummate skill on educating every child. And when one boy brought a gun to school and sold it to another boy, the principal calmly phoned the police and expelled both boys. All academic administrators should have his sense of when forensic language is and is not appropriate.

4.   *Keep the rules clear, fair, and simple; keep policy and procedure manuals short.*

Like all bureaucracies, universities need to codify rules. I have read dozens of different manuals of policy and procedure, some better than others, in the course of studying mobbing cases in varied universities. Yet not a single mobbing in my research is explained by bad policies, faults in written rules. The explanation lies instead in the *ignoring, twisting,* or *misapplication* of reasonable rules by academics who have identified an enemy and aim to get rid of him or her.

Often, after a mobbing hits the news and embarrasses a university, authorities both inside and outside admit that "the matter was handled badly," but they are loath to blame the mob, which after all was composed of respected scholars. They recoil from saying, "Dean A, and Professors B, C, and D got carried away on this occasion and lost their usual good sense; their attack on Professor E was over the top." The blame instead is placed on faulty rules, the poor wording of one policy or the inadequate provisions of another. Committees are therefore struck to revise the rules, and a great flurry of activity ensues, typically resulting in longer policies and more detailed procedures that are said to be far superior to the previous ones. This appears to have occurred at Medaille College, in the wake of the Warden and Watson dismissals.

Ironically, the multiplication of procedural rules may do more harm than good, setting the stage for future mobbings. Once the period of adoption has passed, academics tend not to take time to read long, complicated policies, and their actual behaviour may end up less rule-bound than before. Further, when a dispute arises, it may be exacerbated and its resolution prevented by interminable argument over conflicting interpretations of rules and procedures, while the substance of the dispute is lost. Still worse, a line here or there in a byzantine policy can be lifted out of context and used as a weapon against an enemy.

Rules matter. The current campaign of the Foundation for Individual Rights in Education (FIRE; google its name to access its richly informative website) to get rid of ill-written speech codes that inhibit free expression highlights how important it is to have good rules: clear, fair, short and simple.

5.    *In the face of demands that a professor be punished, entertain not just the null hypothesis but the mobbing hypothesis.*

Often, an issue is already couched in exclusionary, stigmatizing, forensic language by the time one learns of it. Waterloo philosopher Jan Narveson has nicely phrased a request commonly brought to university administrators: "Git my enemies!" Chair or dean receives a delegation that says essentially, "Professor Z is a racist (sexist, plagiarist, thief, bully, abuser, harasser, nutbar, terrorist, or some other discrediting label). This has to stop. Do something."

Faced with this proffered hypothesis of Professor Z's guilt of some offense, an unskilled administrator simply accepts it out of personal respect for its authors or personal aversion to Z: "I'm sorry to hear this about Z, but it does not surprise me. I admire your courage and good faith in coming here. What can I do to help Z's victims and prevent there being more of them?"

A somewhat more skilled administrator acknowledges the proffered hypothesis but weighs it against the contrary or null hypothesis, that Z has not in fact behaved in a way that warrants administrative interference with Z's work: "I understand your concerns and I will look into the matter. Possibly you are right, but possibly there has been some misunderstanding."

A highly skilled administrator entertains the first two hypotheses but also a third one, that this is no mere misunderstanding, that Z's accusers are caught up in a panic or hysteria that prevents them from thinking and seeing straight, that their zealous demand for Z's punishment fits the bill of what researchers call workplace mobbing.

The advantage of knowing this third hypothesis is that it broadens the range of possible interpretations to place on the usually confusing data of disputes. Mobbing is prevented to the extent that administrators and rank-and-file professors know its signs and indicators and keep in mind the possibility that it is happening before their eyes. This helps avoid being naively drawn into an incipient mob, like the unskilled administrator in this example.

6.   *Seek proximate, specific, depersonalized explanations for why some professor is on the outs, as opposed to distant, general, personal explanations.*

Mobbings begin with one professor set apart from and clashing with the majority and with the relevant administrators on what is typically a series of issues: performance evaluation, promotion, course assignments, space allocation, program requirements, mailbox location, and so on and on. (The Richardson case is an archetype in this respect.) As the pattern begins to be obvious, some kind of meeting is likely to be scheduled to try to make things better. This may be at the beleaguered professor's request, or that of a concerned administrator. The meeting is often ad hoc, often in the dean's office, but it may occur as part of a faculty retreat, strategic planning exercise, department meeting, or mediation.

Mobbing is promoted and lasting harm can be done if the meeting yields an explanation of the conflict in terms of some personal characterization of the professor on the outs: his or her sexual or racial identity, an ideological label, traumatic childhood experiences, upbringing, mental health, personality traits, or general disposition. Such an explanation isolates the professor more than ever, no matter whether voiced with sympathy, pity, anger, puzzlement, or dismay.

To nip a mobbing in the bud, the conflict needs to be depersonalized and attention directed to academic objectives. The agenda for such a meeting should be the specific, immediate issues in dispute, even if there are 17 of them. The presider should insist that these issues be reasonably discussed, one by one, with the easiest first, and rule out of order personal characterizations of any of the parties in dispute. This can be hard. Depersonalizing a conflict and breaking it into manageable parts is a skill that must be learned. Exercising this skill when academics are riled up takes discipline and presence of mind. The price for forgetting it in such a meeting can be years of court proceedings, therapy sessions, doctors' visits, and hospital stays. The price can be the chronic disability or death of a scholar who has much to give.

7. *Encourage mindfulness of all the bases on which academic mobbings occur.*

In keeping with a value on human equality, most academics in our time know the vulnerability of women, visible minorities, people with disabilities, and homosexuals to unfair treatment. Today as in the past, a mobbing can be rooted in prejudice against people in any of these categories.

Research shows that a person can also be singled out and ganged up on for a number of other reasons, which need also to be kept in mind as possible explanations when a conflict arises. Any factor that sets a person radically apart from others in an academic unit is a possible basis of mobbing. Whistle-blowing is a common basis: wagons get circled when somebody publicly exposes low conduct in high places.

Envy is a powerful force in human affairs. Any professor who shows others up, even unwittingly, by excellence in teaching, research, credentials, looks, sports, connections, indeed in any way at all, can elicit collegial effort to teach that professor a lesson, trim that colleague down to size.

In the majority of academic mobbings I have studied, one of the leaders of the mob is an administrator – a department chair, dean, vice-president, or president – whose appointment to a position of leadership was opposed by the professor who is targeted. Both the Medaille and Toronto cases exemplify this pattern: Warden had let Donohue know she could not support him as permanent president, and Richardson was on record as opposing Joanne McWilliam as chair of religious studies. A professor who has landed a coveted administrative post sometimes displays almost a compulsion to go after a colleague who supported somebody else, as if to say: "I went out on a limb and risked losing face by letting my name stand. You tried to shame me. Therefore now I will shame you."

The prevention of mobbing in universities depends on us academics doing what we are supposed to be especially skilled at: keeping ourselves conscious of a wide variety of possible factors for explaining what is going on, even for explaining our own initial impulses as to what to do, before we took time to reflect.

8. *Defend free expression and encourage dialogic outlets for it on campus.*

In their important book, *The Shadow University* (Free Press, 1998) Alan Kors and Harvey Silverglate quote approvingly the famous sentiment of Justice Louis Brandeis, that sunlight is the best disinfectant. Like a fungus, mobbing thrives in the dark, hidden by rules of confidentiality, anonymity, secrecy. The prospect of public exposure discourages not only mobbing, but other kinds of nefarious academic shenanigans. Freedom of speech and press are therefore essential to any preventive strategy.

As stewards of an institution dependent on public support, university administrators rightly value good press, and wince at the airing of campus dirty laundry in public media. Yet if a university is to achieve its purpose of seeking and spreading truth, fostering a positive public image must always have lower priority than upholding every professor's right and duty to tell the truth as he or she sees it, arguing points reasonably in light of evidence.

The main technology for free expression is shifting rapidly from print to electronic media. At Waterloo, our campus newspaper, the *Gazette,* ceased publication in June of 2004. Here as elsewhere, academics look increasingly to the web for information and opinion. Websites are commonly used to put before the public cases of allegedly wrongful conviction. To foster an intelligent, dialogic campus climate, universities not only defend individuals' rights to publish websites in the free-for-all of cyberspace, but also supplement personal websites with electronic newspapers and magazines, local counterparts to nation-wide initiatives like insiderhighered.com, that serve freedom of expression at higher calibre.

9. *Keep administration open and loose.*

To the extent the eight measures suggested so far are set in place, they define a campus culture inconducive to mobbing anyone – not a safe or benign culture, since seeking truth is hard and risky work, but an open culture where academics find better things to do than look for witches. Such a culture is a necessarily collaborative creation. It cannot be imposed from the top down. If the senior administration is apart from rather than in solidarity with the professoriate, any trappings of an open culture are fake, and mobbings arise among professors estranged from the administration, also among administrators annoyed by professors who trumpet politically incorrect truths or who claim their right to share in university governance.

The maintenance of an open, participatory campus culture is a challenge for us at Waterloo, as for our colleagues elsewhere. I wish I could say that the first two measures on this list came to be adopted at Waterloo as a result of broad, vigorous dialogue and debate on campus. Not so. The first principle for the UW workplace, so excellent a formulation, was proposed by a management consulting firm. It was announced before the faculty had heard of it. The Board of Governors abolished Waterloo's ethics committee in the midst of a governance crisis, after that committee's decisions had publicly embarrassed the university. Abolition would have been a still more splendid move, had it been rooted in a more democratic process.

The archetypal setting for workplace mobbing, reflected in novels like *Billy Budd*, poems like "The Rhyme of the Ancient Mariner," and films like *The Caine Mutiny*, is the tight ship: intensely hierarchical, strictly disciplined, with little time for reflection, talk or liberty. Historically, survival on the high seas required a closed, rigid organization, and occasional mobbings were a by-product, a cost that few ships escaped. In a university, by contrast, which cannot achieve its scholarly goals except with time for reflection, talk, and liberty, workplace mobbing is not an inevitable cost but senseless waste. By keeping academic administration open and loose, a university not only minimizes this particular form of cruelty but also better serves its intellectual purposes in general.

## 10.  *Answer internal mail.*

Anybody in a position of even a little prominence – as an author of books, for instance, or subject of a news story – is easily overwhelmed by *external* mail: letters, phone calls, or emails from people he or she does not know. He or she must be forgiven for failing to respond to every single communication received. At least I hope so, since I have sometimes failed in this respect, despite my intention to give some brief answer to anyone kind enough to write to me. Nobody has a legal or moral obligation to respond to unsolicited mail from strangers.

It is different with *internal* mail: letters, memos, calls or emails from people in the same network of social relations as the recipient – the same workplace, for instance. The duty to respond applies in particular to communications sent by a co-worker or by a subordinate to a superordinate (student to course instructor, for instance, or professor to dean). And the more heartfelt the communication is, the more important that it receive some kind of response.

One of the early warning signs that a professor is being mobbed is that his or her earnest messages to colleagues or to administrative superiors are simply ignored. They go unanswered. This amounts to the "silent treatment," what is called in German *todschweigen*, death by silence. As a professor and former administrator, I know how often professors get bees in their bonnets and inflict on colleagues and superiors long, unwanted missives that are exceedingly hard to respond to. I have both sent and received such communications. As postmodern influences have penetrated universities, as epistemologies have become more plural, and as power has become more centralized, the problem of not knowing how to respond to messages is probably worse now than in decades past. That is all the more reason to give some kind of respectful response, however brief, if only to affirm the common, collegial bond between sender and recipient that is the academy's one foundation.

## Conclusion

There is nothing sacred about the practical techniques or measures with which this book concludes. The list can be expanded or reduced, the items on it combined or broken down further. The heuristic purpose of this book that was emphasized at the start, bears repeating here at the end. My aim has been to raise questions and provoke thought, more than to answer questions or have any kind of last word. Collectively, the measures listed above reflect the general thrust of my research so far, and outline a practical strategy for lessening the number of horror stories in academe and for making the working lives of all of us – administrators, professors, staff, students – more productive, constructive, fun, and in a phrase from Pope John XXIII, "a little less sad."

# Notes on Authors

**AAUP Committee A** on Academic Freedom and Tenure is a standing committee of the American Association of University Professors in Washington, DC. Its report herein on Medaille College was drafted first by the two investigators, Robert K. Moore, Assistant Professor of Sociology and Criminal Justice at Saint Joseph's University in Philadelphia, and Sandi Cooper, Professor of History at the College of Staten Island, of CCNY. Moore holds JD and PhD degrees from SUNY Buffalo, and is a recipient of his university's Justice Award. Cooper's PhD is from New York University; she has published widely on European peace movements. The Moore/Cooper draft was revised by AAUP staff, sent for comments to the parties in dispute, and revised further. Jonathan Knight is AAUP Associate Secretary and Director of its Department of Academic Freedom and Tenure.

**Jo A. Baldwin** of Kosciusko, Mississippi, is an ordained Itinerant Elder in the African Methodist Episcopal Church and an Assistant Professor of English at Mississippi Valley State University. She has a Bachelor's in English, a Master's in Creative Writing, and a PhD in English from the University of Wisconsin-Milwaukee, a Master's in Speech/Theatre from Marquette University, and a Master of Divinity from United Theological Seminary. When preaching, she uses a style that came out of slavery called "tuning" and is the first to author a book on it, *Seven Signature Sermons By a Tuning Woman Preacher of the Gospel* (Mellen, 2001). Email: revdrjo@bellsouth.net

**Barry W. Birnbaum**, Ed.D., is Associate Professor of Special Education at Northeastern Illinois University. He was named Florida

Gifted Teacher of the Year in 1991, and honored by IBM as Florida Teacher of the Year in 1992. His books include *Foundations and Practices in the Use of Distance Education* (2002) and *Using Assistive Technologies for Instructing Students with Disabilities: A Survey of New Resources* (2005), both from Mellen Press. Email address: b-birnbaum@neiu.edu

**James Gollnick** (PhD Toronto, 1974) is Professor of Psychology of Religion and Director of the Spirituality and Personal Development Program at St. Paul's College, University of Waterloo. He was Dean of St. Paul's from 1995 to 2005. He taught earlier in the Department of Religious Studies at University of Toronto, mainly at Victoria College and Trinity College. Dream analysis has been his major research interest. He draws on Gestalt, Freudian, and Jungian approaches to the psyche. The most recent of his five books are *Religion and Spirituality in the Life Cycle* (Peter Lang, 2005) and *The Religious Dreamworld of Apuleius' Metamorphoses* (Wilfrid Laurier University Press, 1999). Email: jgollnic@uwaterloo.ca

**Anson Shupe** is Professor of Sociology at the joint campus of Indiana University and Purdue University, Fort Wayne. His MA and PhD are from Indiana University. His specialties in research and teaching include social movements, sociology of religion, and elite deviance, which he has managed to combine in recent years into one subdiscipline. He is the author of over 80 book chapters and professional articles, numerous magazine/newspaper assignments and 28 books, including *Agents of Discord: the Cult Awareness Network, Deprogramming, and Bad Science* (Transaction Publishers, 2006). Email: Shupe@IPFW.edu

**James J. Van Patten** received his PhD from the University of Texas, Austin. Professor Emeritus at the University of Arkansas, Fayetteville, he is an adjunct professor at Florida Atlantic University, Boca Raton. Van Patten has served as Visiting Professor at Peabody College, Texas at El Paso, Texas at Austin, and Florida at Gainesville, and as a visiting scholar at UCLA, Michigan at Ann Arbor, and in foundations for higher education. Van Patten has taught and served as consultant in American Cooperative Schools in Bolivia, Columbia, Ecuador, and Greece. The best known of his many books is *History of*

*Education in America* (8<sup>th</sup> edition, Prentice-Hall, 2002, co-authored with J. D. Pulliam); the most recent is *A Case Study Approach to a Multi-Cultural Mosaic in Education* (Mellen, 2003, co-authored with T. J. Bergen). Email: jvanpatt@aol.com

**Stan C. Weeber** earned his PhD from the University of North Texas, and is Assistant Professor of Sociology and Criminal Justice at McNeese State University. His more than fifty publications include contributions to *Sociological Quarterly, Humanity and Society, Contemporary Sociology, Studies in Symbolic Interaction, Sociological Imagination,* and other journals, as well as six books. Recent titles include *Lee Harvey Oswald* (Mellen, 2003) and *Militias in the New Millennium* (University Press of America, 2004). His research interests include political sociology, collective behavior and social movements, comparative criminology, and sociology of sport. Email: sweeber@mail.mcneese.edu

**Kenneth Westhues** (PhD Vanderbilt, 1970) is Professor of Sociology at the University of Waterloo, where he has taught since 1975. A former chair of his department and winner of awards for distinguished teaching in 1985 and 2005, he has been a visiting professor at Fordham University, Memorial University of Newfoundland, and the University of Graz, Austria. He is author or editor of a dozen books, including *First Sociology* (McGraw-Hill, 1982), *Basic Principles for Social Science in Our Time* (St. Jerome's University Press, 1987), *In Search of Community* (Fordham University Press, 1992), and the series on workplace mobbing from Mellen Press: *Eliminating Professors* (1998), *The Envy of Excellence* (2006), *Workplace Mobbing in Academe* (2004), and *Winning, Losing, Moving On* (2005), as well as about fifty book chapters and scholarly articles. He has been associated since 1987 with The Working Centre in Kitchener, Ontario, currently as vice-president of its board of directors. In 2005, through the Waterloo School for Community Development, he helped launch the Working Centre's diploma program in local democracy. Email: kwesthue@uwaterloo.ca